Deindustrialization and Reindustrialization in Romania

"The depth and rigor of this work shows that the Romanian economy has specialists capable of offering a clear, precise and useful diagnosis of the weaknesses, strengths and possibilities of Romanian industry from its origins to its present and future. Luminita Chivu, Constantin Ciutacu and George Georgescu, with the support of Romanian Academy, not only describe reality but also provide alternative guidelines that will serve planners, international investors and European and global governance bodies."

— Jaime Gil-Aluja, President of the Royal Academy of Economics of Spain and author of "Towards an Advanced Modelling of Complex Economic Phenomena"

"The lack of industrial policy in the U.S.A. contributed mightily to the rise of Trumpism, which demonstrates the dangers posed by globalization without thinking creatively about the powerful structural and redistributive forces it unleashes. This valuable case study establishes the foundational principles of such policies for Romania with universal implications. Policy makers keen on helping to establish a decent quality of life with a stable political system can disregard these recommendations only at their peril."

— John Komlos, Professor Emeritus, University of Munich and author of "What Every Economics Student Needs to Know"

Luminița Chivu • Constantin Ciutacu
George Georgescu

Deindustrialization and Reindustrialization in Romania

Economic Strategy Challenges

palgrave
macmillan

Luminiţa Chivu
National Institute for Economic Research
"Costin C. Kiriţescu", Bucharest, Romania

Constantin Ciutacu
National Institute for Economic Research
"Costin C. Kiriţescu", Bucharest, Romania

George Georgescu
National Institute for Economic Research
"Costin C. Kiriţescu", Bucharest, Romania

ISBN 978-3-319-65752-3 ISBN 978-3-319-65753-0 (eBook)
DOI 10.1007/978-3-319-65753-0

Library of Congress Control Number: 2017957569

Cover illustration: Agencja Fotograficzna Caro / Alamy Stock Photo

Printed on acid-free paper

This Palgrave Macmillan imprint is published by Springer Nature
The registered company is Springer International Publishing AG
The registered company address is: Gewerbestrasse 11, 6330 Cham, Switzerland

Preface

The idea of the book originated in the importance we have given in our previous studies to the key economic and social role of the industry sector and the need to investigate the most relevant issues regarding the dynamics of Romania's post-communism deindustrialization, in order to find appropriate answers to new challenges the country faces in the medium and long term in a complex international context.

This book is structured into seven chapters, focusing, in a progressive and analytical manner, on changes generated in the history of industrial revolutions and particularities of Industry 4.0 current trends: Romania's macroeconomic developments during the transition to the market economy, including some adverse effects; the privatization of state-owned companies; the impact of deindustrialization on industrial restructuring, labour market and productivity, looking at relevant international experiences in industrial policies as lessons to be learned by Romania; and concluding with specific actions and measures, both legal and institutional, which could support the country' reindustrialization. Many arguments are based on data series analysis and are illustrated with tables and figures, making the material in the book more accessible by students and academic researchers, policy-makers in the field of industrial policies, investors or entrepreneurs.

We would like to mention that the elaboration of this study is the result of much research, to which, an essential contribution was made by the late professor Constantin Ciutacu, a remarkable personality and economic researcher in Romania, who passed away earlier this year, to whom we pay an emotional tribute. Respected and appreciated by all the researchers and collaborators at the National Institute for Economic Research "Costin C. Kiriţescu", Professor Constantin Ciutacu enjoyed honours, awards and distinctions of excellence, of which, the dearest to his heart was the award of "Academic Merit", the highest distinction awarded by the Romanian Academy.

The study would not have had the actual substance it does and could not have taken the pulse of Romania's industrial realities without the debate and analysis framework offered by the Employers Association of Domestic Investors (PIAROM), for which we would like to thank the President, Mr. Cristian Nicolae Pârvan.

All the work invested in this project could not have been finalized in a book without the constant support of Palgrave Macmillan's editorial teams, to whom we are most grateful for their helpful initiatives, comments and suggestions.

Contents

List of Figures

List of Tables

1

The National and European Context of Industrial Development

Although there are an increasing number of experts, researchers, analysts, journalists and politicians addressing the decline and obsolescence of industry—in other words, deindustrialization—there are other voices which try to demonstrate the contrary: the need to recognise the economic, social and cultural importance of industry.

It is a matter of record that deindustrialisation—defined mainly as widespread and systematic disinvestment in basic production capacity (Bluestone and Harisson 1982, 6)—has been a subject for debate and study in most developed and developing countries, and that real life has offered an abundance of arguments to illustrate the applicability of this concept everywhere, including Romania (Ciutacu and Chivu 2015, 209–216).

In technical writings, industry has always been viewed as the key sector of economic development, and in many countries building industry was almost a centuries-long obsession for the ruling classes.

Industry was regarded as a *sine qua non* pillar for the enhancement, through processing, of the intrinsic value of natural resources, as a better means of capitalising on the knowledge and creative intelligence of human capital, and as an opportunity to further refine that knowledge.

L. Chivu et al., *Deindustrialization and Reindustrialization in Romania*,
DOI 10.1007/978-3-319-65753-0_1

The arguments most often brought forth were the value added to products and the efficiency of production factors, including that of labour.

According to these arguments, the industry has benefited from major support from the state, whose effects—largely generally recognized—have also been the subject of discussions regarding their possible negative long-term impact.

As shown by Grabas and Nutzenadel (2013), the implementation of interventionist industrial policies in most European countries during the post-World War II years, which prevailed until the 1990s, favoured structural economic changes that supported high economic growth rates, but in many cases led to inefficient allocation of resources with a potential adverse effects in the longer run

And, last but not least, industry has always had not only important economic functions, contributing to the development of other economic activities, such as transport, infrastructure, constructions, education and scientific research, but has also performed the social function of creating jobs and providing earnings that made possible increased welfare and quality of life.

The history of industrialisation shows that the economic development of the various states of the world comprised several stages of evolution, from the Stone Age to the Bronze Age the Iron Age, culminating in our times in what we call the industrial revolution.

In fact, three such industrial revolutions have been identified historically, each of them triggered by a certain type of energy, and characterised by a succession of generations of technologies, running from labour-intensive technologies to technologies based on mechanics, electricity, electrical engineering, chemistry, biology and information.

Any industrial revolution is generally preceded and sparked off by scientific, technical and organisational progress. This is also true about the fourth industrial revolution, in progress now under our very eyes: it too requires the existence of three cultural, technological and organisational conditions.

The first industrial revolution started at the end of the eighteenth century; and the drivers were coal, metallurgy, textiles and the steam engine. The second industrial revolution was triggered by electricity, mechanics, crude oil, chemistry, the telegraph, the telephone and collective transport by steam locomotives and steamboats. The third industrial revolution was brought about by the discovery, in mid-twentieth century, of semiconductors and transistors; and its main foci were the development of electronics, telecommunications, information technology, audio-visual media, nuclear technologies, robotics, automation, space technologies and biotechnologies. Lastly, the forth industrial revolution, also known as industry 4.0, has caused a disruption of production processes due to adoption of the internet and data processing and other transmission and communication technologies, which allow new industries to offer their clients intelligent and personalised products with the aid of smart processing techniques.

Professor Klaus Schwab, Founder and Executive Chairman of the World Economic Forum, exploring the dramatic changes in the global environment caused by the new technologies, argues that the world is facing its fourth industrial revolution, but that it is essentially different from the three previous ones in terms of speed, scope and impact. The revolution which we are witnessing is moving at exponential speed, disrupting almost every industry worldwide; and the spread and depth of the changes it is bringing radically are transforming entire production systems, management and governance, with multiplied effects from emerging technology, such as, among others, robotics, self-driving cars, 3-D printing, nanotechnology, biotechnology, energy storage and genetic editing (Schwab 2015). Regarding global concerns about the difficulties of adapting to these changes and capturing their benefits, it is relevant in this context to mention that the central aim of the WEF Forum Annual Meeting 2016 was "Mastering the Fourth Industrial Revolution".

In the long evolution of mankind, particularly in the past two centuries, the focus has been industrialisation, until, after 1990, the reverse concept—deindustrialisation—appeared. In the latest industrial revolution, industrialization and *deindustrialisation* as its corollary are occurring together, both as the result of new materials and of data processing and communication technologies.

We cannot ignore the fact that the foundation of industrial development in the twentieth century, mostly in its middle third, was the *production of metal in general, and of steel in particular.*

Steel production and metal-working have been the basis of the economic systems in the developed countries, and the decline of such systems results in restructuring, deindustrialisation and reindustrialisation by means of 4.0-generation technologies.

After 1950, the developed countries in Europe and North America embarked on what was called at the time the “30 glorious years” or the “Golden Age” (Grabas and Nutzenadel 2013). It was a time when big industrial ventures appeared (for example, the European Coal and Steel Community [ECSC], founded in 1952)—the so-called national champions, which provided jobs for large numbers of workers, whose pay became increasing better (Ciutacu and Chivu 2015, 209–216).

In addition to the workforce directly employed in these companies, this sector favoured the development upstream and downstream of the coal- and mineral-ore-mining industries, the production of energy, transport, construction, education and scientific research. Metal itself provided the raw material that boosted many other manufacturing branches of industry.

The statistics of the time reveal the widespread industrial development that occurred. To quote just a few examples from the European Union (EU) member states, the real index of industrial production during the period 1960–1990 grew 6.5 times in Portugal, 5.8 times in Spain, 4.9 times in Finland, 3.4 times in Austria, 3.1 times in Italy, 3 times in the Netherlands, 2.6 times in France and so on.

Compared to 1990, in 2016 industrial output increased, in real terms, in Spain by 1%, in Portugal by 6%, in France by 7%, in the Netherlands by 17%, in Finland by 74% and in Austria by 112% (output in Italy, in contrast, decreased by 9%).

As for the new EU member states in the Eastern Europe, in the same time frame—1960 till 1990—industrial output increased 10.3 times in Romania, 3.8 times in Poland and 3.2 times in Hungary, while in the period 1990–2016, the industrial output of Romania grew in real terms by 38%, in Poland by 274% and in Hungary by 154%.

Since that time, in general, the industrial sector has contributed less to the creation of the gross value added (GVA) in the economy.

The first signs of the decline of industry’s contribution to the GVA occurred in the Organisation for Economic Cooperation and

Development (OECD) member states in the early 1980s. But the profile of this decline has seen significant variations from one country to another.

A stronger reflection in the reduction of the industry's share in total GVA can be seen in the following countries and periods: in Japan from 1993 in 1997, in Italy from 1992 in 1995 (with a new wave from 1997 to 1999), in the United States in 1991–1994 and after 1990 in Germany. The decline of industry in France was more pronounced between 1993 and 1998.

These developments are a result of public policies and corporate strategies, whose effectiveness has slowed down or accelerated this process (Chatillon 2011).

In 2016, industry, in the EU 28, contributed a share of 19.3% to the overall GVA, as compared with 23.3% in 1995. According to Eurostat data, this average derives from a low of 7.1% in Cyprus (12.6% in 1995), 7.2% in Luxemburg (14.9% in 1995) to a high of 38.9% in Ireland (26.2% in 1995) and 32.3% in Czech Republic (31.4% in 1995).

In 12 EU member states, industry contributed 10% to 19.9% to the GVA (10.6% in Malta, 13.0% in United Kingdom, 13.4% in Greece, 13.9% in France, 15.0% in Netherlands, 16.7% in Belgium and Latvia, 17.8% in Spain, 18.5% in Romania, 18.8% in Denmark, 19.3% in Italy and 19.9% in Sweden); in another 12 EU member states, the contribution of industry was in a range of 20–30% (Finland 20.2%, Estonia 20.7%, Croatia 21.3%, Austria 21.6%, Lithuania 22.1%, Bulgaria 23.8%, Germany 25.7%, Ireland 26.3%, Poland 26.8%, Hungary 27.0%, Slovakia 27.3% and Slovenia 27.6%).

Statistics show that steel production grew significantly in the period from 1960 to 1970 (with the exception of in the United Kingdom).

The rise in the price of crude oil after 1973 brought about major changes in this trend. Between 1990 and 2015, only in 5 of the 19 EU member countries considered for this analysis did, the steel output continued to grow: Austria, from 4.3 to 7.7 mil. tonnes, Finland from 2.9 to 4.0 mil. tonnes, the Netherlands from 5.4 to 7.0 mil. tonnes, Portugal from 0.7 to 2.1 mil. tonnes, and Spain from 12.9 to 14.8 mil. tonnes (Table 1.1).

In the New Member States (NMS), the drop of the steel output has sometimes been very steep: in Romania, for example, the steel production

Table 1.1 Steel production in some of the EU member states (mil. tonnes)

	1960	1970	1980	1990	2015	Maximum output	Year of max output
Austria	3.2	4.1	4.6	4.3	7.7	8.0	2013
Belgium	7.2	12.6	12.4	11.5	7.3	12.4	1980
Bulgaria	0.3	1.8	2.6	2.2	0.5	3.0	1987
Czech Rep. and Slovakia	6.8	11.5	14.9	14.9	9.8	15.4	1987
Denmark	0.3	0.5	0.7	0.6	...	0.8	2000
Finland	0.3	1.2	2.5	2.9	4.0	5.1	2006
France	17.3	23.8	23.2	19.0	15.0	23.2	1980
Germany	37.9	51	51.1	44.0	42.7	51.2	1980
Hungary	1.9	3.1	3.8	3.0	1.7	3.8	1984
Italy	8.2	17.3	26.5	25.5	22.0	31.6	2006
Luxembourg	4.1	5.5	4.6	3.6	2.1	4.6	1980
Netherlands	1.9	5	5.3	5.4	7.0	7.4	2007
Poland	6.7	11.8	19.5	13.6	9.2	19.5	1980
Portugal	...	...	0.7	0.7	2.0	2.1	2013
Spain	1.9	7.4	12.6	12.9	14.8	19.0	2007
Sweden	3.2	5.5	4.2	4.5	4.4	6.0	2004
Romania	**1.8**	**6.5**	**13.2**	**9.8**	**3.4**	**15.0**	**1987**
United Kingdom	24.7	28.3	11.3	17.8	10.9	28.3	1970

Source: *Steel Statistical Yearbook*, World Steel Association, Brussels, various editions, 1960–2015
Note: ... = Not available data

plummeted from a maximum of approximately 15 mil. tonnes in 1987, to 9.8 mil. tonnes in 1990, and to 3.4 mil. tonnes in 2015; in Poland, the steel output shrank from 19.5 mil. tonnes in 1980 to 13.6 mil. tonnes in 1990 and to 9.2 mil. tonnes in 2015 *et cetera.*

According to the *Steel Statistical Yearbook*,[1] world steel production has grown steadily: from 129 mil. tonnes in 1950, to 594 mil. tonnes in 1970, 770.5 mil. tonnes in 1990 and to 1669.9 mil. tonnes in 2014, with a small decrease at 1620.4 mil. tonnes in 2015.

The growth of world steel production is, to a large extent, due to developments in China's industry. There steel production has risen from 47 mil. tonnes in 1985 to 95 mil. tonnes in 1995, 356 mil. tonnes in 2005 and 803.8 mil. tonnes in 2015.

The trade in scrap iron is the most telling proof of ongoing deindustrialisation. After a period of over 30 years of massive investment in the development of industrial platforms and infrastructures, equipment, machinery and equipment specific to "heavy industry", at a time of radical change, progress towards digitization of manufacturing processes and the widespread use of Information and Communication Technology (ICT) generated a rapid moral degradation of old investments and transformed entire generations of technologies into the equivalent of iron scrap.

While the steel industry reversed its growing trend after each of the two shock waves of oil prices hikes in 1973 and 1978, in most of the developed countries, and particularly in the EU member states, after 1990, the reduction in steel output (or its much slower growth) has been accompanied by a rise in the scrap-iron trade (Table 1.2).

In the years 1980–1989, in the EU 15, the trade in scrap iron accounted for 20% of overall steel production, while in the new member states (NMS), scrap iron accounted for only 1%. In the following 25 years (1990–2015), the share of scrap iron in the overall production of steel grew significantly. During the period 2010–2015 it accounted for 44.7%.

The volume of scrap iron trade in the EU 28 has fluctuated from 456 mil. tonnes in 1990–1999 to 701.8 mil. tonnes in 2000–2009 and to 462.7 mil. tonnes in 2010–2015; scrap iron's share of the total steel output followed a rising curve over the same time periods: 24.7% in 1990–1999, 36.7% in 2000–2009, and 45.4% in 2010–2015.

In the aggregate, the balance of the trade in scrap iron in the EU 15 followed a growing curve, from a deficit of some 29 mil. tonnes in 1980–1989 and 23 mil. tonnes in 2000–2009 to a surplus of 39.8 mil. tonnes in 2010–2015.

In the NMS, exports of scrap iron exceeded imports by 20.4 mil. tonnes in 1990–1999, by 52.7 mil. tonnes in 2000–2009 and by 41.6 mil. tonnes in 2010–2015.

As argued by Ciutacu and Chivu (Ciutacu and Chivu 2015, 209–215), in terms of sustainable development, exporting scrap iron is questionable, particularly when paralleled by imports of scrap iron. Importing and exporting the same item, which is facilitated by rules allowing free movement of goods and services, obviously is contrary to the principles of sustainable development, with regard to energy saving and greenhouse gases (GHG)-emission reduction, promoted by the EU 2020 Strategy. The simultaneous existence and encouragement of the manufacture of

Table 1.2 Manufacture of basic steel, and total trade in iron scrap, by time periods

	1990–1999		2000–2009		2010–2015	
	Output (mil. tonnes)	Scrap iron share in steel output (%)	Output (mil. tonnes)	Scrap iron share in steel output (%)	Output (mil. tonnes)	Scrap iron share in steel output (%)
EU 28	**1847.3**	**24.7**	**1914.6**	**36.7**	**1020.3**	**45.4**
Austria	46.1	19.7	65.6	34.5	45.7	**27.3**
Belgium—Luxembourg	139.3	32.3	131.6	74.7	58.7	**98.2**
Denmark	6.9	86.2	1.9	706.2	0.0	...
Finland	33.6	11.2	43.3	22.6	23.1	**16.7**
France	186.4	28.3	190.4	43.6	93.6	**54.9**
Germany	417.3	21.8	446.2	26.5	259.0	**32.1**
Greece	9.6	**56.8**	19.6	62.8	7.9	**50.3**
Ireland	3.1	70.6	0.5	638	0.0	...
Italy	255.4	21.7	278	18	151.5	**21.3**
Netherlands	60	93.9	63.9	88.5	41.2	**90.3**
Portugal	8.2	16.8	13.4	60.4	11.6	**58.0**
Spain	133.8	35.6	170.9	37.5	88.8	**36.0**
Sweden	47.9	14.1	53	22.4	27.3	**35.7**
United Kingdom	172.1	20.3	132.4	47.4	63.6	**72.0**
EU 15	**1519.7**	**27.5**	**1610.8**	**38.2**	**872.1**	**44.7**
Bulgaria	19.6	5.7	18.3	40	3.9	**133.0**
Czech Rep.	72.7	10.1	64	23.5	31.6	**45.1**
Hungary	19.2	32.7	19.6	32.3	8.6	**77.8**
Latvia	2.77	44.2	5.8	59.3	2.2	**240.9**
Poland	107.7	6	93.2	15.9	50.9	**25.6**
Romania	**63.6**	**4.1**	**53.4**	**36**	**19.9**	**54.4**
Slovenia	4.1	105.7	5.5	80.8	3.7	**151.1**
Slovakia	38	7.7	43.9	11.9	27.0	**16.6**
New Member States (NMS)	**327.6**	**11.8**	**303.8**	**28.6**	**148.3**	**49.4**

Source: Authors' own compilation based on data from *Steel Statistical Yearbook*, World Steel Association, Brussels, various editions, 1990–2015

Note: ... = Not available data

basic steel and exports of iron scrap are generated by a systemic inertia. Therefore, this issue requires a broader debate on whether such practices can be substantiated from economic and social perspectives, whether they contradict the principles of sustainable development or whether they are likely to trigger a surge of deindustrialisation.

Until 1989, Romania produced more than 14 mil. tonnes of steel, with some less significant imports of iron scrap. In 2010, with domestic steel production reduced to 3.7 mil. tonnes, Romania exported over 2.5 mil. tonnes of iron scrap.

The statistics for the year 1980 recorded a scrap-iron trade amounting to 53.3 mil. tonnes, and in 2015, world trade volume had reached 167.8 mil. tonnes.

If we start from the assumption that, in the future, China will evolve in the same pattern of the developed countries, the questions to be posed would be where China would be exporting and what countries would import China's scrap iron, considering the fact that China's steel production was 804 mil. tonnes in 2015, which accounted for 50% of all steel global production?

Leaving aside these disturbing implications, which experts and the media often choose to ignore, we cannot help but observe that the advocates of the theory of industrial decline have found arguments in relevant data and statistical information regarding macroeconomic indicators. Most quoted among these are the gross value added, the contribution of industry to the formation of the gross domestic product (GDP) and the curve of the number of workers in the industry.

At global level, according to the development theory, in the case of the old industrialized countries, manufacturing industry diminished its contribution to the creation of the global gross value added.[2]

The data used to support this theory demonstrate that in the time span—1991–2014—the decreasing contribution of old industrialised territories is only relative, but in nominal terms, the value added generated by the manufacturing industry increased in 2014, up from 1991, by 1087 bn. USD in Western Europe and by 1126 bn. USD in North America (Table 1.3).

According to World Bank (WB) data, in 2015, the value added in industry, expressed in billions of USD, totaled 4529 in China, 3327 in

Table 1.3 Contribution of territories to the world added value in the manufacturing industry (%)

	1991	2014
European Union	32	21
North America	24	19
Japan	19	7
Emerging countries	21	53
Total (bn. USD)	4717	6577

Source: Authors' own compilation based on World Bank Data

USA (2014), 1225 in Japan (2014), 923 in Germany, 563 in India, 495 in United Kingdom, 476 in South Korea, 422 in France, 402 in Russia, 385 in Italy, 349 in Mexico and 346 in Brazil. In the same year, the *value added in Romania's industry was 55 bn. USD.*

The relative decline of the manufacturing industry is also reflected in its share of the GDP: In 1991 and 2014, industry generated 16%, and, respectively, 12% of the GDP in the United States, 21% and 16% in the EU, 21% and 15% in Italy, 20% and 16% in Sweden, 17% and 11% in France, 27% and 23% in Germany and 17% and 10% in the United Kingdom. In Romania, the contribution of the manufacturing sector to the GDP was 34% in 1991 and 24% in 2014.

During the same period, we can notice a rise in this share from 15% to 17% in India; in 2013, in China, industry accounted for 30% of the GDP.

Another indicator used as an argument to demonstrate the downward trend in industry is the curve of the number of jobs. In France, for example, in the last 30 years, the industry has lost 2 million jobs, i.e., about one-third of its total employment (Chatillon 2011, 11). In only the last ten years, 500,000–600,000 jobs were eliminated in French industry; whole territories have been devitalized, especially the old mono-industrial regions.

Since 1980 until 2007, the number of jobs in the industrial sector of France dropped by an average of 71,000 jobs/year (17,000 jobs as a consequence of outsourcing, 21,000 jobs as an effect of labour productivity, 9000 by competition), and, with effect from the year 2000, records show an average annual loss of 65,000 jobs (42,000 due to an increasing labour productivity, 3000 due to outsourcing and so on).[3]

Based on a well-documented analysis of the decline in manufacturing employment in Denmark during the period 1994–2007, some authors have demonstrated that it represents not just a story of displaced industries and failing firms, but that deindustrialization involved a transition from manufacturing companies to those engaged in services or more service-linked activities, which raises major questions regarding economic policy (Bernard, Smeets and Warzynski 2017, 31).

Distinguishing three types of manufacturing companies (switchers, stayers and exits), this analysis conclude that the workers separated from either exiting firms or from stayer, have relatively bad short-term labour-market outcomes (lower wages and more likely to be unemployed), but for workers separated from switchers, the long-term prospects are relatively good (Bernard, Smeets and Warzynski 2017, 33).

The traditional strength of industry has been disturbed by the advent the digital technologies, the environmental constraints, global competition, and by the changes in the consumers' behavioural patterns, prompted by increasingly aggressive advertising policies.

An economy that owes its architecture to the first three industrial revolutions is now being gradually ousted, at a growingly faster pace, by the 4.0 generation of industry; the information technology has opened the path to the fourth industrial revolution, creating new configurations between the secondary and tertiary sectors, and leading to the emergence of the new industrial order.[4]

The convergence of the internet, nano- and biotechnologies; robotics/cobotics (collaboration between humans and collaborative robots); the creation of the cyber physical systems (CPS) for data processing, communication and control; and the emergence of cloud computing (remote processing and storage of data) make it possible to use module-structured industrial facilities, which renders them mobile and adjustable, thereby changing radically the traditional image of the factories and industrial parks of a not too distant past. Industry has stepped into an era of smart processing and development.

Industrial companies are now reshaping their functional schemes, the supply and sales lines, as well as the entire economic model, as an effect of the emergence of the international value chains born of a consensual deregulation that requires a new industrial and corporate culture, where the human factor is expected to play an ever greater role.

Despite its dynamic advantage effects, information and communication technology (ICT) is not the only sector where innovation is fast and abundant; other economic sectors are equally important, and seem, at a perfunctory glance, to have lost some of the interest initially vested in them due to the cyclonic changes brought about by ICT (such as the nanomaterials, composites, injection techniques, new forms of energy and so on).

There are also voices claiming that the relocation of manufacturing processes leaves industrial parks deserted and destroys skills, weakens the middle class, and cleaves an ever deeper divide between highly paid positions and low-competence jobs (concentrated especially in travelling services and the big distribution chains).

New theories have arisen about how states must respond to these new challenges posed by growing tensions between post-industrial labour markets and industrial welfare states (Häusermann and Palier 2008, 559–586). The challenges that they face regarding new employment policies are can summed up as follows: massive unemployment that began in the early 1970s; difficulties in entering the labour market for newcomers; the expansion of atypical/precarious forms of work; increasing income inequality and feminisation of the labour market.

But if these are developments caused by market demands, the question that arises is whether education should be remodelled to respond to such requirements.

The services produced, also called out-of-factory goods, are, most of the time, consumed on the spot, and therefore rarely exported; or if they are, it is as part of exported industrial ware, which, also indirectly, spares them from competition; part of the services belongs to the intermediate consumption for industry (in 2011, consumed services accounted for 39% of the European value added to the export of manufactured goods to non-European countries).

In general, industry is the sector where 80% of all innovations happen, and 75% of Europe's exports; a quarter of the purchasing transactions in industry are for services; 80% of the manufacturing costs arise from how a product was envisaged in its design stage; in 2010, 80% of the in-house spending for research and development in France was concentrated in industry, and only 18% was in services.

In most of the developed countries, industry is the main source of monetary externalities and *knowledge*; research is a pillar of sustainable development; industrial ventures can cope with competition thanks to research, which is a source of new knowledge, of new products, of new manufacturing technologies, at a low cost and yet with the possibility to ensure the diversity and quality of goods, which, in turn, translates into productivity and better living standards.

In 2013, in France for example, industrial ventures spent 24.1 bn. euro for research, distributed as follows: 3.95 bn. euro in car manufacturing, 3.5 bn. euro in spacecraft industry, 3.1 bn. euro in pharmaceuticals, 1.8 bn. euro in the chemical industry, 1.6 bn. euro in the manufacture of measuring apparatuses, 1 bn. euro each on the manufacture of telecommunication, electrical and other machinery and equipment. The total number of researchers in France grew from 100,000 in 1985 to 266,000 in 2013.

In the same reference year, 2013, Romania spent 558 mil. for all of its research activity (0.4% of the GDP), compared to 79.7 bn. euro in Germany, 47.5 bn. euro in France, 34 bn. euro in the United Kingdom, 21 bn. euro in Italy, 14.4 bn. euro in Sweden, 13 bn. euro in Spain, 9.6 bn. euro in Austria and Belgium, 7.8 bn. euro in Denmark, 6.7 bn. euro in Finland, 3.4 bn. euro in Poland, 3 bn. euro in the Czech Republic, 935 mil. euro in Slovenia *et cetera*.

Industrial decomposition in Romania rendered useless dozens of institutes for research and technological development and forced tens of thousands of researchers to resort to petty business schemes for survival, such as selling second-hand clothing or dealing in scrap iron, among others.

It is very unlikely that reindustrialisation by way of innovation and smart processing, or, in general terms, the competitive development of industry, would be possible without investment in research and development.

But small and medium companies cannot afford to invest in research and development, which is why the only sources of money for industrial innovation are the public budget, and the European funds.

The new products resulting from research and development will generate growth and competitiveness in other sectors, so as computers (for example, boosted productivity, helped the diversification and celerity of banking services, brought radical changes in the health system, and in the production of pharmaceuticals *et cetera*).

Gradually, the loss of property over the raw materials and natural resources has been exacerbated by the loss of intellectual property. The deindustrialisation of Romania has meant not only the physical disappearance of more than 1000 industrial platforms and of the physical possession thereof; it has meant the disappearance of drawings, schemes, blueprints and all the technical knowledge and know-how related to the goods and products that the Romanian industry used to manufacture, and which formed *an enormous wealth of intellectual property, now lost*, because it wasn't even considered as an asset in the negotiation of the privatisation agreements.

The view of the German Government is that industry is the economic and social engine of Europe, and Gary P. Pisano and Willy C. Shih (Harvard) explained, in 2009, why America needs" a manufacturing renaissance", if it seeks prosperity (Pisano and Shih 2012).

The purpose of industry is not to create companies that are highly priced on the stock exchange, to bring quick money into the pockets of a few shareholders; sadly, however, many companies make more and faster money by means of financial speculation than by production proper.

Such a money-centred, short-term vision prefers to sacrifice profitable operations if investment therein fails to fetch super-financial gains; this thinking is detrimental to capital assets, which are one of the pillars of economic development, and a fundamental component of investments and intermediate consumption in any economy.

A new type of accounting has been proposed which cuts the value chain into separate items, so that low-paid jobs that cannot be outsourced are deleted; very often, in industry, the logical connection between the upstream and downstream jobs, which is indispensable for the integration as early as the design phase of a product features that require the consistency between all the links in the chain—manufacturing, logistic, sales, post-sales—is all but gone.

One is at risk of failing to see that advanced automation, though capable of provide high performance, may, if not properly integrated with design, generate losses. On the average, 80% of the manufacturing cost arises from how the product is designed.

The new goals—centred directly to profit—make managers from industry to ignore sometimes the medium and long-term perspectives; more attention is paid to decrease variable costs (salaries and operation costs), to the detriment of fixed costs (which are also an expression of the quality of management).

An analysis of downsizing announcement, drawing on 714 large, publicly held US firms, between 1981–2006, shows that pressure from institutional investors and the new decision context encouraged firms to downsize more frequently, due to the strong link between the rise of shareholder value and the recent prevalence of downsizing. Under these circumstances, shareholder-value-oriented managers are using downsizing as a strategy to manage shareholder value and to signal to investors their commitment to increasing value (Jung 2015). Building on resource-dependence theory and demonstrating these firm-level processes that have led to the rise of downsizing as a shareholder-value strategy, Jung (2015) has pursued the sociological research on growing job insecurity and income inequality over the past three decades.

Organisation and cultural factors may cause costs to rise by 30% when a product is made in segments, by different manufacturers. (Toyota's product quality does not derive from the number of robots used in the manufacturing process, but from the management of their human resources, where people are not treated as mere robots).

Information and communication technology provides an advantage for those companies that have modelled their internal organisation to fit the requirements of the new technologies and that have the necessary culture, governance, vision and collaborative attitude between their subsystems and corresponding job chart, because results are never linear.

The decisive factors for the future are not necessarily technical or financial, they are mostly immaterial in nature—strategies, innovation and adequate anticipation necessary to make an industrial venture viable and competitive.

Competitiveness factors and indicators cannot be developed and applied globally for an entire industry or for all territories. There are big differences among sectors, branches, products and territories; therefore the effort must be made to adjust to them specifically.

From the regional policy perspective, as highlighted by Meliciani and Savona (2015, 387–416), it is extremely important to have the ability to build on regions' existing specialisation, ensuring technological rejuvenation of traditional sectors and moving towards knowledge-based sectors. Under these circumstances, an appropriate mix of innovation and industrial policy might favour the revamping of old manufacturing and rural areas, which would entail an increasing demand for knowledge-based services and an upgrading of the sectoral specialisation, enhancing knowledge spillovers and innovation.

There is a dedicated literature which analyses the intensity of competitiveness factors and indicators by groups of industries, branches and sub-branches which can serve as useful reference. A good example are the contributions to the *Manufacturing the Future* (Global McKinsey Institute 2012) (Tables 1.4 and 1.5).

A quick glance at the drivers behind the industrial strategies of various states reveals what they have in common: a move towards industry 4.0, through renewal of the means of production and development of technologies based on ICT, robotics, automation and vocational training.

For several decades—the past three, to be more exact—global economic organisations and institutions, including the EU, have viewed industrial policies as a way to distort market trends as a barrier against the efficient allocation of resources in a market economy, which is why the state's top-to-bottom (vertical) interventions (through subsidies, state shareholding, customs revenues or public markets) have been replaced by horizontal measures (putting in place favourable conditions for innovation and company formation).

Surprisingly, the European Commission (EC), in 2010 and 2012, the World Bank (WB) in 2013 and the OECD in 2013 radically changed their position on these topics.

The EC reviewed its stance with regard to the place of industry in the economy, and to public intervention, stressing that a highly competitive manufacturing sector can provide the resources and many potential

Table 1.4 Manufacturing factor intensity level, by groups of industries

Group of industries	Industrial sub-branches/branches	Intensity of research and develop ment (%)	Intensity of labour	Intensity of capital (%)	Intensity of energy (%)	Intensity of trade (%)	Density of value
Industries generating global innovation for local markets (34% of GVA in the manufacturing industry worldwide, 2010)	Chemical products	High	Low	High	Medium-high	Medium-high	Medium-low
	Motor vehicles, trailers, and-trailers	Medium-high	Low	Medium-low	Medium-low	Medium-high	Medium-high
	Other means of transport	High	Medium-high	Low	Low	Medium-high	Medium-high
	Electric machinery	Medium-high	Medium-low	Low	Medium-low	Medium-high	Medium-high
	Machines, machinery and equipment	Medium-high	Medium-low	Low	Medium-low	Medium-high	Medium-high
Regional manufacturing industries (28%)	Rubber and plastics	Medium-high	Medium-high	Medium-low	Medium-high	Medium-low	Medium-high
	Metal structures and metal products	Low	High	Low	Medium-high	Low	Medium-low
	Food, beverages, tobacco	Medium-low	High	High	Medium-high	Low	Low
	Publishing and printing	Medium-low	Medium-high	Medium-low	Medium-low	Low	Medium-low

(*continued*)

Table 1.4 (continued)

Group of industries	Industrial sub-branches/branches	Intensity of research and develop ment (%)	Intensity of labour	Intensity of capital (%)	Intensity of energy (%)	Intensity of trade (%)	Density of value
Energy- and Resource-intensive industries (22%)	Products of wood	Low	High	Medium-high	High	Low	Low
	Oil refining, coking coal, and nuclear industries	Low	Low	High	High	Medium-low	Low
	Paper and pulp	Medium-low	Medium-high	Medium-high	High	Medium-low	Low
	Other, non-metallic, mineral products	Medium-high	Medium-high	Medium-high	High	Low	Low
	Metallurgical products	Low	Low	High	High	Medium-low	Medium-low
Innovative global industries and technologies (9%)	Computers and office machinery	High	Medium-low	High	Low	High	High
	Semiconduc-tors and electronics	High	Low	Medium-high	Low	High	High
	Medical, optical, and high-precision apparatuses	High	Medium-low	Medium-high	Low	High	High

(continued)

Table 1.4 (continued)

Group of industries	Industrial sub-branches/branches	Intensity of research and develop ment (%)	Intensity of labour	Intensity of capital (%)	Intensity of energy (%)	Intensity of trade (%)	Density of value
Labour-intensive industries (7%)	Textiles, footwear and leather goods	Medium-low	High	Low	Medium-high	High	Medium-high
	Furniture, jewellery, toys, etc.	Medium-low	High	Medium-low	Low	High	Medium-high

Source: Based on *Manufacturing the Future*, Global McKinsey Institute, SUA, 2012

Note: Intensity of research and development = Research and development spending/Gross value added × 100 (USA, 2007); Intensity of labour = Work hours per 1000 USD gross value added (EU 15, 2007); Intensity of capital = Gross operating surplus/Gross value added × 100 (world average 2006–2010); Intensity of energy = Cost of purchase of fuels and electric power/Gross value added × 100 (USA, 2010); Intensity of trade = Exports/Gross production × 100 (world average 2006–2010); Density of value = Worth of shipped goods/quantity of shipped ware (USD in thousands/tonne, USA, 2007)

Table 1.5 Manufacturing factor intensity, by groups of industries

Group of industries	Industrial sub-branches/branches	Intensity of research and development (%)	Intensity of labour	Intensity of capital (%)	Intensity of energy (%)	Intensity of trade (%)	Density of value
Industries generating global innovation for local markets (34% of GVA in the manufacturing industry worldwide, 2010)	Chemical products	25	10	50	5	42	1
	Motor vehicles, trailers and semi-trailers	16	14	32	2	39	8
	Other means of transport	25	19	29	1	42	8
	Electrical machines	6	17	30	2	46	7
	Machines, machinery and equipment	8	18	32	2	48	8
Regional manufacturing industries (28%)	Rubber and plastics	3	21	33	5	21	3
	Metal structures and metal products	1	23	28	3	14	3
	Food, beverages, tobacco	2	23	40	4	15	1
	Publishing and printing	2	19	33	3	4	3
Resource-and energy-intensive industries (22%)	Wood products	1	31	35	7	13	0.5
	Refining of crude oil, coal coking, nuclear industries	1	6	56	10	21	0.4
	Pulp and paper	2	18	37	10	24	1
	Other, non-metallic, mineral products	3	20	39	11	14	0.1
	Metal products	1	14	41	14	26	1

(continued)

Table 1.5 (continued)

Group of industries	Industrial sub-branches/branches	Intensity of research and development (%)	Intensity of labour	Intensity of capital (%)	Intensity of energy (%)	Intensity of trade (%)	Density of value
Innovative global industries and technologies (9%)	Computers and office equipment	25	15	41	1	91	72
	Semi-conductors and electronic equipment	33	15	38	1	60	
	Medical, optical, and precision apparatuses	35	17	40	1	57	
Labour-intensive industries (7%)	Textiles, footwear, and leather products	2	35	31	5	50	5
	Furniture, jewellery, toys, etc..	2	30	33	1	69	4

Source: Base on *Manufacturing the future*, Global McKinsey Institute, 2012

Note: Intensity of research and development = Research and development spending/Gross value added × 100 (USA, 2007); Intensity of labour = Work hours per 1000 US Dollars gross value added (EU 15, 2007); Intensity of capital = Gross operating surplus/Gross value added × 100 (world average 2006–2010); Intensity of energy = Cost of purchase of fuels and electric power/Gross value added × 100 (SUA, 2010); Intensity of trade = Exports/Gross production × 100 (world average 2006–2010); Density of value = Worth of shipped goods/Quantity of shipped ware (USD in thousands/tonne, USA 2007)

solutions to the societal challenges that EU is facing, such as climate change, the health of the ageing population and the development of a healthy, safe and secure society.[5] This EU key document speaks of merging vertical and horizontal policies into a uniform approach to sectors like aerospace engineering, environmental goods and services, health, security and energy-intensive sectors with high exposure to international competition. In 2012, the EC clearly spelled out its interest in advanced technologies for bio-industry, construction, use of environment-friendly materials and smart development and vehicles.

The concept of "new industrial policy and innovation in enterprises" proposed by the WB is intended not only to create a favourable environment (horizontal policy), or to render support to certain industrial sectors (vertical policy), but also to encourage restructuring and dynamic technological advance.

Another dimension of this new policy is a straightforward approach to the elements of political economy involved in public interventions in industry. This new approach is designed to replace the traditional opposition between horizontal and vertical through corrections of various types of "coordination and market failures", by designing modes of action by the public authorities in consideration of the principles of political economy.

The *first coordination failure* is the correlation between public and private research, between universities and enterprises or between the large corporations and the small enterprises. Some experts claim that cluster policies can address the coordination issue between corporate research activities.

The *second market failure* is private companies' inability to valorise, on the market, the externalities of research, because analysts claim that from a social perspective, private companies do not integrate externalities in their economic calculus.

The *third market failure* regards trans-border mergers and acquisitions: some hold that the market is not always able to distinguish between socially desirable and socially non-desirable international transactions.

Another market failure is that access to finance, particularly in the case of small and medium enterprises (SMEs), and intermediate-sized enterprises, is closely connected to the fact that everybody is interested in drawing benefits from the existing innovative potential rather than investing in new research projects, which are viewed more like a complement to, rather than a substitute for, public involvement.

And, finally, related to value chains, new challenges have brought about the fragmentation of the production chain for the manufacture of certain products[6]; this causes changes in revenue formation, growth and the very nature of competition between countries; it generates a closer interdependence and a stronger need for cooperation, which, in turn, render the governance of world trade more and more complex.

For a variety of reasons, we are witnessing a process of *relocalisation and desegmentation* of the value chains (growing salaries and the need for qualified labour in emerging countries, higher transportation costs, volatile foreign exchange rates, political risk, difficulties in ensuring quality control, protection of intellectual property and the decline or stagnation of the price of energy at world level). Regarding this trend, Patrick Artus (2014) warned that countries that lose their production apparatus are at risk of becoming economies based on domestic services, with a low living standard.

Notes

1. *Steel Statistical Yearbook*, World Steel Association, various editions, 1960–2015.
2. *L'avenir de l'industrie*, in Problemes economiques, France, No. 3137/August 2016, p. 5.
3. *Problemes economiques*, France, No. 3137/August 2016, p. 6.
4. See also (Szirmai 2011) and (Szirmai et al. 2013).
5. Communications from the Commission to the European Parliament, the Council, the European Economic and Social Council, and the Committee of the Regions, *An Integrated Industrial Policy for the Globalisation Era. Putting Competitiveness and Sustainability at Centre Stage* and *A Stronger European Industry for Growth and Economic Recovery*, COM (2010) 614 final and COM (2012) 582 final, p. 4.
6. *Problemes economiques*, France, No. 3137/2016, p. 33.

References

Artus, Patrick. 2014. Une nouvelle vague des delocalisations se profile. *Natixis*, 425.

Bernard, Andrew B., Valerie Smeets, and Frederic Warzynski. 2017. Rethinking Deindustrialization. *Economic Policy* 32 (89): 5–38.

Bluestone, Barry, and Bennett Harisson. 1982. *The Deindustrialization of America*. New York: Basic Books. http://www.d.umn.edu/~epeters5/Cst1201/Articles/Deindustrialization%20of%20America.pdf.

Chatillon, Alain. 2011. *Rapport d'information sur la deindustrialisation des territories*. No. 403, Senat France. http://www.senat.fr/notice-rapport/2010/r10-403-1-notice.html

Ciutacu, Constantin, and Luminiţa Chivu. 2015. Romania's Deindustrialisation. From the "Golden Age" to the "Iron Scrap Age". *Procedia Economics and Finance* 22: 209–216. http://www.sciencedirect.com/science/article/pii/S2212567115002646?via%3Dihub.

Grabas, Christian, and Alexander Nutzenadel. 2013. *Industrial Policies in Europe in Historical Perspective*. Working Paper No. 15, Work Package 306, European Commission, WWW for Europe Project, July.

Häusermann, Silja, and Bruno Palier. 2008. The Politics of Employment-Friendly Welfare Reforms in Post-industrial Economies. *Socioecon Review* 6 (3): 559–586. https://doi.org/10.1093/ser/mwn011.

Jung, Jiwook. 2015. Shareholder Value and Workforce Downsizing, 1981–2006. *Social Forces* 93 (4): 1335–1368.

L'avenir de l'industrie. 2016. In Problemes economiques, France, No. 3137/August 2016, pp. 5–6.

Manufacturing the Future. 2012. Global McKinsey Institute, SUA.

Meliciani, Valentina, and Maria Savona. 2015. The Determinants of Regional Specialisation in Business Services: Agglomeration Economies, Vertical Linkages and Innovation. *Journal of Economic Geography* 15 (2): 387–416. https://doi.org/10.1093/jeg/lbt038.

Pisano, Gary P., and Willy Shih. 2012. *Producing Prosperity: Why America Needs a Manufacturing Renaissance*. Boston, MA: Harvard Business Review Press.

Schwab, Klaus. 2015. The Fourth Industrial Revolution. What It Means and How to Respond. *Foreign Affairs*. https://www.foreignaffairs.com/articles/2015-12-12/fourth-industrial-revolution

Steel Statistical Yearbook. World Steel Association, various editions, 1960–2015.

Szirmai, A. 2011. *Manufacturing and Economic Development*. UNU-WIDER Working Paper No. 2011/75, Helsinki, November.

Szirmai, A., et al. 2013. *Pathways to Industrialization in the Twenty-First Century—New Challenges and Emerging Paradigms*. WIDER Studies in Development Economics, Oxford University Press.

2

Macroeconomic Changes in Romania During the Transition Period

2.1 The Macroeconomic Picture of Transition

Since 1990, Romania's economy has undergone a transition from the centralized economic system to an economy based on free initiative and market mechanisms.

The mutation from a private sector contribution to GDP of 16.4% in 1990 to more than 75% in 2015 was achieved through complex transformations across society and all sectors of the economy. During this period decision-makers, state institutions, companies, and individuals experienced a process of learning and permanent adaptation.

At the beginning of 1990, the Romanian economy was an overwhelming state-owned and super-centralized economy; the economy comprised almost exclusively state-owned enterprises and production cooperatives that were extremely large, and most of their output was destined for investment and export goods.

The sudden dismantling of CMEA (Council for Mutual Economic Assistance) in October 1991 and the dissolution of Eastern European market; the collapse of the domestic market, which had been dominated by economic agents with low flexibility; the liberalization of prices

L. Chivu et al., *Deindustrialization and Reindustrialization in Romania*,
DOI 10.1007/978-3-319-65753-0_2

(November, 1990) and the loss of significant export market segments caused a severe economic recession.

During the first decade post-communism, the transition to a market economy brought some economic reforms and restructuring, especially in terms of privatization and fundamental changes in economic and employment structures. The process itself was notably complex, complicated and difficult, as it was hard to harmonize and synchronize the individual components—economic, institutional-legal, social, political, cultural-educational, mental, and psychological among others. Often, the economic and technological sides of the restructuring outpaced the institutional, legal, political and social-cultural components and have resulted in the first decade in a dramatically decreased GDP, substantial changes in the structure of gross added value and employment, galloping and persistent inflation and high unemployment (Ciutacu and Chivu 2010).

Among other essential elements in the process of law building, the institutions of the market economy had a special importance. In this regard, the first interim government in 1990 dismantled the centralized economy, transforming the former State Committee of Planning into the Ministry of National Economy.

In 1990, a decree for the promotion of free initiative was promulgated, followed by the institution of Law No. 31, which transformed state-owned enterprises into commercial companies; in 1991 Law No. 58 on the privatization of commercial companies was promulgated, followed by a whole series of laws (Law No. 77/1994 and Law No. 55/1995, etc.) which fundamentally changed the property-ownership structure of the Romanian economy.

Prior to 1990, the economic environment had been based on the fundamentals of vertical (enterprise, central unit, ministry), but also horizontal, integration and value chains (e.g., mining industry—primary processing industry—secondary processing industry—trade enterprise, or agriculture—agro-food industry—trade). That economy, in which the workers were common owners of companies' assets, did not necessarily focus on the profit of each link, but rather the value added to the whole value chain and "full employment". The new legal framework laid the foundations for a competitive environment in which each link, company or person had the freedom to handle its own business.

Despite the enthusiasm for the new climate of freedom and initiative brought about by these profound changes, in the context of mass privatization, lack of experience, coupled with a lack of financial liquidity and specific support mechanisms, in many borderline cases lead to heavy layoffs, loss of assets or even dismantling of companies. In fact, in most countries in transition, repercussions on wealth and income distribution and on social structure caused by large-scale privatization have been unavoidable (Chilosi 1996, 75–93).

The property destructuring and restructuring that took place in Romania can be summarized as follows: starting from a total of 197,000 enterprises (more than 90% of them large) in 1989, in 2015 a total of 513,989 companies (out of which 95% were small and medium-sized enterprises) were registered.

In agriculture, the land law (Law no. 18/1991) laid the foundations for a dual mechanism of land reform and the reestablishment of land ownership rights. The result of retrocession can be summarized as follows: at the beginning of the transition, 85% of the agricultural land was owned by the state or agricultural cooperatives; in 2015, a total of 93.6% of the agricultural lands were private property, divided into 3,629,656 agricultural holdings, of which 3,601,776 were without legal status (subsistence farms with an area of less than 5 hectares, divided into two to three plots separated by large distances). The remainder, 27,880 holdings, had legal status. The excessive fragmentation of land, the advanced age and the lack of financial resources of the new landowners (necessary for the efficient exploitation of the land) and the lack of support mechanisms for setting up networks for collecting and selling agricultural products led to a gradual loss of important segments of the internal market for agro-food products.

In the service sector, under-dimensioned in the centralized economy in Romania, in addition to the privatization or concession of large electricity transport and distribution companies, the concession of local interest services; the transfer of educational, health and cultural services to private operators; and the expansion of financial and banking services and telecommunications led to an increase in the number of service companies from 190,000 in 1989 to 463,460 in 2015 (of which over 200,000 had no employees). Most businesses in the service sector—171,959 (of which 99.9% were small to medium-sized enterprises [SMEs])—were in commerce, followed by construction with 48,341 companies (99.8% SMEs), transport and storage with 41,746 companies (99.7% SMEs), hotels and restaurants with 25,497 companies (99.9% SMEs) and IT with 20,619 companies (99.6% SMEs).

In 2015, a total of 297,148 private entrepreneurs were active in the economy, including 15,869 family businesses and 274,065 independents.

The magnitude and complexity of the transformations have always been reflected in the evolution of institutional architectures: the Romanian Agency for Investment and International Technical Assistance (1990), then the Romanian Agency for Foreign Investments and, since 2014, the Department for Foreign Investments and Public-Private Partnership, within the government's internal structure; the National Agency for Privatization and Small and Medium Enterprises Development (1991), the Department for Reform and Economic Integration (1991), the Coordination, Strategy and Economic Reform Council and the European Integration Department (1992), the Ministry of Integration, Local Public Administration (1991), later Ministry of Administration and Interior and Ministry of Internal Affairs; the State Property Fund, transformed in 2001 into the Authority for Privatization and State Ownership Management and merged in 2004 with the Authority for the Capitalising of Banking Assets (established in 1998) and transformed into the Authority for the Valuation of the State Assets in 2012; five Regional Private Property Funds, transformed into five Financial Investment Companies (1996); the Romanian Development Agency, merged in 2000 with the National Agency for Small and Medium Enterprises and the National Agency for Regional Development; Restructuring Agency (1994), Department for Relations with Trade Unions and Employers (1994), Stock Exchange (1995), National Securities Commission, Court of Accounts, Competition Council, National Authority for Consumer Protection, among others.

The institutional construction—referring both to the rule of law and to the specific aspects of the functioning of the market economy—has seen two distinct periods, not only from the point of view of the architecture of the institutions, but also from the perspective of the mechanisms of action, the content and the way of functioning.

After the events of February 1, 1995, when the Agreement for Romania's Association to the EU was promulgated, and June 22, 1995, when Romania officially submitted its application for the EU membership, with the support of all its political forces, the pace and content of the reforms changed significantly. In December 1999, Romania was invited by the EC to the accession negotiations; and, from 2000 to 2005, all the negotiation files were closed.

This process, besides the efforts for the proper transposition of the Acquis Communautaire, has involved another kind of transformation and restructuring that has had an impact especially on the level of administrative, managerial and anticipatory capacity.

In accordance with the EC timetable, Romania signed the Accession Treaty in 2005 and, on January 1, 2007, became a full member of the EU.

Since April 1, 2004, Romania has also been a full member of NATO.

A retrospective look at the processes of transition and economic reforms in Romania shows that a gradual strategy has been adopted, in which the economic shocks were less drastic in the first years, later becoming more and more painful. Although initially it seemed that the transition would take place at most over the medium term, it has had a long-term impact. The internal processes of the institutions' profound restructuring and the market economy mechanisms overlapped with the efforts required by the political and institutional–legal reforms necessary for NATO and EU integration.

In the first decade of transition, the GDP experienced dramatic falls (Table 2.1). Only after 2000, did the GDP reach, in real terms, the pre-transition level, though obviously in a significantly different structure.

Starting in 2000, the economy has grown, sometimes even spectacularly, and consumption—supported by loans—has boosted expansion since 2008. Starting with 2008, the effects of the global economic and financial crisis have made their presence felt, highlighting the fragility of macroeconomic balances. Against the backdrop of the global economic downturn, it has been noticed that Romanians consume more than just products; and for macroeconomic balance, new sectoral restructurings and reductions in the number of employees, especially in the public sector, are needed.

Table 2.1 The macroeconomic indicators, 1990–2015

		1990	1995	2000	2005	2007	2010	2011	2012	2013	2014	2015
GDP (bn. euro, current prices)		31.26	29.09	40.58	79.75	124.65	126.80	133.34	133.90	144.28	150.63	160.37
GDP index in euro (%)		100.0	93.1	129.8	255.1	398.8	405.6	426.6	428.3	461.5	481.9	513.2
Real GDP index (%)		100.0	89.7	87.9	116.1	133.2	132.0	134.9	135.7	140.3	144.4	149.9
Industrial production (bn. euro, current prices)		42.38	22.94	31.67	58.25	82.73	80.62	89.01	86.4	88.2	…	….
Gross value added in industry (bn. euro, current prices)		12.7	8.7	10.1	20.0	29.0	35.5	38.0	33.5	36.3	37.4	…
Real value index of the production (%)	Industry (%)	100.0	65.4	58.1	72.7	82.1	89.7	94.7	90.5	99.7	102.9	105.7
	Manufacturing industry (%)	100.0	62.7	57.9	76.4	87.7	98.5	104.0	96.1	107.5	112.4	116.3
	Mining/extraction industry (%)	100.0	83.0	65.1	65.7	67.1	81.1	56.7	97.3	97.9	101.9	89.2
	Electricity, heating, gas and water (%)	100.0	79.2	58.5	53.2	55.0	59.4	63.2	71.5	74.1	68.8	69.7
Added value index (%)	Manufacturing industry	100.0	75.9	74.9	100.8	115.5	117.2	114.5	108.7	117.3	…	…
	Mining/extraction industry	100.0	64.5	50.4	49.0	49.9	51.9	42.8	35.0	24.6	…	…
	Production of electricity, heating, gas, and water	100.0	420.3	281.0	275.6	286.0	316.4	387.6	356.6	342.3	…	…
Total net investment (bn. euro, current prices)	National economy	6.1	4.9	6.3	13.2	25.1	17.2	20.7	20.0	18.3	19.4	…
	Industry	2.8	2.1	2.5	4.9	8.2	6.5	7.8	7.97	7.84	7.89	…

Source: Authors' own compilation based on the NIS and NBR data
Note: … = Not available data

These changes have also overlapped with the effects of the four freedoms of the internal market of the EU, for which the Romanian economy and, in particular, the economic agents, have not been sufficiently prepared. The years following the transition have been marked by increased public and private external debt; growing external trade deficits (especially in relation to the EU member states); the loss, mainly by the domestic companies, of important segments of the domestic market; and the migration of important population contingents (especially young and highly skilled people), leading to skilled labour shortages in many sectors of the economy.[1]

In recent years, following macro-stabilization efforts, the economic indicators have resumed their upward trend. Starting in 2013, macroeconomic statistics signal an exit from the crisis, and investors' perceptions about the risk of businesses in Romania have improved further since then.

In 2015, Romania's GDP, expressed in euro, totalled approximately 160.4 bn. euro, compared to 31.3 bn. euro in 1990, 40.6 bn. euro in 2000 and 124.6 bn. euro in 2007, which was the year of Romania's accession to the EU (Table 2.6).

In constant prices, compared to 1990, the GDP index for 2015 stood at 149.9%. In current euro, the nominal value of the GDP was 5.1 times bigger in 2015 than in 1990.

As to the GDP per capita, in purchasing power standards, Romania's convergence process is on the rise: 34% of the EU 28 average in 2004, and 57% in 2015 (Table 2.2).

In addition to the information provided by the Table 2.2, the convergence can be also demonstrated by the share Romania holds of the total GVA generated by the EU 28 member countries. While in 2000, Romania's share of the overall EU GVA was only 0.44%, this share had grown to 1% in 2007, and to 1.09% in 2008; the onset of the economic crisis pushed this ratio down to approximately 1% in 2010; it then rose again slightly, reaching 1.08% in 2015. Eurostat detailed statistics indicate that Romania's share of the total EU GVA was higher in agriculture (2.4% in 2000, 4.3% in 2006, 4.8% in 2008, 3.9% in 2010 and 3.6% in 2015), while Romania's share of the EU 28 GVA in industry was 0.6% in 2000, 1.4% in 2007, 1.7% in 2010 and 1.6% in 2015.

Table 2.2 The GDP per capita, in purchasing power standards (EU 28 = 100.0)

	2004	2007	2010	2011	2012	2013	2014	2015
EU 28	100	100	100	100	100	100	100	100
Belgium	121	115	120	120	120	120	118	117
Bulgaria	34	40	43	44	46	46	47	46
Czech Rep.	79	84	81	83	82	83	84	85
Denmark	125	122	126	126	124	124	126	125
Germany	116	116	119	122	124	124	126	125
Estonia	55	69	63	68	74	75	76	74
Ireland	143	147	129	130	131	131	134	145
Greece	95	91	87	77	74	74	73	71
Spain	100	103	98	95	92	91	91	92
France	110	107	108	108	107	108	107	106
Croatia	57	61	59	60	60	59	59	58
Italy	108	105	104	103	101	98	96	95
Cyprus	97	100	102	96	91	84	82	81
Latvia	48	60	53	57	60	62	64	64
Lithuania	50	61	60	65	70	73	75	74
Luxembourg	246	254	254	265	258	264	266	271
Hungary	62	61	65	65	65	66	68	68
Malta	81	78	86	84	84	86	86	89
Netherlands	133	136	135	135	132	132	131	129
Austria	128	123	126	128	131	131	129	127
Poland	49	53	62	64	66	67	68	69
Portugal	77	79	81	78	77	77	78	77
Romania	**34**	**42**	**50**	**51**	**54**	**54**	**55**	**57**
Slovenia	86	87	83	83	81	80	82	83
Slovakia	57	67	73	73	74	76	77	77
Finland	117	118	115	117	115	113	110	108
Sweden	129	128	126	127	127	124	123	123
United Kingdom	125	118	108	106	107	108	109	110

Source: Eurostat data

2.2 Developments in Sectoral Structures

In the past 25 years, the *sectoral structure* of the national economy has undergone significant changes. The data in the *National Accounts* system indicate that, for the entire economy, the gross production expressed in current euro (by converting into euro the annual production expressed in lei, at the annual average leu/euro exchange rate published by the National Bank of Romania, NBR) moved from 76.2 bn. ecu in 1990 to 302.79 bn. euro in 2014 (Table 2.3, Appendix A.1).

Table 2.3 The evolution of the gross production, intermediate consumption and gross value added, by economic sectors (current bn. euro)

Branch	Indicator	1990	1995	2000	2005	2007	2008	2009	2010	2011	2012	2013	2014
National economy, total	Gross production	76.22	60.86	78.63	151.21	234.92	267.65	230.57	244.74	266.90	268.60	288.73	302.79
	Intermediate consumption	47.50	33.45	42.18	80.77	124.55	143.14	124.14	133.96	149.90	151.00	162.42	169.77
	Gross value added	28.72	27.41	36.45	70.44	110.37	124.51	106.43	110.78	117.00	117.60	126.31	133.02
Agriculture, forestry, fishing	Gross production	11.14	9.62	8.53	13.70	15.86	19.90	15.92	15.31	17.20	13.40	16.46	15.67
	Intermediate consumption	4.32	4.37	4.14	6.99	8.68	10.63	8.30	8.21	8.60	7.10	8.72	8.56
	Gross value added	6.82	5.25	4.39	6.71	7.18	9.27	7.62	7.10	8.60	6.30	7.75	7.10
Industry and construction	Gross production	49.98	32.01	37.34	70.74	112.16	125.16	108.64	115.87	126.00	124.40	130.42	130.03
	Intermediate consumption	35.64	21.47	24.81	45.74	70.48	78.86	68.48	70.98	79.40	81.70	85.58	83.78
	Gross value added	14.34	10.54	12.53	25.00	41.68	46.30	40.16	44.89	46.60	42.70	44.84	46.24
Services	Gross production	15.1	19.23	32.76	66.77	106.9	122.59	106.01	113.56	123.70	130.8	141.85	157.09
	Intermediate consumption	7.54	7.61	13.23	28.04	45.39	53.65	47.36	54.77	61.90	62.20	68.12	77.42
	Gross value added	7.56	11.62	19.53	38.73	61.51	68.94	58.65	58.79	61.8	68.6	73.72	79.67

Source: Authors' own compilation based on data from Romania's *Statistic Yearbook*, NIS, Bucharest, various editions, and NBR data

The gross value added in agriculture grew from 6.8 bn. euro in 1990 to 7.1 bn. euro in 2014. The highest value of this indicator was reached in 2008 (9.27 bn. euro), and the lowest was recorded in 2000 (4.39 bn. euro).

Services was a sector that contributed to GAV with 7.6 bn. euro in 1990, 68.9 bn. euro in 2008, 58.8 bn. euro in 2010 and 79.7 bn. euro in 2014.

From a relative point of view, agriculture lost part of its share in the total gross production of the economy, from 14.6% in 1990 to 6.3% in 2010 and to 5.2% in 2014, with intermediate consumption following a descending trend, from 9% to 6% in 2010 and to 5.0% in 2014, with a similar decline in its contribution to the total GVA from 23.7% in 1990 to 12.1% in 2000, 6.4% in 2010 and 5.3% in 2014 (Table 2.4).

Industry and construction also reduced their contribution to gross production (from 65.6% in 1990 to 42.9% in 2014), to intermediate consumption (from 75% to 49.4%) and to the GVA (49.9% in 1990 and 34.8% in 2014, after a low of 34.4% in 2000).

The growth in the services sector is visible for all the three indicators, particularly for intermediate consumption (from 15.9% in 1990 to 45.6% in 2014), and the GVA (from 26.3% in 1990, to 55.7% in 2007 and to 59.9% in 2014).

On the other hand, the statistical data above reveal that the services sector was more exposed to the negative effects of the economic and financial crisis than was the industrial sector.

The real index of gross production, intermediate consumption and GVA shows that, from 1990 to 2014, overall growth in the economy was 2.8 times for intermediate consumption, 2.13 times for gross production and 1.53 times for the GVA (Appendix A.2).

In real terms, the highest increase of the GVA compared to 1990 took place in 2014: production and supply of electricity, heating, gas and hot water (3.71 times); followed by commerce (3.14 times); construction (2.58 times); and transport, warehousing and communications (1.48 times), while in the manufacturing industry, the GVA increased only 1.25 times.

During the same interval, the GVA underwent a downward trend in the extraction/mining industries (to 16.0% less than the GVA in 1990), the hotel and restaurant sector (down to 70.2% of the 1990 level), as well as in agriculture, forestry and fishing (down to 92.5% of the 1990 level). (Appendix A.2).

Table 2.4 The structure of the gross production, intermediate consumption and gross value added, by economic sectors (%, prices for each year, total economy = 100.0)

Branch	Indicator	1990	1995	2000	2005	2007	2008	2009	2010	2011	2012	2011	2012	2013	2014
Agriculture, forestry, fishing	Gross production	14.6	15.8	10.9	9.1	6.8	7.4	6.9	6.3	6.4	5.0	6.44	4.99	5.70	5.17
	Intermediate consumption	9.1	13.1	9.8	8.7	7.0	7.4	6.7	6.1	11.5	8.9	5.74	4.70	5.37	5.04
	Gross value added	23.7	19.2	12.1	9.5	6.5	7.4	7.2	6.4	7.4	5.4	7.35	5.36	6.13	5.34
Industry and constructions	Gross production	65.6	52.6	47.5	46.8	47.7	46.8	47.1	47.3	47.2	46.3	47.21	46.31	45.17	42.94
	Intermediate consumption	75.0	64.2	58.8	56.6	56.6	55.1	55.2	53.0	53.0	54.1	52.97	54.11	52.69	49.35
	Gross value added	49.9	38.5	34.4	35.5	37.8	37.2	37.7	40.5	39.8	36.3	39.83	36.31	35.50	34.77
Services	Gross production	19.8	31.6	41.7	44.2	45.5	45.8	46.0	46.4	46.3	48.7	46.35	48.70	49.13	51.88
	Intermediate consumption	15.9	22.7	31.4	34.7	36.4	37.5	38.2	40.9	41.2	41.2	41.29	41.19	41.94	45.61
	Gross value added	26.3	42.4	53.6	55.0	55.7	55.4	55.1	53.1	52.8	58.3	52.82	58.33	58.36	59.89

Source: Authors' own compilation based on data from Romania's *Statistic Yearbook*, NIS, and Bucharest

Intermediate consumption grew at a much faster pace than gross production in the overall economy (up 279.87% in 2014 from the 1990 level of intermediate consumption, and 213.48% for gross production). In agriculture, gross production in 2014 rose to 111.81% of the 1990 level and the level of intermediate consumption grew to 157.4%; in the extraction/mining industries, intermediate consumption was approximately equal, and gross production fell to 46.4% of the reference year; in the processing industry, intermediate consumption was 188.9% and gross production was 164.0%.

Energy is the only sector where intermediate consumption grew less that gross production (intermediate consumption in 2014 was 75.8% of the 1990 level, and the gross production was 91.1%).

Viewed from the perspective of the real indices of gross production, intermediate consumption and GVA, for the period 1990–2014 (where 1990 = 100.0), Romania's economy had a very modest (not to say alarmingly poor) evolution.

In 25 years, the total value of the GVA increased by only 53.4%, which represents annual average growth of less than 2%; at such a growth rate, it is hard to imagine that in the following 50–100 years Romania could take such spectacular leaps forward to compensate for the lag in economic development compared to other EU member states.

In spite of big debates during the past 20–25 years regarding the potential for the development of agriculture, tourism and other services, the results have disappointing: in 2014, gross agricultural production represented 111.8% of the production level of 1990, and the GVA of agriculture barely achieved 92.5% of the same reference year. During the same period, gross production in the hotels, restaurants and the catering sector dropped to 85.7% of the 1990 level, and the GVA declined to 70.2%.

2.3 Inflation and the Exchange Rate of the National Currency

Inflation has been one of the persistent characteristics of the economic transition in Romania: if we take consumer prices in 1990 as a reference of 1.0, inflation increased by a factor of 2.892 between 1990 and 2007, and 3.977 between 1990 and 2015.

After Romania's accession to the EU, the average annual growth of consumer prices increased more slowly: from 7.85% in 2008 against 2007, and to 3.14% in 2011 against 2010; prices increased by 4.95% in 2012, by 1.55% in 2013 and by 0.83% in 2014. In 2015, consumer prices dropped by 0.93% (December 2015 against December 2014).

An analysis of the indices of the main prices in the economy reveals a lack of strategic thinking at times, be it at micro-, mezzo- or macroeconomic level (Table 2.5).

The most spectacular growth in an economy that, at least at a declarative level through all information channels, was seeking to achieve competitiveness and a resettlement of its values in consonance with the market requirements, and with the principles of supply and demand—and was doing this in many ways, including with the assistance of the International Monetary Fund (IMF), WB and other internationally known consultants—was in the sector of *catchment, treatment and distribution of water*, where prices in 2015 were 37,564.3 times higher than in 1990!. Following closely behind were the prices in the extraction/mining industries, which grew more than 11,530 times (accompanied by a correspondingly high growth of the subsidies received every year), and the prices for the production, transport and distribution of energy, gas and hot water: 7555.5 times, which, in one word, spells plunder.

The much faster rise in input prices (energy, water, raw materials and so on) compared to output prices has generated tensions and bottlenecks that have affected both companies and the general population.

The GDP deflator shows that prices have risen by a factor of 5830; the price of 1 gram of gold increased to 3792 times its previous level, and the national currency (leu) depreciated relative to euro 1620 times.

In an attempt to understand these flabbergasting developments, we used the following method[2]: we converted the GDP into the equivalent tonnes of gold, and we found that Romania produced, based on the GDP and the price of gold, 2177.4 tonnes of gold in 1990, 1224 tonnes in 1991, 3378 tonnes in 1995, 2680.9 tonnes in 1998, 7686.5 tonnes in 2007, 3207 tonnes in 2012 and 4771.7 tonnes in 2015 (down from 4901 tonnes in 2014).

This raises the question whether it wouldn't have been more profitable for the country to deal only in gold mining from its national natural reserves and trade the gold production on the international stock

Table 2.5 Price index during 1990–2015 (1990 = 100.0)

Year	GDP deflator	Rate of exchange (leu/euro)	Price of 1 gram of gold	Consumer prices	Price of industrial production	Prices in mining industry	Prices in manufacturing industry	Prices for the prod., transp and distrib of energy, gas, hot water	Catchment and distribution of water
1991	295	320	457	27	857	1058	449	1372	1820
1992	885	1458	816	839	1786	2141	1436	2174	1759
1993	2897	3223	1914	2987	4359	5436	3508	5025	4686
1994	6926	7168	4989	7072	11,387	12,242	9446	11,998	14,365
1995	9948	9582	5752	9353	15,383	14,576	13,106	14,313	22,893
1996	14,334	14,076	9609	12,983	23,054	21,536	19,849	19,812	33,071
1997	34,210	29,483	24,321	33,077	58,256	74,753	46,188	63,952	88,564
1998	52,117	36,400	24,436	52,624	77,575	87,783	62,722	81,703	156,294
1999	78,548	59,380	34,939	76,278	110,288	135,205	88,069	116,729	229,745
2000	112,373	72,717	49,239	111,767	167,253	217,689	133,860	166,813	345,626
2001	154,780	94,840	64,358	150,291	227,297	325,227	180,577	231,537	470,743
2002	189,962	113,892	83,614	184,162	278,309	398,153	214,175	334,460	657,727
2003	235,149	136,851	98,501	212,291	330,325	462,589	257,144	375,663	811,530
2004	271,231	147,696	108,846	237,504	393,881	524,848	304,397	470,746	980,887
2005	303,978	132,035	105,829	258,912	426,161	661,121	324,476	524,126	1,193,447
2006	336,532	128,430	138,302	275,900	467,305	821,123	355,531	550,482	1,504,510
2007	381,595	121,608	138,109	289,246	502,596	946,729	380,831	589,683	1,728,822
2008	445,874	134,195	178,311	311,949	579,532	1,055,356	448,697	615,206	1,888,501
2009	464,758	154,404	241,128	329,380	590,403	969,369	455,658	657,910	2,117,306
2010	491,429	153,405	318,798	349,450	627,868	989,178	487,784	682,765	2,278,713

(continued)

Table 2.5 (continued)

Year	GDP deflator	Rate of exchange (leu/euro)	Price of 1 gram of gold	Consumer prices	Price of industrial production	Prices in mining industry	Prices in manufacturing industry	Prices for the prod., transp and distrib of energy, gas, hot water	Catchment and distribution of water
2011	514,503	154,426	391,062	369,674	672,525	1,031,845	527,675	699,780	2,540,352
2012	540,019	162,373	472,156	382,002	708,820	1,067,329	557,391	726,803	3,151,073
2013	557,412	161,025	383,032	397,221	723,704	1,100,200	561,273	787,690	3,418,588
2014	566,749	161,958	345,703	401,464	722,825	1,154,206	557,907	792,811	3,643,486
2015	583,014	161,972	379,153	397,666	712,706	1,153,051	553,444	755,549	3,756,434

Source: Authors' own compilation based on data from Romania's *Statistic Yearbook*, NIS, Bucharest, various editions, and NBR data

exchanges. Even if, by a *reductio ad absurdum*, Romania would have gained more in terms of wealth, a national economy and a national industry means a lot more than just gambling with demand and supply in certain markets.

Another constant of the economic evolution was the *rise of the amounts transacted on the interbank currency market*. More specifically, in 1996, the national gross production was 65.6 bn. euro, the GDP totalled 29.5 bn. euro, and the volume of foreign exchange transactions was 3.41 bn. euro (8.65 euro GDP per 1 euro of Forex transactions); in 2004, the gross production was 119.4 bn. euro, the GDP had a value of 61 bn. euro, and the annual volume of Forex transactions exceeded, for the first time, the value of the GDP, reaching the level of 64.2 bn. euro.

Going further, we see that, in 2007, the annual volume of foreign exchange transactions of 356.6 bn. euro was higher than both the gross production of overall economy (232 bn. euro), and then the GDP (124.65 bn. euro). In spite of the economic crisis, in 2008, the total value of the foreign exchange transactions was higher than the amount of 465 bn. euro, while the GDP was less than three times less, i.e. 139.8 bn. euro, and the gross production hardly reached 267.7 bn. euro (Table 2.6). Finally, in 2015, the value of the Forex transactions was more than 2.4 times higher than the GDP.

The exponential growth of foreign exchange transactions is a reflection of potential economic and financial stability, and of the imbalances at the macroeconomic level caused by pressure on the exchange rate and by other factors, visible or invisible. The relevance of these evolutions is more important as we know that over 95% of the bank capital is not domestic, and that the share of the Romanian goods exchange is irrelevant, not to mention the fact that many other transactions may exist which are not entered in the official records of the banking system.

One other thing we might add is that an important part of the intermediate consumption and of the gross production derives from imports, which have grown from 4.7 bn. euro in 1991, to 32.6 bn. euro in 2005, 57.2 bn. euro in 2008 and to 63.0 bn. euro in 2015.

Imports accounted for approximately 12.3% of the foreign exchange transactions in 2008 and 16.4% in 2015; if added to the worth of exports, they total an aggregate 30.6% of the overall foreign exchange transactions.

Table 2.6 Gross production, the GDP, and the annual worth of transactions on the inter-bank foreign exchange market (bn. euro)

	1996[a]	2000	2005	2007	2008	2009	2010	2011	2012	2013	2014	2015
Gross production	65.6	78.6	151.2	232.0	267.7	230.6	246.8	266.9	268.6	290.4	299.7	314.3
GDP	29.5	40.6	79.8	124.7	139.8	183.3	126.8	133.3	133.9	144.3	150.6	160.4
Volume of Forex transactions	3.4	24.8	97.3	356.6	465.0	352.8	397.9	440.6	414.9	388.3	363.1	384.4

Source: Authors' own compilation based on NIS and NBR data
[a]For the year 1996, the quotations are in ecu

In general, Forex transactions generate short-term analyses and reactions, most often with regard to the daily rate of exchange and short-term anticipations. Long-term analyses and anticipations are less often used, mostly by academic researchers.

Consultancy and economic and financial prognosis services work mostly with monthly, quarterly or semester aggregations of such data, losing sight of the curve of real indices of some of the macroeconomic indicators that are crucial for economic policy-making, and of genuine strategies for growth and sustainable development.

This may explain why the gross production of the overall economy has grown by only 1.73 times, while in commerce the gross production has increased 3.44 times, and why the highest growth of value added is also in commerce (2.81 times) and in energy (3.42 times), although the production and the consumption of energy are constantly declining.

2.4 International Trade in Goods

During the entire transition period, Romania has been confronted with growingly severe *trade balance deficits*. Practically, from 1997 until 2014, the cumulative trade deficit (export FOB–import CIF) totalled over 154.3 bn. euro, which is equal to the GDP for the year 2014.

While in 2004 the trade deficit was approximately 7.3 bn. euro, in 2006 it had doubled to 14.9 bn. euro and soared to over three times this level in 2007 and 2008 (21.7 bn. euro in 2007, and 23.5 bn. euro in 2008). Romania's accession to the EU may also have been an element that favoured this growth of the trade deficit as an effect of the Romanian economy's opening to the EU internal market. The economic crisis that started in 2008 somewhat slowed the increase of the trade deficit, which was approximately 10 bn. euro until 2012 and then dropped to 5.7 and 6.0 bn. euro in 2013 and 2014, respectively, only to then rise again to 8.4 bn. euro in 2015.

In fact, the trade balance deficit of 23.5 bn. euro in 2008 was higher than the total annual amount of 21.523 bn. euro of net salaries paid to the 5.046 mil. employees on record in that year.[3]

The deficit decreased as an effect of the faster growth of exports (from 33.7 bn. euro in 2008, to 45.3 bn. euro in 2011 and to 52.5 bn. euro in 2014); after the value of imports went down to 39 bn. euro in 2009, imports started growing again in 2010, and they reached 55 bn. euro per year in the period 2011–2013 and 58.5 bn. euro in 2014. In 2015, exports totalled 54.6 bn. euro, and imports jumped to 63.0 bn. euro.

The share of the trade balance deficit in the GDP followed an ascending curve, from 5% in 1991 to 10.3% in 2001 and 17.5% in 2007; then it dropped to 3.9% in 2013 and 2014 and went up again to 5.3% in 2015 (Table 2.7).

While Romania was in the pre-accession seven-year phase the overall worth of the country's imports was 171.3 bn. euro and exports totalled 121.3 bn. euro;[4] in the following seven post-accession years (2007–2013), the overall imports totalled 359.4 bn. euro, compared to only 269.6 bn. euro worth of exports, which resulted in a deficit of 89.7 bn. euro (Table 2.8).

The balance of imports, exports, and the balance of foreign trade transactions by groups of industrial products, and by EU member countries, spanning the time intervals 2000–2006 and 2007–2014 are illustrated in Appendix A.3.

The data therein indicate that, overall, for the transactions with the EU members, the sections of industrial products (according to Standard

Table 2.7 Romania's foreign trade balance in 1991–2015 (bn. euro, %)

	1991	1995	2000	2005	2008	2010	2011	2014	2015
Exports	3.5	6.1	11.3	22.3	33.7	37.4	45.3	52.5	54.6
Imports	4.7	7.9	14.2	32.6	57.2	46.9	55.0	58.5	63.0
Surplus/deficit	−1.2	−1.8	−3.0	−10.3	−23.5	−9.5	−9.7	−6.0	−8.0
GDP	25.1	29.1	40.6	79.7	139.8	124.4	131.5	150.6	160.4
% exports in GDP	13.9	21.0	27.8	27.9	24.1	30.0	34.4	34.9	34.0
% imports in GDP	18.9	27.3	35.1	40.9	40.9	37.7	41.8	38.8	39.3
% surplus/deficit in GDP	−5.0	−6.3	−7.3	−12.9	−16.8	−7.6	−7.3	−3.9	−5.3

Source: Authors' own compilation based on Tempo online, NIS data

Table 2.8 Trade balance during the periods 2000–2006 and 2007–2013 (bn. euro)

	2000	2001	2002	2003	2004	2005	2006	2000–2006	2007	2008	2009	2010	2011	2012	2013	2007–2013
Import	14.2	17.4	18.9	21.2	26.3	32.6	40.7	**171.3**	51.3	57.2	39.0	46.9	55.0	54.7	55.3	**359.4**
Export	11.3	12.7	14.7	15.6	18.9	22.3	25.9	**121.3**	29.5	33.7	29.1	37.4	45.3	45.1	49.6	**269.6**
Balance	−3.0	−4.7	−4.2	−5.6	−7.4	−10.3	−14.8	−50.0	−21.8	−23.5	−9.9	−9.5	−9.7	−9.6	−5.7	−89.7

Source: Authors' own compilation based on NIS data

International Trade Classification SITC REV3) have recorded a deficit balance of 17.7 bn. euro in 2000–2006, accounting for 82.5% of the total trade deficit with the EU countries, and an even higher deficit—57.7 bn. euro—in 2007–2014, representing some 76.2% of the entire trade balance deficit with these countries.[5]

Romania had a positive trade balance for industrial products with six of the EU member countries: Belgium, Cyprus, Croatia, Estonia, Malta and the United Kingdom (with the last of them, the positive trade balance stood at 1.4 bn. euro in 2000–2006, and at 2.6 bn. euro in 2007–2014).

The biggest trade balance deficit was recorded in the exchange of industrial products with Hungary, more specifically 122.3 mil. euro in 2000–2006 and 14.98 bn. euro in 2007–2014, followed, in decreasing order, by Germany, with a deficit of 6.4 bn. euro in 2000–2006 and 12.5 bn. euro in 2007–2014, and Poland, with a deficit of 1.5 bn. euro in 2000–2006 and 8.7 bn. euro in 2007–2014.

The industrial product groups for which Romania has the largest deficits in the period 2007–2014 with the other EU member states are chemicals products (21.94 bn. euro), electrical machinery, appliances and equipment (21.32 bn. euro) and metal and related products (10.35 bn. euro); it has the biggest surpluses for shoes and other similar products (6.66 bn. euro), followed by other goods and products (+5.90 bn. euro) and textiles and related products (3.88 bn. euro).

The analysis of Romania's trade balances with each of the 28 member states (Appendix A.3) reveals that deficits generally tend to be in the area of high-technology and processing groups, and surpluses are mainly generated by products requiring less processing or those that are labour intensive. The only positive exception for Romania in the surplus area is the transport group.

2.5 External Debt and Public Indebtedness

A high level of indebtedness is not a problem in itself as long as loans are intended to finance investment projects in industrial sectors that support economic growth and provide increased financial resources that allow compliance with the debt-reimbursement schedule, either by the private sector or by the state. However, if the borrowings are misdirected or discretionary, especially in the case of sovereign loans, and do not support an increase in the efficiency of industrial activities and the services sector in terms of the economy competitiveness as well as GDP growth, sooner or later debt sustainability is affected, and companies encounter difficulties in meeting repayment commitments. The struggle to repay debt, through adverse spillbacks, has a negative impact on growth and its potential in the medium and long term.

The global financial crisis of 2008–2009 dramatically highlighted, in addition to its effects on the real economy and its rapid spread through all markets—transmitted in particular via banking and commercial channels—that debt sustainability is determined, decisively, by the particular situation of each country as well as the specific factors of influence.[6] The effects of the financial crisis, which still persist, have repercussions on sovereign risk due to the rise in public debt, not only in developing countries but also in advanced ones, which has affected their financial soundness and threatens the macroeconomic and financial balances at the regional, continental and global level.

The major lesson from international developments and experiences, including the impact of the global financial crisis, in terms of maintaining external financial stability, is that each state must ensure its own framework of sovereign debt sustainability, increase its capacity for absorbing potential external shocks, properly assess vulnerabilities and take steps to effect timely correction and carefully monitoring the systemic risk.

In the case of Romania, it should be noted that at the beginning of the transition to the market economy the country was in external financial balance. Under the circumstances of the foreign debt liquidation in March 1989 by the communist regime, about 2.5 bn. dollars remained to be recovered from external debtors, especially third world countries.

This exceptional financial situation of Romania, unburdened by debts—a unique case among the countries of Southern and Eastern Europe—could have been a valuable asset in accelerating the nation's transition, which began in 1990 with a series of reforms, from a super-centralized command economy to the market economy.

One of the biggest challenges during Romania's transition to a market economy and its integration into the EU was the accelerated growth of internal and external indebtedness (the most dynamic of all macroeconomic indicators), accentuated by the effects of the global financial crisis, which were not anticipated and counterbalanced and instead became excessive in relation to the requirements of sustainable development, macroeconomic efficiency, debt repayment capacity and cost-bearing support.

Based on WB data,[7] it was estimated that, in 1990–2000, Romania's external debt stock increased moderately, by about one billion dollars on average annually; in the pre-accession period (2001–2006) it increased to about 6 bn. dollars annually; and in the post-accession period (2007–2014) to almost 10 bn. dollars annually. Thus, the share of external debt in GNI (Gross National Income) increased from 3% in 1990 to 30% in 2000, to 45% in 2006 and to over 67% in 2014. Romania's external debt burden, represented by its annual debt service relative to exports of goods and services, increased from 0.3% in 1990 to 20% in 2000 to 27% in 2006 and to 38.3% in 2014.

Unlike the pre-accession period, in which the increase in external debt occurred, in particular, due to the autonomous financial flows required to cover the increasing trade and current account deficits, which exceeded 10% of GDP (largely funded by massive inflows of foreign investments, including "hot money"), the explosive rise in the external debt after 2007 (Table 2.9), occurred during the global financial crisis circumstances, as a result of compensatory financial flows, mainly the IMF–EU loan of 20 bn. euro in April 2009, which was granted as financial assistance in order to avoid a major imbalance in Romania's external balance of payments.

The increase in external debt during the transition period, motivated by the need to recapitalize the economy, was intended to cover the costs of industrial restructuring and upgrading, including attracting foreign investments, and should have resulted in sustainable economic growth, including increasing Romania's capacity for external payments, in particular because of the increase in foreign exchange earnings from exports of goods and services, in such a way that reimbursement of the due external debt outstanding so be smooth and without affecting the development prospects.

Table 2.9 The external debt of Romania during the period 2007–2016 (mil. euro)

External debt	2007	2008	2009	2010	2011	2012	2013	2014	2015	2016
I. Long-term external debt	38,526	51,762	65,746	72,909	75,929	78,760	76,894	75,829	70,558	69,116
I.1 Public debt[a]	10,197	10,749	19,057	26,948	31,312	33,833	34,284	35,427	32,984	33,494
I.2 Private debt[b]	28,329	41,013	46,559	45,961	44,617	44,927	42,610	40,402	37,574	35,622
II. Short-term external debt	20,103	20,592	15,417	19,549	22,795	20,921	19,166	18,915	19,876	23,416
Total external debt (I+II)	58,629	72,354	81,163	92,458	98,724	99,681	96,060	94,744	90,434	92,532

Source: For the period 2007–2013, based on NBR-Interactive database. For the period 2014–2016: Press releases on balance of payments and external debt, NBR

[a]Including direct public debt and publicly guaranteed debt, including IMF loans (Ministry of Public Finance and Monetary Authority, including DST allocations from IMF)

[b]Including long-term deposits of non-residents

The decoupling, which became ever more pronounced, of Romania's external indebtedness from economic growth led to a deterioration in the effectiveness of foreign borrowings and, implicitly, Romania's resilience to external shocks, increasing the vulnerabilities and risks associated with debt sustainability (Zaman and Georgescu 2012, 228–265).

In real terms, in the post-accession period, the ratio GDP/long-term external debt decreased from 3.2 in 2007 to 2.2 in 2015, a trend reflecting the weak macroeconomic performance of Romania. In terms of the long-term external debt burden, the share of debt service relative to the GDP reached more than 14% in 2015 compared to 7% in 2007 (Zaman and Georgescu 2016, 99–114).

The vulnerabilities of the external financial situation are also evident from the analysis of the net international investment position (NIIP), an indicator included in the EC's scoreboard under the Macroeconomic Imbalance Procedure [MIP]). In the case of Romania, the NIIP deteriorated sharply, its deteriorating from −29.4% to GDP in 2005 to −70.4% in 2012, mainly due to the increase in external debt in the debt instrument segment FDI, portfolio investment, other investment), followed by an slight improvement trend, reaching −57.2% in 2014 and −50.2% in 2015, a level that remained well above −35%, the alert threshold of MIP scoreboard (European Commission 2015).[8]

Romania's net debtor's position vis-à-vis the rest of the world entails a number of risk factors, both on the external assets side, supported by about two-thirds of the international reserves pillar (with low immediate liquidity and coming partly from minimum reserve requirements due by commercial banks, most of them with foreign capital), and on the external liabilities side, given the volatility of capital flows, including FDI, as well as the maintenance of a high degree of dependence on external financing (Georgescu 2016, 361–381).

Not only is Romania's external financial situation under pressure, mainly as a result of the imbalances generated by the accumulation of trade and current account deficits, but so is its internal financial framework, with fiscal deficits (representing more than 5% GDP annually in 2008–2011 and reaching a peak of 9.1% in 2009), exacerbated by expansionary budget policies funded by sovereign and private loans, which were also used for repayments and debt refinancing. Additionally, the effects of the global financial crisis and the financial assistance package granted to Romania by the IMF and the EU in 2009 lead to an explosive increase in public indebtedness.

In nominal terms, in lei, between 2000 and 2016, Romania's public debt stock (government and local authorities) increased more than 12 times, and in euro, more than 8 times, reaching 339.2 bn. lei (74.7 bn. euro) on December 31, 2016.[9] Expressed in euro *per capita*, the public debt increased from 370 euro in 2000 to 3790 euro in 2016. The debt-to-GDP ratio rose from 6.6% in 1995 to 19.8% in 2007, and to 36.4% in 2010 and 44.5% in 2016.[10] The almost sevenfold increase of the public debt share in GDP over the past two decades is by far the most significant of all EU 28 countries, an unenviable record for Romania.

Romania's high internal and external public indebtedness, as well as the deterioration of debt sustainability parameters, hinder the recovery and sustainable growth of the economy, diminish the country's investment capacity, maintain the vicious circle of outstanding payments—debt rollover—borrowing costs—sovereign risk—unsustainable growth, combined with neglecting the hidden debt surfaces and violating the principle of intergenerational equity, has lead to an increase in the unpredictability of the business environment associated with overhang effects, as well as to the worsening of the frictions between the various components of the debt (short-term versus long-term, internal versus external, public versus private).[11]

Rehabilitating Romania's financial position and, above all, ensuring debt sustainability, requires firm action by governmental and monetary authorities in order to promote coherent macro-economic policies aimed at recoupling the internal and external indebtedness of the economic cycles, mainly in industrial sectors; respecting the fundamental correlation between economic growth and indebtedness level, conditioned by getting below the prudential threshold of 40% debt-to-GDP ratio in the long run; as well as keeping all risk factors under control, whether generated by domestic vulnerabilities or by more or less predictable events of the international economic, financial and geopolitical environment.

Notes

1. See Chivu and Ciutacu (2016).
2. The method is not new, and in the context of the analysis of the relationship between GDP and gold prices, at global and country levels, to help demonstrate the idea, sometimes the GDP is converted to tonnes of gold, as, for example in the case of United States (http://pricedingold.com/us-gdp/) or in international comparisons (https://www.quora.com/Comparing-the-GDP-according-to-tonnes-of-gold-according-to-the-gold-rate-in-those-years-how-much-have-each-country-progressed).
3. Calculations based on NIS data regarding the average number of employees, and the average net monthly salary earnings, multiplied by 12 months (1309 lei × 12 months × 5.046 mil. persons).
4. See Ciutacu and Chivu (2015, 216–221).
5. In this evaluation, the expansion of inward/outward processing trade operations, which accounted for over one-third of Romania's international trade in 2004 and 2005, should also be considered (for more on this see Georgescu 2006, 24–31).
6. See Stiglitz and Heymann (2014), Darvas and Huttl (2014), Cecchetti, Mohanty and Zampolli (2011), Belhocine and Dell'Erba (2013).
7. The WB database provides long-time data series on external debt stocks for more than 200 countries. The gross external debt (including long-term external debt and short-term external debt) is expressed in USD. http://datatopics.worldbank.org/debt/ids/country/ROU
8. European Commission, *Macroeconomic imbalances. Country Report Romania 2015*, in: "European Economy Occasional Papers", No. 223, EC-DGECFIN, Brussels, June, 2015, pp. 12–26.
9. Public debt registered according to Romanian methodology (OUG 64/2007), including state guarantees.
10. Structure of the public debt 31 of March 2017, Ministry of Public Finance, Romanian Government. http://discutii.mfinante.ro/static/10/Mfp/buletin/executii/Structuradatorieipublice2000-2017martieRo.pdf
11. See Georgescu (2013, 353–361).

References

Belhocine, N., and S. Dell'Erba. 2013. The Impact of Debt Sustainability and the Level of Debt on Emerging Markets Spreads. *IMF Working Paper*, WP/13/93, May.

Cecchetti, S.G., M.S. Mohanty, and F. Zampolli. 2011. *The Real Effects of Debt*. Symposium "Achieving Maximum Long-Run Growth", Jackson Hole, Wy (USA), August 25–27.

Chilosi, Alberto. 1996. *Distributional Consequences of Privatisation in the Economie in Transition: An Analytical Framework*. Netherlands: Kluwer Academic Publishers. https://doi.org/10.1007/BF02430939.

Chivu, Luminița, and Constantin Ciutacu. 2016. Romania and the Four Freedoms: From Theory to Practice. In *Proceedings of ESPERA 2015*. Frankfurt am Main: Peter Lang Academic Research.

Ciutacu, Constantin, and Luminița Chivu. 2010. *Anticipating and Managing Restructuring—National Background Paper Romania. 27 National Seminar on Restructuring*. International Training Center-International Labour Office, European Commisssion/DG Employment, Social Affairs and Equal Opportunities. http://ec.europa.eu/social/main.jsp?catId=819&langId=en

———. 2015. Non-competitive Evolutions of the Foreign Trade in Romania. *Procedia Economics and Finance* 22: 216–221. https://doi.org/10.1016/S2212-5671(15)00265-8.

Darvas, Z., and P. Huttl 2014. *The Long Haul: Debt Sustainability Analysis*. Bruegel Working Papers, June.

European Commission. 2015. *Macroeconomic Imbalances. Country Report Romania 2015*. In European Economy Occasional Papers, No 223, EC-DGECFIN, Brussels, June, pp. 12–26.

Georgescu, George. 2006. Inward Processing Trade and Implications for the Balance of Payments Current Account (The Case of Romania). *Journal for Economic Forecasting* 8 (1): 24–31. March. http://www.ipe.ro/rjef/rjef1_06/rjef1_06_2.pdf

———. 2013. Public Debt, Sovereign Risk and Sustainable Development of Romania. *Procedia Economics and Finance* 8: 353–358. https://doi.org/10.1016/S2212-5671(14)00101-4.

———. 2016. *Prospects of Romania's International Investment Position and Financial Stability Risks*. Frankfurt am Main: Peter Lang Academic Research.

Stiglitz, J.E., and D. Heymann. 2014. *Life after Debt. The Origins and Resolutions of Debt Crisis*. IEA Conference, Vol. 152, Palgrave Macmillan.

Structure of the Public Debt, 31 of March. 2017. Ministry of Public Finance, Romanian Government. http://discutii.mfinante.ro/static/10/Mfp/buletin/executii/Structuradatorieipublice2000-2017martieRo.pdf

Zaman, Gheorghe, and George Georgescu. 2012. Sovereign Risk and Debt Sustainability—Warning Levels for Romania. In *Non-Linear Modelling in Economics. Beyond Standard Economics*, 228–265. New York: Addleton Academic Publishers.

———. 2016. Provocări în perioada tranziției la economia de piață în România. Creșterea gradului de îndatorare internă și externă. *Revista Studii de Istorie Economică și Istoria Gândirii Economice*, September, Vol. XVII.

3

Privatization-Driven Transformation of Romania's Industrial Landscape

3.1 Privatisation and Fixed Assets

During the first years of the economic transition in Romania, the concept of restructuring was used for the state-owned companies put up for privatisation. The Privatisation Law no. 58/1991 provided—in Sect. 3.2: The establishment and operation of the State Ownership Fund (Fondul Proprietatii de Stat—FPS), Art. 25 (c)—that FPS was authorised to take measures towards the restructuring and technological updating of state-owned companies or towards the liquidation of the non-profitable ones.

Privatisation was regarded as a means to make companies profitable, first by "clearing" them of debts, and then by their reorganising them as sources of profit. To attain this goal, some of the companies' loss-generating operations were eliminated; and some of their equipment was sold as scrap iron, which fetched the investor handsome and immediate revenues as export merchandise, thereby sparing the investor the trouble of maintaining jobs by means of investment and technical upgrading, product innovation and the design of new market strategies and so on.

Moreover, the agencies in charge of state-owned companies privatization—FPS, its successor, the Authority for the Privatisation and Management of the State's Capital Participations (Autoritatea pentru

L. Chivu et al., *Deindustrialization and Reindustrialization in Romania*,
DOI 10.1007/978-3-319-65753-0_3

Privatizarea şi Administrarea Participaţiilor Statului—APAPS), later renamed as the Authority of Valuation of the State Assets (Autoritatea pentru Valorificarea Activelor Statului—AVAS)—were compelled, by law, to take steps to diminish the involvement of the State and the local public administration authorities in the economy. According to provisions of Law no. 58/1991 (art 25[a]) and the Government Emergency Ordinance (GEO) no. 88/1997 (articles 5[1], 10[2] and 10[3]), the legality of the clauses of the privatisation contracts would not be subject to inspection by the Comptrollership, and the members of the boards of directors and the employees (of the FPS, APAPS, AVAS) would not be liable for the transactions made by such agencies. Provisions of this type were intended to eliminate any social accountability of the State with respect to its own enterprises, and to discourage any partnership and cooperation with the local actors (Ciutacu and Chivu 2010).

According to Law no. 58/1991, the privatization process in Romania included the free transfer of 30% of the state's shares through the mass privatization program, and, institutionally, through five private equity funds (now financial investment companies). Privatization and restructuring have been supported by WB programs (FESAL, ASAL, PSAL I and PSAL II), the IMF (stand-by agreements), PHARE, USAID among others.

Between 1992 and 2015 more than 7700 state-owned companies were privatized, with total revenues estimated at about 15 bn. euro, several times lower than the total nominal value of the shares sold by the state. A short list of the most important privatizations and the related proceeds is presented in Table 3.1.

In addition to these privatizations many smaller state-owned companies were privatized by domestic investors (in some cases even by the employees). Some state-owned companies were privatized by the MEBO (Management Employee Buyouts) method, considered by analysts as the most relevant privatization method during the first decade of transition in Romania. Until 2000, a total of 2632 companies (one third of the total companies to be privatized) were included in MEBO privatization, and in more than half of them (62.8%) the employees were majority shareholders. The annual number of companies privatized by this method grew from 19 in 1992 to 249 in 1993, 565 in 1994, 479 in 1995, 509 in 1996, 378 in 1997, 267 in 1998, 336 in 1999 and 46 in the year 2000. Of the companies privatized by this method, 29.0% were

Table 3.1 Most important privatisations in Romania, during 1992–2015

State-owned company/Purchaser foreign company[a]	Year of privatization	Privatization proceeds[b]
Banca Comerciala Romana/Erste Group (Austria)	2006	2200 mil. euro
Petrom/OMV Group (Austria)	2004	700 mil. euro
Romtelecom/OTE Hellenic Telecommunication Organization (Greece)	1998	675 mil. USD
Romcim/Lafarge (France)	1997	214 mil. USD
Banca Romana de Dezvoltare/Societe Generale (France)	1999	188 mil. USD
Banc Post/General Electric Capital Corporation and Banco Portugues de Investimento (USA and Portugal)	1999	93 mil. USD
Sidex/ArcelorMittal (Luxembourg-India)	2001	70 mil. USD
Rompetrol Rafinare/Rompetrol Group BV Rotterdam	2000	63 mil. USD
Automobile Craiova/Ford Motor Company (USA)	2007	57 mil. euro
Casial Deva/Lasselberger/HeidelbergCement (Austria/Germany)	1997	52 mil. USD
Banca Agricola/Raiffeisen Bank (Austria)	2001	52 mil. USD
Automobile Dacia/Renault Group (France)	1999	49 mil. euro
Rulmenti Grei Ploiesti/Timken (USA)	1997	41 mil. USD
Otelinox Targoviste/Samsung Deutschland (South Korea—Germany)	1997	40 mil. USD
Phoenix Baia Mare/Allied Deals (United Kingdom)	1998	37 mil. USD
COST Targoviste/Conares Trading—Mechel (Switzerland—Russia)	2002	35 mil. USD
Alro/Marco International (USA—Russia)	2002	11.5 mil. USD

Source: Based on data of the State Property Fund and Ministry of Public Finance
[a]generally, by purchasing the majority stake
[b]excluding the investments committed in privatization contracts and equity raisings

in industry, of which 0.9% were in extraction and energy, 18.0% in light industry and 10.1% in heavy industry (Telegdy 2002, 14).

Although many privatizations proved successful, especially those made with the participation of strategic foreign investors, which hold a significant ownership share in many industrial sectors (*Foreign Direct Investments in Romania in 2015*, NBR 2016)[1] process was complicated by the multiplication of laws that regulated the change of property—more than 100—and the overall process was marked by delays, poorly prepared offers for sale, intentional deterioration of the financial situation of some companies in order to sell them in pieces, accompanied by corruption scandals, post-privatization diversion of the production or services activities performed before the change in ownership, including by demolition of buildings, dismantling of equipments and abusive layoffs.

It is worth mentioning that, according to a study by Chiriac (Chiriac 2016), only one-fifth of all privatized companies throughout the period after 1990 are still active and have more than 10 employees.

Currently, 616 companies remain in the portfolio of the Authority for State Assets; half of them are insolvent or are in bankruptcy procedures.

The economic and institutional restructuring that continued uninterrupted every year of the transition period, which was paralleled by widespread and successive repositioning of economic values, influenced the economic development and growth processes, as well as the framework permitting the emergence of concepts, strategies, and the definition of targets/objectives for each particular domain.

This dramatic course of events is reflected in the evolution of all macroeconomic indicators, the references for which changed daily.

Fixed assets, an indicator of critical importance for any economic growth strategy, have been regarded as a parameter of interest only for statistical purposes. In terms of worth, fixed assets, expressed in euro, at the prevailing prices for each year, rose from 127 bn. ecu in 1990 to 354 bn. euro in 2014. The ratio of the value between fixed assets and the GDP deteriorated from 0.24 in1990 to 0.42 euro in 2014.

Despite the incompleteness of information and methodological changes, which may give rise to disputes as to accuracy and magnitude, one cannot fail to notice that the *fixed assets index* (1990 = 100.0) reveals a growth of value of only 8.87 times until 2007. If we compare this to the GDP deflator for the same time period (1990–2007), we observe that it reflected a rise in GDP prices of 3815.9 times; industrial production prices grew 5025.95 times; consumer prices grew more than 2892 times, and so on. In other words, the value of the fixed assets grew more slowly and became progressively smaller compared to other indicator values; and this depreciation triggered a tendency to destroy companies and to derive profit from them by trading their assets—as, among other things, scrap iron; what happened was a gross and serious devaluation of the fixed capital in the economy, for the sake of being "competitive" as exporters of scrap iron (Table 3.2).

Table 3.2 Index of fixed assets in the economy

	Total	Public administration*	Industry total	Mining industry total	Manufacturing	Prod., transp. and distrib. of electricity, heating, hot water	Water supply and distribution	Agriculture, forestry
	1990 = 100.0							
1991	103.8	195.9	104.1	101.6	104.5	103.6	106.0	96.0
1992	106.7	208.2	106.3	105.7	106.8	104.8	114.0	100.8
1993	115.1	234.7	112.2	114.2	112.7	109.5	121.2	106.9
1994	125.9	400.9	117.6	117.4	120.3	110.6	125.5	111.6
1995	143.6	1002.2	127.2	124.1	133.8	113.2	131.0	121.1
1996	150.3	947.3	132.2	127.4	137.7	120.8	132.8	119.0
1997	153.7	1490.0	133.5	121.6	143.2	118.2	133.1	121.4
1998	205.0	1780.0	173.4	82.7	168.7	181.2	399.0	136.8
1999	258.0	3130.0	249.3	156.5	241.6	258.4	481.2	129.4
2000	364.6	16,450.0	326.1	205.5	303.5	376.8	479.9	128.3
2001	457.2	21,615.3	401.8	230.8	373.3	454.4	759.2	131.3
2002	502.1	18,966.9	456.5	281.1	432.2	503.0	793.3	171.0
2003	685.8	46,273.9	477.7	299.8	464.4	506.0	815.4	192.5
2004	564.0	29,560.7	502.5	290.8	529.3	485.7	872.5	176.5
2005	624.9	32,521.7	546.5	343.2	570.0	534.7	858.1	202.3
2006	703.7	35,367.5	600.4	388.6	667.4	525.3	878.7	254.2
2007	887.8	43,526.7	707.0	457.6	808.8	587.1	949.2	335.2
	2008 = 100.0							
2009	110.2	122.5	103.6	100.8	106.1	110.3	119.5	126.6
2010	117.7	142.8	106.4	101.7	110.3	116.8	140.1	120.1
2011	124.2	157.3	109.6	102.2	117.0	125.0	148.2	134.2
2012	123.2	146.7	110.1	102.5	122.1	120.2	139.6	144.0

Source: Authors' own compilation based on NIS data

*Including defence and compulsory social security, since 2008

The structure of fixed assets by branches of the national economy reveals that the share of industry dropped from 47.6% in 1990, to 26% in 2014; and the share of the manufacturing industry diminished from 31% in 1990, to 13.6% in 2014; during the same period of time, the *public administration sector* (and defence and compulsory social security since 2008) increased its share from 1.0% of the total fixed assets in 1990 to 43.7% in 2014 (!) (Table 3.3).

Many arguments could be invoked to sustain claims that certain macroeconomic indicators—of exceptional strategic importance for the accuracy and solidity of the transition, restructuring, and economic growth strategy—followed an unpredictable curve.

One of the causes could be the statistical artifacts; but even more than this, the blame lies with the concerted multidimensional aggression against Romania's national wealth and values endorsed by all the media channels. In addition we must include the so-called scientific studies and the blatant lack of professionalism that have caused the demonisation of industry and contributed to industrial decapitalisation, disinvestment and depreciation, all of which have resulted in the deindustrialisation of Romania.

3.2 Industrial Companies' Landscape

The results of the restructuring and privatisation of economic ventures, and particularly of those in industry, is reflected, in the first phase, in the number and size of the newly emerged companies.

In brief, from the records of the Romanian Register of Companies, we know that while in 1991 there were 1712 industrial companies, with a total of 3.052 mil. employees, which resulted in an average of 1783 *employees per company,* in 2011 the records showed 47,084 industrial companies, with a total of 1.259 mil. employees, which meant an average of 27 *employees per company.*

In 2015, a total of 54,020 industrial companies employed 1.335 mil. persons, which meant an average number of 24.7 employees per company.

In 1991 Romania had only 79 companies employing fewer than 100 persons, and 127 companies with an average number of 130 employees; as an effect of the new Companies Act no. 31/1990, the composition and

Table 3.3 Structure of fixed assets (total economy = 100.0)

	Total	Public administration*	Industry total	Mining industry total	Manufacturing	Prod., transp. and distrib. of electricity, heating, hot water	Water supply and distribution	Agriculture, forestry
1990	100.0	1.0	47.6	6.0	31.0	8.3	2.3	10.5
1991	100.0	1.6	50.5	6.4	32.9	8.8	2.4	8.3
1992	100.0	0.6	62.0	7.4	36.6	15.1	2.9	8.8
1993	100.0	0.7	60.7	7.4	35.9	14.6	2.8	8.7
1994	100.0	1.2	57.3	7.0	34.6	13.2	2.6	8.9
1995	100.0	1.0	58.8	6.4	30.4	17.8	4.2	12.0
1996	100.0	1.0	58.3	6.4	30.5	17.6	3.9	10.9
1997	100.0	2.2	60.1	9.9	30.8	15.8	3.6	8.0
1998	100.0	2.1	58.4	5.3	26.8	17.5	8.9	6.4
1999	100.0	2.7	69.1	7.8	29.4	24.7	7.1	4.0
2000	100.0	29.4	47.2	6.0	21.4	16.5	3.1	2.1
2001	100.0	30.1	45.2	5.2	20.3	15.9	3.9	1.5
2002	100.0	21.1	41.5	4.9	19.0	14.6	3.1	1.5
2003	100.0	57.9	22.1	2.5	10.3	7.9	1.4	1.3
2004	100.0	41.4	29.9	3.2	14.9	9.9	1.9	1.4
2005	100.0	41.1	29.1	3.1	15.1	9.2	1.7	1.4
2006	100.0	40.4	27.5	3.1	15.7	8.1	0.5	1.5
2007	100.0	39.9	25.7	3.0	15.3	7.0	0.4	1.7
2008	100.0	27.7	44.5	26.8	11.9	5.1	0.3	1.9
2009	100.0	31.1	41.7	24.5	11.4	5.2	0.4	2.3
2010	100.0	34.7	40.7	23.4	11.2	5.3	0.5	1.8
2011	100.0	21.8	63.8	53.3	6.6	3.4	0.3	1.4
2012	100.0	42.4	26.3	3.7	14.2	7.5	0.5	2.3
2013	100.0	43.9	25.6	3.7	13.7	7.1	0.6	2.7
2014	100.0	43.7	26.0	3.9	13.6	7.3	0.9	2.8

Source: Authors' own compilation based on NIS data

*Including defence and compulsory social security, since 2008

reshuffling of Romanian industrial enterprises by size classes changed radically (Table 3.4).

Similarly, the trend has continued in recent years: in 2011 over 90% of the industrial companies had less than 50 employees, and approximately 70% of the companies operated with less than 10 employees; in 2015, a total of 92.1% of all companies had fewer than 50 employees and 72.8% of them had fewer than 10 employees.

The second most important change was the *transfer of property*.

In 2015, a total of 98.9% of all industrial companies had a majority of private shareholders, and only 1.1% were under the majority ownership of the state; in the same year, 8.0% of all industrial companies were under the full ownership of foreign capital (Table 3.5).

Table 3.4 Distribution of industrial companies by size range

			Size ranges by number of employees			
	Year	Total	0–9	10–49	50–249	250 and over
Total industry	**1995**	**34,850**	**27,566**	**4014**	**1653**	**1617**
	2001	**43,454**	**29,162**	**9046**	**3851**	**1395**
	2011	**49,715**	**34,299**	**11,051**	**3496**	**869**
	2015	**54,020**	**39,327**	**10,412**	**3386**	**895**
Extraction and mining industries	1995	170	74	32	14	50
	2001	321	151	88	42	40
	2011	1108	800	240	51	17
	2015	1107	789	248	48	22
Manufacturing industry	1995	34,404	27,455	3946	1523	1480
	2001	42,787	28,950	8897	3678	1262
	2011	45,052	30,914	10,184	3223	731
	2015	48,404	34,974	9527	3132	771
Electric power, heating, gas and water	1995	276	37	36	116	87
	2001	346	61	61	131	93
	2011	3555	2580	616	238	121
	2015	4509	3564	637	206	102
Total economy	**1995**	**304,359**	**283,997**	**13,400**	**4384**	**2578**
	2001	**311,260**	**271,713**	**29,888**	**7702**	**1957**
	2011	**430,608**	**375,479**	**45,221**	**8335**	**1573**
	2015	**488,210**	**433,075**	**45,177**	**8277**	**1681**

Source: *Romania's Statistic Yearbook*, NIS, Bucharest, various editions, and *Results and Performances of Industrial and Construction Companies*, NIS, Bucharest, various editions

Table 3.5 Distribution of companies by ownership, 2015 (%)

		Of which:		
	Total	State ownership majority	Private ownership majority	Companies fully owned by foreign capital
National economy, of which:	**100.0**	**0.3**	**99.7**	**5.4**
Industry, of which:	**100.0**	**1.1**	**98.9**	**8.0**
Extraction/mining industry	100.0	1.9	98.1	11.2
Manufacturing industry	100.0	0.2	99.8	7.9
Production and supply of electricity, heating, gas and water	100.0	9.8	90.2	9.0

Source: Authors' own compilation of NIS data

Table 3.6 Distribution of employees by structure of ownership, 2015 (%)

		of which:	
	Total	State ownership	Private ownership
National economy, of which:	**100.0**	**26.6**	**73.4**
Industry, of which:	**100.0**	**10.0**	**90.0**
Extraction/mining industry	100.0	43.9	56.1
Manufacturing industry	100.0	1.8	98.2
Production and supply of electricity, heating, gas and water	100.0	56.4	43.6

Source: Authors' own compilation of NIS data

In 2015, 90.0% of all the employees in industry were working in private companies, and only 10.0% of the workers held a job in a state-owned company (Table 3.6).

The contribution of the various forms of ownership to the generation of turnover in the industrial branches of Romania, in 2014 (Table 3.7), indicates the substantive contribution of foreign capital, the share of which in the total turnover fluctuates from 34% to 100%; foreign capital held the largest shares in the turnover of the following industries: tobacco (100%), crude oil processing (97%), vehicle manufacturing (96%), manufacture of electrical equipment and production of beverages (82%).

Table 3.7 Distribution of turnover and number of employees by origin of capital, in 2014

Industry	State capital	Romanian private capital	Foreign capital	State capital	Romanian private capital	Foreign capital
Oil and gas extraction	21	1	78	25	2	73
Manufacture of coke and of refined petroleum products	0	3	97	0	21	79
Manufacture of road vehicles, trailers and semi-trailers	0	4	96	0	9	91
Manufacture of tobacco products	0	0	100	0	0	100
Metallurgy	0	17	83	0	24	76
Manufacture of pharmaceuticals	9	35	56	16	43	42
Manufacture of electrical equipment	0	18	82	0	25	75
Manufacture of beverages	0	18	82	0	33	67
Manufacture of other means of transport	2	37	61	5	56	39
Manufacture of chemicals	9	29	62	21	35	43
Manufacture of machinery and equipment	0	28	72	1	49	50
Manufacture of computers	0	26	74	0	29	71
Manufacture of rubber products	0	29	71	0	50	50
Manufacture of paper	0	46	54	0	61	39
Food industry	0	66	34	0	62	18

(*continued*)

Table 3.7 (continued)

Industry	State capital	Romanian private capital	Foreign capital	State capital	Romanian private capital	Foreign capital
Manufacture of other products from non-metallic minerals	0	48	52	0	70	30
Manufacture of textiles	0	34	66	0	45	55
Tanning and dressing of hides	0	31	69	0	52	48
Manufacture of metal structures, and metal products	3	51	46	5	65	29
Wood processing, except for furniture	0	42	58	0	70	30
Manufacture of clothing	0	49	51	0	59	41
Manufacture of furniture	0	52	48	0	67	33
Production and supply of electricity, heating, gas and water	25	11	64	67	12	21

Source: Authors' own compilation based on data from the National Trade Register Office (ONRC)

Competitiveness in industry depends on a number of other factors, and on the company's status in respect of turnover and market share. Bearing this in mind, both experts and decision-makers are aware of the difficulties encountered by small and medium-sized enterprises when attempting to access financing sources; undertake research, development and innovation; and stay informed of the latest developments in the market and competitive conditions among others.

According to the EC Recommendation of 2003, effective from 2005, companies fall into the following size classes[2]: micro-enterprises—with less than 10 persons employed and with a turnover of up to 2 mil. euro; small enterprises—with 10–49 employees and up to 10 mil. euro turnover; medium-sized enterprises—with 50–249 employees and up to 50 mil. euro turnover[3]; and large enterprises—with 250 or more employees.

The distribution of companies in Romanian industry by size classes forms a picture that is far from that in the old EU member states.

NIS data for the time interval 2008–2014, indicate that the average number of employees per industrial company has fluctuated between 24 and 28 persons; the great majority of micro-enterprises had an average of 2–3 employees. In companies ranked as large, with more than 250 employees, the average number of personnel was 770 (Table 3.8).

The general trend in 2014 was for micro-enterprises and small companies with up to 20 employees to reduce the average number of personnel.

The trend towards a decreasing average number of employees continued in the mining and the manufacturing industries; in the production and supply of electricity, heating, gas and hot water we can notice a tendency to concentration: that is, reducing the number of employees in the small companies and increasing the number of personnel in the very large companies.

From a European perspective, in 2014, according to the data published by the Ministry of Public Finance (MFP), a classification of companies operating in the Romanian economy and industry, from the turnover point of view, places the overwhelming majority in the category of *micro-enterprises* or, at most, *small enterprises*,.

NIS data indicate that over all industries, the average size of a company, with respect to turnover, was 1.4 mil. euro in 2008 and 1.68 mil. euro in 2011 and 2014. In 2014, companies of 50 to 249 employees recorded an average turnover of approximately 5.5 mil. euro; and companies with more than 250 employees reported, the same year, a turnover of more than 65 mil. euro (Table 3.9).

The table shows that, from the point of view of turnover, the average size of a company in the manufacturing industry is four to six times smaller than that of a company in the extraction/mining industry or in the energy production sector.

Table 3.8 Average number of employees by company size range in the industry, 2008–2014

NACE Rev. 2 (activities in the national economy of Romania—sections)	Company size-class	2008	2009	2010	2011	2014
Total industry	Total	27	24	25	28	26
	0–9 employees	3	2	3	3	2
	10–19 employees	14	14	14	14	14
	20–49 employees	31	31	31	31	31
	50–249 employees	105	107	106	106	105
	250 employees and over	799	807	791	792	771
Extraction/ mining industry	Total	79	62	58	59	42
	0–9 employees	3	3	3	3	3
	10–19 employees	14	14	14	14	14
	20–49 employees	30	30	29	29	30
	50–249 employees	115	117	116	111	103
	250 employees and over	3271	3350	3466	3087	1779
Manufacturing industry	Total	24	22	23	26	24
	0–9 employees	3	2	3	3	3
	10–19 employees	14	14	14	14	14
	20–49 employees	31	31	31	31	31
	50–249 employees	105	106	106	106	105
	250 employees and over	699	696	687	698	700
Production and supply of electricity, heating, gas, hot water and air conditioning	Total	176	141	91	86	50
	0–9 employees	2	2	2	2	1
	10–19 employees	14	13	13	14	14
	20–49 employees	34	32	30	30	30
	50–249 employees	129	120	122	121	113
	250 employees and over	1460	1458	1433	1391	1874

Source: Authors' own compilation based on data from *Results and Performances of Industrial and Construction Companies*, NIS, Bucharest, various editions

It also shows that, in the production and supply of electricity, heating, and so on, the average size of companies shrank by a factor of 3 t in 2014, compared to 2008, particularly in micro- and small enterprises. This does not apply to companies with more than 50 employees, where the turnover per company is considerably higher.

A detailed presentation of company sizes, by industrial branch, in relation to the average turnover recorded in 2014, is given in Table 3.10.

Table 3.9 Average turnover by size-class of industrial enterprises (thou. euro/enterprise)

NACE Rev. 2 (activities in the national economy of Romania—sections)	Company size-class	Year				
		2008	2009	2010	2011	2014
Total industry	Total	1424	1143	1433	1679	1684
	0–9 employees	86	75	100	122	110
	10–19 employees	552	446	519	491	587
	20–49 employees	953	892	933	1046	1252
	50–249 employees	4098	3841	4372	4490	5490
	250 employees and over	56,427	51,102	61,582	65,544	64,433
Extraction/mining industry	Total	7012	4196	5082	5596	5594
	0–9 employees	126	140	132	94	142
	10–19 employees	736	564	507	756	943
	20–49 employees	1836	1371	1692	1703	1810
	50–249 employees	6168	5414	5623	5959	6632
	250 employees and over	311,165	240,616	332,412	326,982	274,857
Manufacturing industry	Total	1101	880	1125	1331	1432
	0–9 employees	67	55	72	85	77
	10–19 employees	457	361	410	380	464
	20–49 employees	892	839	854	890	1057
	50–249 employees	3823	3608	4103	4193	4587
	250 employees and over	42,142	37,924	47,172	51,370	57,189
Production and supply of electricity, heating, gas, hot water, and air conditioning	Total	26,013	18,547	13,654	13,935	8262
	0–9 employees	2439	1806	1481	1739	835
	10–19 employees	13,957	13,054	10,276	10,241	9777
	20–49 employees	7757	7033	9432	14,172	14,649
	50–249 employees	22,504	16,972	18,973	22,181	58,447
	250 employees and over	189,061	168,163	183,007	183,875	200,783

Source: Authors' own compilation based on data from *Results and Performances of Industrial and Construction Companies*, NIS, Bucharest, various editions

Table 3.10 Classification of industrial branches by company average turnover, in Romania, in 2011 and 2014

Branch	Number of companies		Total turnover (mil. euro)		Average turnover/ company (mil. euro)		Share of the turnover recorded by foreign capital companies (%)		Leading company 2011/2014	Leading company's turnover (mil. euro)	
	2011	2014	2011	2014	2011	2014	2011	2014		2011	2014
Total manufacturing and mining industry	**46,160**	**53,864**	**69.143**	**90.710**	**1.50**	**1.68**	..	…	…	…	…
Oil and gas extraction	15	38	4.949	4.902	329.90	128.99	80.0	78.9	OMV Petrom	3.909	3.715
Manufacture of coke and petroleum products	44	47	4.186	4.746	95.13	100.99	100.0	33.7	Rompetrol Rafinare	2.401	3.035
Manufacture of road vehicles, trailers and semi-trailers	373	450	8.838	13.181	23.69	29.29	98.0	96.6	Automobile Dacia SA	3.110	4.237
Manufacture of tobacco products	10	8	555	214	55.51	26.69	100.0	100.0	JTI Manufacturing	467	123
Metallurgical industry	369	431	4.876	3.925	13.21	9.11	95.0	87.6	ArcelorMittal Galati	1.100	808

(*continued*)

Table 3.10 (continued)

Branch	Number of companies		Total turnover (mil. euro)		Average turnover/ company (mil. euro)		Share of the turnover recorded by foreign capital companies (%)		Leading company 2011/2014	Leading company's turnover (mil. euro)	
	2011	2014	2011	2014	2011	2014	2011	2014		2011	2014
Manufacture of pharmaceuticals	114	136	648	816	5.69	6.0	65.7	56.5	Terapia SA	99	117
Manufacture of electrical equipment	569	612	2.557	3.182	4.49	5.2	85.0	79.8	Coficab Eastern Europe/Arctic SA	268	341
Manufacture of beverages	560	678	1.864	2.172	3.33	3.20	80.0	70.6	Coca Cola Hbc	410	412
Manufacture of other means of transport	385	466	1.304	1.484	3.39	3.18	63.7	73.6	Daewoo Mangalia	407	206
Manufacture of chemicals	768	879	2.575	2.217	3.35	2.52	53.3	60.9	Azomures SA	384	378
Manufacture of machines, machinery, and equipment	1169	1266	2.238	3.090	1.91	2.44	71.3	76.3	Schaeffler Romania	350	391
Manufacture of computers	811	854	2.606	1.779	3.21	2.08	90.0	72.3	Nokia/SC Celestica SRL	968	208

(*continued*)

Table 3.10 (continued)

Branch	Number of companies		Total turnover (mil. euro)		Average turnover/company (mil. euro)		Share of the turnover recorded by foreign capital companies (%)		Leading company 2011/2014	Leading company's turnover (mil. euro)	
	2011	2014	2011	2014	2011	2014	2011	2014		2011	2014
Manufacture of rubber products	2472	2769	3.742	4.370	1.51	1.58	75.0	66.8	Continental Automotive Products	525	461
Manufacture of paper	649	730	752	879	1.16	1.20	65.0	55.4	Rondocarton	54	58
Food industry	6951	8120	8.000	8.968	1.15	1.10	35.0	36.9	Agrana Romania/SC Bunge Romania SRL	220	283
Manufacture of other products from non-metallic materials	2189	2410	2.511	2.592	1.15	1.08	64.0	56.6	Holcim Romania SA	223	219
Coal mining	26	32	396	33	15.21	1.03	0.0	0.003	SNLO/National Company for Mine Closures	256	19
Manufacture of textiles	1245	1313	928	1.214	0.75	0.92	77.0	58.8	Rifil SA/SC Coindu Romania	64	87

(continued)

Table 3.10 (continued)

Branch	Number of companies		Total turnover (mil. euro)		Average turnover/ company (mil. euro)		Share of the turnover recorded by foreign capital companies (%)		Leading company 2011/2014	Leading company's turnover (mil. euro)	
	2011	2014	2011	2014	2011	2014	2011	2014		2011	2014
Tanning and dressing of hides	1336	1567	1.062	1.158	0.79	0.74	79.0	60.2	Rieker România	80	81
Construction of metal structures and metal products	5414	5777	3.671	3.686	0.68	0.64	47.0	46.0	Sews Romania/ Bamesa Otel SA	214	98
Wood processing, except for manufacture of furniture	4786	5345	2.449	2.991	0.51	0.56	65.1	55.4	Hozl-industrie Schweighofer SRL	375	451
Manufacture of clothing	3719	4584	1.987	2.242	0.53	0.49	61.0	46.4	Benrom SRL/SC Rosco Textil SRL	150	70
Manufacture of furniture	3048	3347	1.741	1.827	0.57	0.13	56.0	35.5	Johnson Controls Romania/SC Aramis Invest SRL	264	128

(*continued*)

Table 3.10 (continued)

	Number of companies		Total turnover (mil. euro)		Average turnover/company (mil. euro)		Share of the turnover recorded by foreign capital companies (%)		Leading company	Leading company's turnover (mil. euro)	
Branch	2011	2014	2011	2014	2011	2014	2011	2014	2011/2014	2011	2014
Total 23 industrial branches	**37,022**	**41,859**	**64.435**	**71.668**	**1.74**	**1.71**	**–**	**–**	**–**	**16.298**	**15.926**
Share of the 23 branches in total mining and manufacturing industries (%)	**80.20**	**77.7**	**93.19**	**79.00**	**...**	**...**	**72.9**	**65.6**	**Share of leading companies in total turnover of extraction and processing industries**	**25.3**	**22.2**

Source: Authors' own compilation based on data from: (Mereuță et al. 2013) and *Results and Performances of Industrial and Construction Companies*, NIS, Bucharest, 2016

Note: ... = Not available data

As Table 3.10 shows, the average *turnover per company in the overall mining and manufacturing industries* was, in 2014, 1.68 mil. euro.

The largest industrial companies deal in crude oil and gas extraction, scoring an average turnover of approximately 128.99 mil. euro, with OMV Petrom holding the top position with a turnover of 3.7 bn. euro in 2014.

In parallel with the increase in the number of companies in industry, another trend that appeared after 1996 was the *concentration of industrial companies*, which became obvious when the turnover of the top five companies and the number of employees of the top 20 companies grew significantly. In general, most of the leading companies are involved in the manufacture of *coking coal and related products, and oil processing*—the topmost five companies had, in the aggregate, a turnover of 85.6% in 1996, 97.8% in 2011, and 98.9% in 2015, with a employees that accounted for 81.6%, 83.6%, and, respectively, 89.0% of the entire employment in the sector (Chivu and Ciutacu 2014, 157–166).

Coming second from the point of view of concentration was the *metallurgical industry*, which accounted for 51.2% in 1996, 50.2% in 2011, and 50.9% in 2014 of the aggregate turnover of the top five companies.

The *concentration trend* is also visible in the *manufacture of textile products*, where the top five companies had a share of 6.3% of the sector's turnover in 1996, 24.5% in 2011, and 17.1% in 2015.

In the sector of *production and supply of electrical power, heating, gas and water*, where the market has been continuously opening to companies that are investing in renewable sources of energy, the level of concentration has followed a reverse tendency, so that the turnover of the top five companies accounted for 92.5% of the sector's total in 1996 but only 29.3% in 2011 and 14.2% in 2015 (Table 3.11).

A similar *decreasing concentration trend* can be noticed in the manufacture of *road transport motor vehicles*, due to the growing number of manufacturers of car parts (the top five companies generated 67% of the sector's turnover in 1996, 50% in 2011, and 39.7% in 2015).

In light of the current situation, it is obvious that the actions and supportive policies of the Romanian government, such as the encouragement of an industrial policy in line with the aims and targets of Europa 2020 Strategy, cannot ignore the present situation, which requires an approach based on dialogue, cooperation and public–private partnership.

Table 3.11 Concentration of production companies in industry

Sub-branch	Year	Total number of enterprises	Average number of employees	Aggregated as share of the turnover (%)		Aggregated as a share of the number of employees (%)	
				Top 5	Top 20	Top 5	Top 20
Food industry	1996	8636	250,040	10.3	16.5	7.4	15.7
	2001	9920	199,763	8.1	17.3	5.1	12.7
	2011	7508	164,440	10.1	26.0	5.7	13.1
	2015	8149	160,370	4.6	16.2	5.6	13.1
Manufacture of textiles	1996	2462	185,891	6.3	23.2	8.8	24.5
	2001	4930	308,116	3.7	13.9	4.8	14.0
	2011	1317	28,862	24.5	51.1	12.7	33.3
	2015	1325	31,861	17.1	46.3	17.2	42.1
Manufacture of clotting	1996	3479	20,277	7.2	23.4	11.5	29.9
	2001	1732	108,177	6.0	16.3	8.8	23.9
	2011	4111	159,784	15.2	27.7	3.7	11.9
	2015	4759	156,256	6.9	20.6	4.0	12.4
Manufacture of coking coal and other products, and petroleum products	1996	14	29,258	85.6	100.0	81.7	100.0
	2001	25	13,686	90.1	100.0	82.8	100.0
	2011	40	3392	97.8	100.0	83.6	98.7
	2015	44	2549	99.1	100.0	89.0	98.9
Manufacture of chemicals	1996	811	133,881	31.9	62.4	24.4	59.1
	2001	1024	68,986	28.3	56.6	27.9	61.8
	2011	827	31,179	48.3	71.7	37.3	63.7
	2015	871	24,044	29.7	56.1	28.0	54.5
Manufacture of other products from non-metallic minerals	1996	959	124,281	23.4	47.9	16.4	41.7
	2001	1593	84,480	20.7	40.5	12.3	39.8
	2011	2359	41,703	31.3	50.9	11.1	28.0
	2015	2412	38,613	12.6	41.9	12.2	30.3
Metallurgical industry	1996	322	163,847	51.2	80.0	46.6	75.9
	2001	412	102,014	48.9	82.7	51.6	77.8
	2011	426	37,559	50.2	83.2	44.8	74.1
	2015	407	29,908	54.0	76.9	43.2	70.9
Manufacture of machines, machinery and equipment	1996	674	284,663	24.9	48.0	25.7	49.2
	2001	1016	170,637	3.9	32.1	19.7	46.6
	2011	1270	54,809	39.2	58.2	20.1	41.4
	2015	1236	51,474	32.1	57.4	19.3	41.8

(continued)

Table 3.11 (continued)

Sub-branch	Year	Total number of enterprises	Average number of employees	Aggregated as share of the turnover (%)		Aggregated as a share of the number of employees (%)	
				Top 5	Top 20	Top 5	Top 20
Manufacture of road motor vehicles, trailers and semi-trailers	1996	152	107,270	67.1	87.5	56.0	85.2
	2001	311	73,630	56.6	75.1	44.1	74.9
	2011	425	124,336	50.0	76.0	31.2	64.4
	2015	456	168,349	39.7	68.1	25.1	60.6
Production and supply of electricity, heating, gas, hot water, and air conditioning	1996	146	177,030	92.5	95.6	73.3	84.6
	2001	151	127,601	80.5	96.3	68.7	85.4
	2011	924	79,239	29.3	63.3	27.9	65.2
	2015	1460	71,754	14.2	44.5	45.0	78.7

Source: *Romania's Statistic Yearbook*, NIS, Bucharest, various editions

In other words, the effort to achieve competitiveness; to boost research, development and innovation; to upgrade production and products; to promote new generic and advanced technologies capable of saving resources; to expand the use of renewable energy and energy-saving devices; to reduce green-house emissions; and, not least, the effort to generate well-paid jobs for quality work are both directly dependent on companies' own policies.

When we say this, we have in mind one of the topmost sectors of Romanian manufacturing industry: the manufacture of road transport motor vehicles. In 2012, for example, the landscape in this sector consisted, in addition to the two large manufacturers with 100% foreign share-holding (Automobile Dacia, which belongs to Renault Group, and Ford Romania), there are a considerable number of multinationals that manufacture various components, both for the two large car manufacturers in Romania, but also, or even more so, for other manufacturers in Europe or outside Europe.

They all choose to operate in Romania due to the competitive edge they derive from the low labour costs. In many cases, however, this competitive edge does not translate into more advanced technologies, or into a technical competency and higher quality of the component parts made in Romania. Many times these products are questionable if analysed from the perspective of sustainability, innovation, research and development and the competitiveness and upgrading requirements that the new industrial revolution makes imperative.

In 2012, the two car manufacturers represented some 34% of the overall turnover of the entire sector, and provided employment for 14.5% of the total number of workers in this sector. The companies that manufactured car parts represented 66% of the turnover and 85.5% of the whole sector's employment (Appendix A.4). Multinationals held 95.8% of the turnover and Romanian companies sonly 4.2%.[4]

Notes

1. At end 2015, the FDI stock in Romania amounted to 64.4 bn. euro, out of which 28.7 bn. euro were channeled to industry, mainly in manufacturing and electricity, gas and water supply (See National Bank of Romania, *Foreign Direct Investments in Romania in 2015*, NBR, 2016, Bucharest, p. 9. file:///E:/Downloads/eFDI2015.pdf).
2. In France, the Economic Modernisation Act covers also the intermediate sized companies (ISC) with up to 5000 employees and a turnover of 1.5 bn. euro, as well as large enterprises. For the bedrock of industry, the ISCs are viewed as a fundamental element for the viability and sustainability of industrial structures.
3. Authors' own compilation based on data from Results and Performances of Industrial and Construction Companies, NIS, Bucharest, various editions.
4. See Ciutacu and Chivu (2010).

References

Chiriac, Cristina. 2016. *Marea privatizare. Restructurarea proprietății*. Bucuresti: Editura Paideia.

Chivu, Luminița, and Constantin Ciutacu. 2014. About Industrial Structures Decomposition and Recomposition. *Procedia Economics and Finance* 8: 157–166. https://doi.org/10.1016/S2212-5671(14)00076-8.

Ciutacu, Constantin, and Luminița Chivu. 2010. *Anticipating and Managing Restructuring—National Background Paper Romania. 27 National Seminar on Restructuring*. International Training Center-International Labour Office, European Commisssion/DG Employment, Social Affairs and Equal Opportunities, 2010. http://ec.europa.eu/social/main.jsp?catId=819&langId=en

Foreign Direct Investments in Romania in 2015. 2016. Bucharest: NBR, p. 9. file:///E:/Downloads/eFDI2015.pdf

Mereuță, Cezar, Ionuț Pandelică, and Amalia Pandelică. 2013. *The Foreign Majority Shareholding in Nodal Companies in the Main Markets of Romania—A Compendium*. Bucharest: Editura Economică.

Results and Performances of Industrial and Construction Companies. 2016. Bucharest: NIS.

Telegdy, Álmos. 2002. *Management—Employee Buyouts in Romania. Privatization Process And Ownership Outcomes*. Budapest: University of Economic Sciences and Central European University. http://www.efesonline.org/CEEEONet/REPORTS%202002/National%20Report%20Romania%20EN.pdf.

4

Industrial Production Restructuring

In the past two decades, Romanian industry has been the object of unprecedented restructuring, which caused an enormous amount of turmoil, the real magnitude of which, with regard to economic and social effects, to the changes in the industrial landscape of the country and to the loss of a wealth of knowledge and skills, is far greater than statistics can express.

Below we analyse the restructuring process by considering the developments, in real terms, of the total industrial production and that of its three subsectors (mining and quarrying, manufacturing and the production and supply of electricity, heating, gas and water) from the perspective of the indicators of System of National Accounts and also from the physical production perspective.

4.1 Industrial Production Developments in Real Terms

If we were consider value indicators in current prices, it would be difficult to create an accurate and coherent picture of the level of some of the industrial sectors, due to inflation, which, in itself, was a factor that

L. Chivu et al., *Deindustrialization and Reindustrialization in Romania*,
DOI 10.1007/978-3-319-65753-0_4

contributed to the defragmentation and rebuilding of economic and industrial structures and sometimes did much more than the necessary reconfigurations brought about by technological developments, innovation, promotion of new products among other factors.

The *indices of the industrial production in constant prices* is the most relevant statistical instrument for the measurement of the magnitude of a restructuring process, although these indices, like any average unit of measure, may conceal significant details.

A careful analysis of the indices of industrial production as a whole, and also by branches, sub-branches, activities and products, reveals that, particularly during the first ten years of Romania's transition to a market economy, more than half of the country's industrial production simply vanished, along with the technical infrastructure, knowhow, competence and skills and ultimately the workforce employed in industry.

In 2000, for example, the total industrial production, in constant prices, had diminished to 58% of that in 1990; the most drastic losses were registered by the sub-branches rubber and plastic materials (down to 24.4% of the production in 1990), metal construction (31.9%), chemical substances and products (32.4%), textile products (35%), machinery and equipment (36.1%) (Appendix A.5).

The only rise on the production side in 2000, compared to 1990, was in the manufacture of furniture and other industrial activities (141.1%), clothing (137.6%) and electrical machinery and apparatuses (120.6%).

As for total industrial production—including the sectors extraction/mining industry; manufacturing industry; and the production and supply of electricity, heating, gas and hot water (Table 4.1)—the indices show that, compared to the 1990 level, it stood at 94.7% in 2011, at 106.5% in 2013 at and at 116.1% in 2015.

Even during the economic crisis, the *manufacturing industry* managed to exceed its 1990 output, following a curve that dropped to 98.5% in 2010 but then rose to 104.0% in 2011 and 132.1% in 2015.

The output in the extraction/mining industry continued to drop, compared to 1990—from 65.1% in 2000 to 56.7% in 2011—though it

Table 4.1 Real indices of the industrial production (1990 = 100.0)

	1995	2000	2005	2007	2010	2011	2012	2013	2014	2015
Real index of total industrial production	65.4	58.1	72.7	82.1	89.7	94.7	98.8	106.5	112.9	116.1
Real index of manufacturing industry	62.7	57.9	76.4	87.7	98.5	104.0	108.7	118.7	127.6	132.1
Real index of extraction/ mining industry	83	65.1	65.7	67.1	81.1	56.7	92.1	94.2	102.1	83.2
Real index of electricity, heating, gas and hot water	79.2	58.5	53.2	55	59.4	63.2	63.1	62.3	59.3	60.1

Source: Authors' own compilation based on data from *Romania's Statistic Yearbook*, NIS, Bucharest, various editions

managed to recover to 83.2% in 2015; meanwhile in 2000 the *production and supply of electricity, heating, gas and hot water* plunged to 58.5% of the 1990 level, increased slightly to 63.2% in 2011, and dropped again to 60.1% in 2015.

The period after 2005 saw remarkable growth in the *manufacture of road transport vehicles*, mainly cars, expressed in terms of the 1990 level—from 86.6% in 2000, to 387.3% in 2011 and to 485.0% in 2014, an almost fivefold increase (Appendix A.5).

Another thriving sector has been the *manufacture of tobacco* products: after a slight a decline in 2000 to 99.6% of 1990 levels, it rose to 162.1% in 2011 and 192.8% in 2014.

Wood processing has been another standout sector, although the main operations consisted of primary processing: up in 2011 to 134.7% of 1990 levels and 158.7% in 2014, after a slump to 49.5% in 2000. *Electrical machinery and apparatuses* surged to 192.5% in 2007, then slumped to 106.9% in 2011, only to rise again to 152.9% in 2014.

Practically speaking, the best hope for Romania to have a modern and competitive industry lies in the car manufacturing sector, because the upgrading of industry cannot be led by the tobacco manufacturers or by the export of processed wood products or scrap iron (of which there isn't much left anyway).

The four big branches of production which experienced the biggest declines, compared again to 1990 levels, were the *mining and preparation of metallic ores* (in 2008 it was only 1.5% of the production of 1990); the *metallurgical industry*, which went down in 2011 to 46.9% and in 2014 to 42.1% of 1990 levels; the *manufacture of textile products*, the output of which, in 2011, had diminished to 36.9%, and in 2014 to 47.1% of 1990 levels; the production of *means of transport other than road transport, such as air, rail, sea- and river-going vessels* was reduced to 39.8% in 2011 and 70.1% in 2014 of 1990 levels.

Taking as reference the month of December 2005, and in line with the latest NACE aggregation, the indices of industrial production in the past decade (2005–2015) for the overall domestic market and external market, appear as in Table 4.2.

The figures in Table 4.2 indicate that the highest price rises occurred in the water supply and sanitation and tobacco sectors.

The course followed by Romania's industry is not an exception by comparison to other EU member states.

Taking the year 2005 as reference, we can see that the output of the mining industry in Romania had grown 1.60 times, by 2015, which was less than the growth of the same industry in Slovakia—1.94 times, or Poland—1.61 times, but higher than in all the other EU member states (Appendix A.6).

In the manufacturing industry, output grew 1.73 times during the same reference period, 2005–2015, which places Romania the third among the EU member countries, after Slovakia and Poland (Appendix A.7). The production of electricity, heating, gas and hot water in Romania grew 1.13 times, which was slightly below the figures for Bulgaria (1.16 times) and Austria (1.15 times) (Appendix A.8).

At a time when the EC's policy is targeting competition in the field of energy and raw materials and the efficient use of the member countries' resources, the extraction/mining industries of Romania still are experiencing positive developments.

Table 4.2 Price indices of industrial production by activities (CAEN Rev. 2) and large groups of industries (December 2005 = 100.0)

Branch/Sub-branch	2005	2006	2007	2008	2009	2010	2011	2012	2013	2014	2015
TOTAL	**100.0**	**106.9**	**116.1**	**125.5**	**128.6**	**137.6**	**145.9**	**152.9**	**152.8**	**150.8**	**148.2**
Mining industry	**100.0**	**121.0**	**143.0**	**136.3**	**136.2**	**139.6**	**146.9**	**147.9**	**157.1**	**153.1**	**143.9**
Mining of hard coal and lignite	100.0	111.3	123.7	127.2	135.5	136.1	141.5	153.9	147.1	144.4	141.5
Extraction of crude oil and natural gas	100.0	124.2	151.1	137.6	136.9	136.1	138.5	142.8	163.8	154.2	135.4
Other extraction/mining activities	100.0	107.3	115.4	128.9	131.3	131.8	137.9	142.6	144.4	146.7	146.1
Activities ancillary to extraction/mining activities	100.0	124.2	151.1	137.6	132.6	147.0	176.6	158.2	151.1	158.8	174.5
Manufacturing industry	100.0	106.2	116.0	126.7	130.5	141.2	149.9	158.2	155.8	152.2	150.0
Food industry	100.0	106.4	123.1	135.1	136.5	148.0	159.4	177.5	170.8	167.9	169.0
Manufacture of beverages	100.0	108.5	111.8	128.0	139.4	143.8	149.6	155.8	167.4	170.8	176.7
Manufacture of tobacco products	100.0	124.2	134.8	155.6	189.4	223.6	215.6	221.9	230.6	240.3	245.7
Manufacture of textile products	100.0	101.4	110.2	119.0	122.4	132.4	140.8	152.0	159.7	163.0	168.3
Manufacture of clothing	100.0	109.8	125.4	141.0	152.6	162.6	171.9	185.1	193.3	203.3	211.5
Tanning and dressing of hides; manufacture of travelling bags and luggage, leather items, saddlery and harness, and footwear; dressing and dyeing of furs	100.0	115.7	131.6	148.1	161.7	174.2	190.7	201.6	201.1	210.0	215.0
Processing of wood; manufacture of wooden and cork products, except for furniture; manufacture of straw items and other plaiting vegetal materials	100.0	104.6	113.5	126.7	124.1	128.8	136.9	143.8	148.0	151.2	157.3
Manufacture of paper and paper products	100.0	105.3	115.1	130.0	127.3	142.3	156.7	163.6	169.1	170.5	170.7

(*continued*)

Table 4.2 (continued)

Branch/Sub-branch	2005	2006	2007	2008	2009	2010	2011	2012	2013	2014	2015
Printing and reproduction of recorded media	100.0	105.0	117.8	124.9	136.4	139.9	159.9	175.5	177.6	178.8	179.3
Manufacture of coking products and of petroleum-based products	100.0	113.6	140.8	103.1	135.0	182.7	210.6	226.7	213.2	152.5	124.2
Manufacture of chemical substances and products	100.0	103.9	108.4	123.1	122.8	130.7	144.5	155.7	149.4	146.2	130.8
Manufacture of basic pharmaceutical products and pharmaceutical preparations	100.0	105.7	101.8	113.6	135.9	159.3	163.1	172.6	179.9	185.0	197.0
Manufacture of rubber and plastic products	100.0	116.5	114.8	120.7	122.8	127.4	134.7	144.1	143.9	144.6	146.1
Manufacture of other of non-metallic mineral products	100.0	105.6	112.1	124.9	123.2	122.0	121.3	126.5	124.0	123.6	121.0
Metallurgical industry	100.0	111.0	114.8	141.9	130.4	156.2	164.5	165.9	149.8	152.3	133.1
Industry of metal structures and metal products, except for machines, machinery, and equipment	100.0	100.8	119.3	136.4	134.5	138.9	148.0	152.7	146.0	142.6	138.2
Manufacture of computers, of electronic and optical devices	100.0	101.1	114.9	117.1	112.4	128.3	133.0	135.1	130.3	125.1	122.7
Manufacture of electrical equipment	100.0	115.5	125.1	135.0	135.7	145.3	150.9	153.1	152.1	150.4	148.4
Manufacture of machines, machinery, and equipment n.e.c.	100.0	107.4	110.7	130.0	133.8	138.7	140.3	147.9	149.1	146.8	149.4
Manufacture of road transport vehicles, trailers and semi-trailers	100.0	98.6	106.0	119.6	124.6	128.7	135.3	141.0	140.8	139.3	141.9
Manufacture of other means of transport	100.0	103.5	106.8	121.5	135.2	138.1	143.9	153.3	153.7	154.1	148.9
Manufacture of furniture	100.0	104.8	111.4	122.2	129.4	132.0	135.1	139.7	143.6	146.6	151.4
Other industrial activities n.e.c.	100.0	101.3	104.2	124.6	133.9	139.3	147.9	153.8	160.2	169.4	178.4

(continued)

Table 4.2 (continued)

Branch/Sub-branch	2005	2006	2007	2008	2009	2010	2011	2012	2013	2014	2015
Repair, maintenance and construction of machines and equipment	100.0	107.8	115.9	129.9	134.8	143.1	148.3	149.9	150.5	150.5	153.0
Production and supply of electricity, heating, gas, hot water and air conditioning	100.0	106.6	110.9	117.8	118.1	121.0	127.0	129.6	136.2	140.0	137.1
Water supply, sanitation, waste management; decontamination activities	100.0	124.3	137.6	148.7	167.6	181.7	230.9	245.8	273.3	283.2	292.8
Industry of intermediate products	100.0	110.3	117.6	131.7	128.9	140.2	148.1	154.3	149.6	150.1	145.5
Industry of capital goods	100.0	100.3	109.8	122.0	124.8	131.2	136.7	141.8	140.0	137.5	137.9
Industry of durables goods	100.0	90.9	95.4	104.1	109.2	110.1	115.4	120.3	121.5	122.7	124.4
Industry of goods for current use	100.0	107.3	117.0	131.5	139.6	147.7	157.6	170.8	173.1	174.7	178.1
Energy industry	100.0	109.5	119.4	117.7	123.6	133.7	144.0	149.2	154.0	146.4	138.6

Note: n.e.c - not elsewhere classified
Source: Authors' own compilation based on data from Tempo online, NIS

4.2 Evolution from the Perspective of the System of National Accounts

The *analysis of the national accounts (National Accounts 2012–2013*, NIS 2016) provides a complementary perspective of how some industrial indicators have changed.

Appendix A.9 displays the figures regarding the *gross production, intermediate consumption and the gross value added*, expressed in euro for the three industrial sectors; and Appendix A.10 displays the same parameters for sub-branches and activities in the manufacturing industry.

Of great importance are the indices of the gross production, intermediate consumption and gross value added based on data provided by *Romania's Statistic Yearbook*, NIS, various editions (Table 4.3).

In 2013, compared to 1990, the gross production in the manufacturing industry increased by 51.4%, while in the extraction/mining industry, gross production dropped to 53.6%; the production and supply of electricity, heating, gas and water dropped to 96.2%.

In the past 24 years, the gross value added grew in the manufacturing industry by 17.3%, but diminished in the extraction/mining industries to less than a quarter (24.6%) (Fig. 4.1).

Although gross production and intermediate consumption diminished, the gross value added in the energy sector had a spectacular growth spurt of 4.2 times by 1995 and 3.42 times by 2013 as compared with 1990 (Fig. 4.2).

This growth, which was generated by the policies designed to align internal prices to global prices for the sake of competition and not necessarily in line with domestic production costs, presented a major challenge, representing as it did a significant effort to increase competitiveness of the entire Romanian economy and manufacturing industry, regardless of global market trends.

The data for the years 1991, 2002, 2005, 2010 and 2013 for the balance of resources/use per product (the System of National Accounts) (Appendixes A.11, A.12, A.13, A.14 and A.15) prompt us to draw the following important conclusions.

On the *resource* side:

Table 4.3 Indices of gross production, intermediate consumption and gross value added, in industry (1990 = 100.0)

Branch	Indicator	1995	2000	2005	2007	2008	2009	2010	2011	2012	2013
Mining industry	Gross production	82.9	65.0	70.8	73.0	58.8	61.5	68.2	83.1	66.2	53.6
	Intermediate consumption	99.3	77.6	92.0	95.2	75.0	78.1	83.3	133.3	105.0	95.5
	Gross value added	64.5	50.3	48.9	49.9	41.7	44.1	51.9	42.8	35.0	24.6
Manufacturing industry	Gross production	79.9	84.1	119.7	138.7	143.6	135.7	137.7	142.5	141.5	151.4
	Intermediate consumption	81.8	88.5	129.6	151.0	157.4	147.1	148.2	159.0	162.2	172.9
	Gross value added	75.9	74.9	100.9	115.6	118.4	114.0	117.3	114.6	108.8	117.3
Electricity, heating, gas and water	Gross production	95.4	75.3	80.7	84.5	96.6	110.4	93.2	109.2	108.1	96.2
	Intermediate consumption	77.9	65.3	72.0	75.5	87.4	99.5	83.2	95.1	98.0	84.9
	Gross value added	420.3	281	275.6	286.0	311.5	361.6	316.4	387.6	356.6	342.3

Source: Authors' own compilation based on data from *Romania's Statistic Yearbook*, NIS, Bucharest, various editions

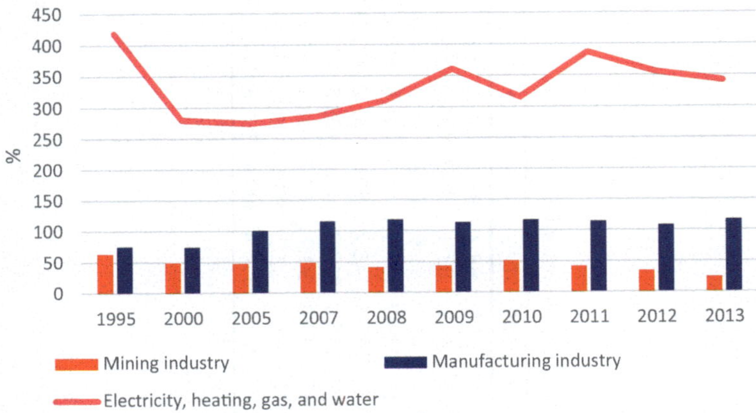

Fig. 4.1 Indices of gross value added, in industry, by subsectors (1990 = 100.0). Source: Authors' own compilation based on data from *Romania's Statistic Yearbook*, NIS, Bucharest, various editions

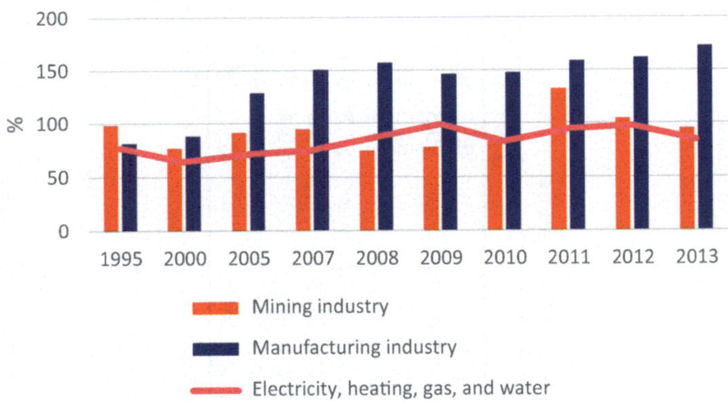

Fig. 4.2 Indices of intermediate consumption, in industry, by subsectors (1990 = 100.0). Source: Authors' own compilation based on data from *Romania's Statistic Yearbook*, NIS, Bucharest, various editions

- *Imports* increased their share from a *minimum of 3.1%* for rubber and plastic material products and a *maximum of 14.1%* for the extraction/mining industry products *in 1991*, to shares between a *minimum of 0.6%* for electric power and a *maximum of 49.7%* for machine building, household appliances and spare parts; *44.3%* for textile products, and *39.6%* for chemical products, *in 2002. In 2010,* the share of imports versus total resources stood at *54.4%* for computers and electronic products; at *54.1%* for machines, machinery and equipment; *52.3%* for electrical equipment; *48.6%* for chemical products; *47.4%* for basic pharmaceutical substances and pharmaceutical preparations. In 2013, imports accounted for *57.2%* of the resources for the manufacture of computers, electronic and optic products; *53.6%* for the manufacture of machines, machinery and equipment; and over *50%* for the manufacture of electrical equipment and products of the chemical industry.

- *The share of the commercial and transport margins in overall resources* went from a *minimum of 0.3%* in energy, *2.7%* for the means of transport, *3.5%* for the products of the chemical industry, *3.6%* for the products of the electro technical industry *in 1991* to *37.5%* for the products of the extraction industry, *36.3%* for pharmaceutical substances and preparations, *24.5%* for products obtained from processing of crude oil, *23.7%* for products of the food industry, beverages, tobacco, *in 2010. In 2013*, the share of commercial and transport margins was *37.9%* for pharmaceuticals, *27.2%* for the extraction industry, *18.1%* for crude processing and *17.6%* for the products of the chemical industry.
- *Subsidies per product* represented *10.0%* of the resources for energy, *3.2%* for products of the food industry, *1.1%* for textiles and clothing and *0.5%* for products of the extraction/mining industry *in 1991*; *in 2010,* they accounted for only *0.6%* of all resources for electricity, heating, gas and steam, and 0.1% for the extraction industry, electrical equipment, a share that increased to *1.5%* in 2013:

On the *utilisation* side:

- in *1991*, *exports* held maximum shares of *18.0%* for wood, paper and cardboard products; *15.7%* for the means of transport, *15.2%* for the products of the metallurgical industry and *12.9%* for chemical products; in *2010*, exports accounted for a share of *55.4%* for electrical equipment; *42.0%* for textile products and clothing; *38.0%* for means of transport; *30.4%* for machines, machinery and equipment; *26.8%* for metallurgical products and metal structures; *22.3%* for wooden products; *in 2013*, exports had reached shares of *55.3%* for electrical equipment, *53.9%* for furniture, *46.6%* for the production of means of transport, and *39.9%* for wooden products; large shares were also held by rubber products, machines and equipment.

- The *rate of intermediate consumption as a share of overall use* tended to diminish; *in 2013*, the intermediate consumption accounted for over *92%* in the extraction industry, *81.8%* for the production of electricity and gas, *71.7%* in the metallurgical industry, *67%* in the textile industry, *65%* in the chemical industry, *60%* crude processing and *58.8%* for rubber and plastic materials. On a similarly descending path in 2010 was the *production remaining on stock*: the largest stocks that year were recorded in the extraction/mining industries (*2.9%*) and in the production of furniture, and other industrial goods (*2.4%*), compared with *17.9%* in the means of transport industry, *9.4%* in the manufacture of machines, *9.0%* in the extraction/mining industries and *8.4%* in the industry for textile products, compared to levels in 1991. *In 2013*, the tendency for stocks to decrease continued, with the largest of them (*2.2%*) being recorded in the pharmaceutical industry.

The economic restructuring process can also seen in the changes in the shares held by certain groups of industrial products in the main macroeconomic indicators of the national accounts (Appendixes A.16, A.17, A.18, A.19 and A.20).

Even if the groups of products are not entirely comparable, the revisions brought to the classification of activities in the national economy for the purpose of aligning it to the methodology and standards of international classification and the basic structure of the groups allows for a comparative study:

- the share of the main groups of industrial products in the *total production of goods and services in the economy* dropped from 71.9% in 1991, to 36.0% in 2010 and 36.8% in 2013;
- *in the total intermediate consumption for overall economy, these groups of products accounted for* 88.9% in 1991, 59.5% in 2010 and 43.1% in 2013;

- the shares of industrial products in the *gross value added* diminished from 39.8% in 1991 to 31.9% in 2010 and to 28.6% in 2013; and the share in the total compensation of employees dropped from 45.6% in 1991, to 26.9% in 2010 and to 27.1% in 2013;
- in the total amount of *subsidies per product*, these groups of products accounted for 83.4% in 1991, 18.6% in 2010 and 42% in 2013;
- the shares held in *production-related taxes* grew from 42.9% in 1991, to 67.3% in 2010 and 62.7% in 2013; and in the *gross operating surplus* the shares of the groups of industrial products dropped from 36% in 1991, to 34.6% in 2010 and to *28.8%* in 2013.

It would also be interesting to see the *share of exports and imports in the production of goods and services* by main groups of industrial products (Table 4.4, Fig. 4.3).

In 2010 and 2013, the statistical data show that, in some of the groups of products, imports exceeded the production of goods and services within the group: while in 2010 this was the case in the group of basic pharmaceuticals, the chemical industry, processing of crude oil and the manufacture of computers, electrical equipment, machines and machinery, in 2013 this happened also in the extraction/mining industry, where imports exceeded the domestic production by 70 mil. euro. The one exception: coking products obtained from crude processing, where imports were much below levels of domestic production. In this group, the ratio between domestic production and imports displayed a thorough reversal: from domestic production of 2.8 bn. euro and imports of 3.95 bn. euro in 2010 to domestic production of 7.37 bn. euro, and imports of only 1.7 bn. euro in 2013. This leads us to believe that Romania is being steered to import when prices are high and to export when prices on the domestic market are low.

In 2013, the greatest *surplus in the foreign-trade* transactions was seen in the manufacture of road transport vehicles (over 4 bn. euro), followed by the manufacture of furniture and other industrial goods n.e.c. (approximately 950 mil. euro); wooden products; paper (779 mil. euro), textile and clothing products; water supply and products obtained from crude oil processing.

But in the case of the other eight groups of industrial products, the foreign trade balance was negative; the highest *deficit* was recorded in

Table 4.4 Share of imports and exports in the production of goods and services in some of the groups of industrial products, in 2013

Group of products	Production of goods and services (mil. euro)	Import (mil. euro)	Share of imports in the production of goods and services (%)	Export (mil. euro)	Share of exports in the production of goods and services (%)	Balance of foreign trade operations (mil. euro)
Products of the mining industry	3257.8	4070.4	124.9	337.2	10.3	–3733.3
Textile, footwear and leather products	6481.6	3175.4	49.0	3669.3	56.6	494.0
Food, beverages and tobacco products	20,046.2	3711.8	18.5	2127.6	10.6	–1584.2
Wooden products, paper, printing services	5200.5	1181.4	22.7	1960.2	37.7	778.8
Coking products and products obtained from processing of crude oil	7374.6	1731.3	23.5	2073.5	28.1	342.2
Products of the chemical industry	2612.4	4490.0	171.9	1829.3	70.0	–2660.6
Basic pharmaceutical products and pharmaceutical preparations	630.8	2818.8	446.9	1028.3	163.0	–1790.5
Products made of rubber and plastic materials and products made of other non-metallic minerals	6621.2	3228.3	48.8	2799.8	42.3	–428.5
Products of the metallurgical industry, metal structures and metal products (except for machines, machinery and equipment)	9125.2	5715.7	62.6	4281.5	46.9	–1434.1
Computers, electronic and optical devices	2344.3	4505.4	192.2	2430.6	103.7	–2074.8
Electrical equipment	3659.7	4474.8	122.3	4785.0	130.7	310.1

(continued)

Table 4.4 (continued)

Group of products	Production of goods and services (mil. euro)	Import (mil. euro)	Share of imports in the production of goods and services (%)	Export (mil. euro)	Share of exports in the production of goods and services (%)	Balance of foreign trade operations (mil. euro)
Machines, machinery and equipment	3179.9	5420.2	170.5	3786.9	119.1	−1633.3
Means of transport	12,634.0	4468.3	35.4	8509.6	67.4	4041.4
Furniture, other industrial goods, repair, maintenance, and construction services	5288.2	1197.7	22.6	2147.5	40.6	949.8
Electricity, gas, steam and air conditioning	14,754.8	16.7	0.1	104.5	0.7	87.7
Water supply, sanitation, waste management, decontamination services	3613.3	122.9	3.4	858.4	23.8	735.5
Total 16 groups of industrial products	106,824.3	50,329.0	47.1	42,729.1	40.0	−7599.9

Source: Authors' own compilation based on data from *National Accounts 2012–2013*, NIS, Bucharest, 2016

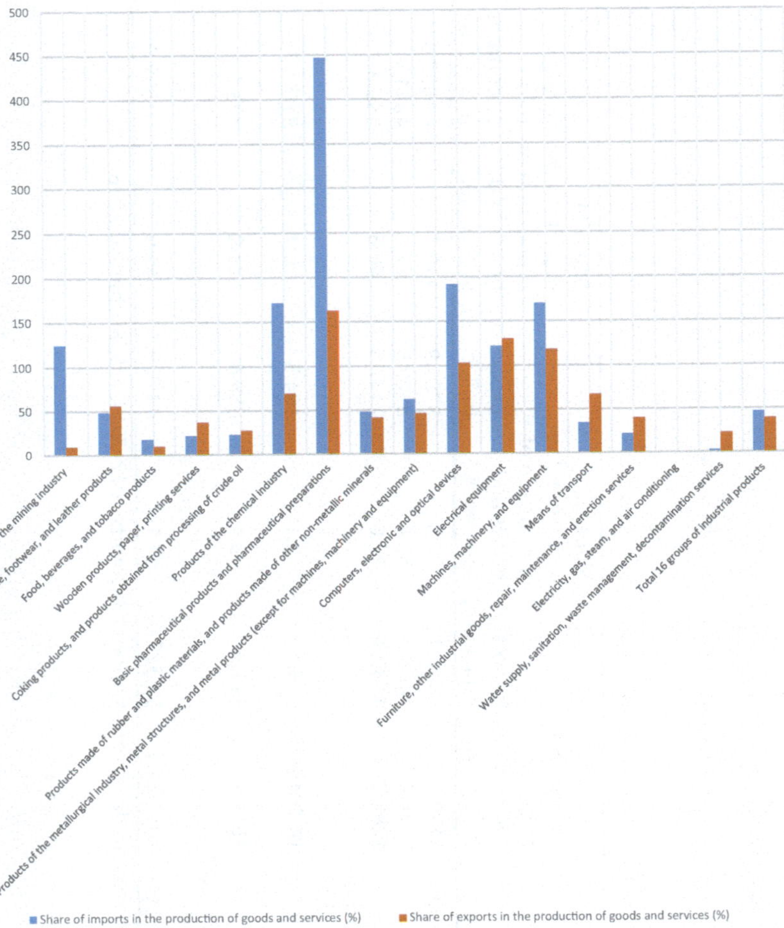

Fig. 4.3 Share of imports and exports in production, by groups of industrial products, in 2013 (%). Source: Authors' own compilation based on data from *National Accounts 2012–2013*, NIS, Bucharest, 2016

the mining industry at over 3.7 bn. euro; the chemical industry, over 2.66 bn. euro; the manufacture of computers and electronic products, 2.07 bn. euro; the manufacture of pharmaceuticals, 1.8 bn. euro; the manufacture of machines, machinery and equipment; over 1.6 bn. euro; and the food industry, 1.58 bn. euro.

4.3 The Slumping Curve of Physical Production

The decline of industries based on the technologies and market principles specific to previous industrial revolutions—which some experts, journalists, and political decision-makers prefer to call "*deindustrialisation*"[1]—can be seen to be in full swing if we analyse the graph showing the physical production of the main industrial products (Appendix A.21).

Although this decline is real, it will not completely put an end to certain industrial products, which will continue to be manufactured in the context of the new industrial revolution (NIR).

If we take a look at Tempo database (*Tempo Online*, NIS) the products generically included in the *group of raw materials and energy*, we will notice that in 2014, the production of electric power diminished by some 13%, which translates into 10 bn. Kwh, with 1989 as year of reference; the production of heating in 2014 represented 15.6% of the production of heating in 1988 (28.5 bn. Kcal, six times less than 182.4 bn. Kcal); the total quantity of mined coal dropped by some 42 mil. tonnes (which was 37% of what had been in 1989), and the production of iron ore practically ceased to exist.

The production of other essential raw materials—extracted crude oil and natural gas—is declining mainly because of the depletion of some of the natural reserves: the quantity of extracted crude, for example, went down from more than 13.3 mil. tonnes in 1970 to some 3.9 mil. tonnes per year in 2013 and 2014, and the volume of extracted natural gas has steadily declined—from 40.8 bn. cm in 1980 (when the peak of domestic production was reached), to 28.3 bn. cm in 1990, 14.6 bn. cm in 2000 and 11.4 bn. cm in 2014.

Similarly, a concomitant, dramatic decrease in the production of diesel oil occurred: after a drop from 8.5 mil. tonnes in 1988 to 3.8 mil. tonnes in 2011, production rose in 2014 to 5.1 mil. tonnes; the production of fuel oil diminished from 10.2 mil. tonnes in 1980 and 8.1 mil. tonnes in 1990 to 320,700 tonnes in 2014; mineral oils declined from 664,000 tonnes in 1980 and 85,000 tonnes in 2006 to 24,200 tonnes in 2014.

In the *metal production* group, the output of steel dropped from 14.4 mil. tonnes in 1989 to 3.8 mil. tonnes in 2011 and 3.2 mil. tonnes in

2014; the production of cast iron decreased from 9.3 mil. tonnes to 3.9 mil. tonnes in 2006; and the production of finished rolled products went down from 9.3 mil. tonnes to 4 mil. tonnes in 2011 and 3.2 mil. tonnes in 2014. As for the mining of ores like iron, copper, lead, zinc and gold among others, statistics have not been reported.

Industrial products show drastic reductions in the manufacture of electric motors (19.2 mil. Kwh in 1980, then dropping to 0.7 mil. Kwh in 2011 and 0.3 mil. Kwh in 2014) and electric generators—from 1.1 mil. KwA in 1980 to 0.1 mil. KwA in 2000, after which this category leaves is left blank in Romania's statistics. The production of electric transformers dropped from 15.9 mil. KwA in 1980, to 5.4 mil. KwA in 2011 and 2.7 mil. KwA in 2013.

The production of machine tools (lathes, milling machines, metal-cutting machines, rectifying machines, boring machines) plummeted from 13,000 items in 1980 to 71 items in 2011. The production of *machinery and equipment for exploration and drilling* decreased from 166,000 tonnes in 1986 to 49,000 tonnes in 2008; similarly, the *production of machines and equipment for various industries* was reduced from 689,000 tonnes in 1986, to 12,000 tonnes in 2011. For the subsequent years, no statistics are provided. While in 1980, Romanian industry manufactured 71,000 tractors, 1612 excavators and road rollers, 276 locomotives, 14,060 freight cars (in 1987), 601 passenger cars, 35,000 lorries (in 1970) and 144 sea- and river-going vessels, nothing was reported in subsequent years on the production of excavators, tractors, locomotives, lorries, ships/boats, road-rollers and passenger railway cars.

In the *group of chemical products*, in 1986, Romanian industry manufactured 2.4 mil. tonnes of sulphuric and chlorhydric acid, as against 0.2 mil. tonnes in 2011 and 0.1 mil. tonnes in 2013 and 2014, respectively; in 1985, Romania produced 3.1 mil. tonnes of chemical fertilisers (100% equivalent active substance—eas), a level of production which then declined to 1.3 mil. tonnes in 2011 and to 0.785 mil. tonnes in 2014.

On the rise, however, was the production of car tyres, from 5 mil. pieces in 1990, to 28 mil. pieces in 2011 and 23,5 mil. pieces in 2014; the production of detergents (100% eas) from 11,600 tonnes in 1990, to 206,700 tonnes in 2011 and 230,900 tonnes in 2014.

In the *building materials* category, the production of cement diminished from 14.6 mil. tonnes in 1980, to 8.1 mil. tonnes in 2011 and

7.6 mil. tonnes in 2014; the production of glass plunged from 77.5 mil. sqm in 1980 to 16 mil. sqm in 2006; and the production of timber went up from 2.9 mil. cm in 1990, to 5.1 mil. cm in 2011 and 5.9 mil. cm in 2014.

Other industries, such as the *production of textiles*, simply nosedived: cotton and cotton-like yarns from 183,000 tonnes in 1980, to 18,100 tonnes in 2011 and 12,500 tonnes in 2014; wool and wool-type yarns from 75,800 tonnes in 1987, to 29,100 tonnes in 2011 and 27,900 tonnes in 2014; linen and hemp yarns from 45,500 tonnes in 1980, to 1400 tonnes in 2008 and 500 tonnes in 2011; fabrics from 1.154 mil. sqm in 1980, to 44.2 mil. sqm in 2011, with a modest comeback to 70.8 mil. sqm in 2014; knitwear from 296 mil. items in 1980, to 27.6 mil. items in 2011 and 23 mil. items in 2014; the *production of footwear* from 118 mil. pairs in 1989, to 45.9 mil. pairs in 2011, with a slight increase to 51.6 mil. pairs in 2014.

A similar downward trend occurred in a number of industries, which, after 2011, went through a slight recovery: in the *food industry*, the production of meat fluctuated from 993,000 tonnes in 1980, to 259,000 tonnes in 2000, and up again to 579,700 tonnes in 2011 and 680,300 tonnes in 2014; fresh milk from 5.9 mil. hl in 1980, to 2.2 mil. hl in 2011 and to 2.6 mil. hl in 2014; edible oils from 392,000 tonnes in 1987, to 203,800 tonnes in 2011 and to 273,700 tonnes in 2014; sugar from 716,000 tonnes in 1989, to 384,200 tonnes in 2011 and 437,500 tonnes in 2014; canned meat from 77,000 tonnes in 1980, to 25,500 tonnes in 2011 and to 33,700 tonnes in 2014; tinned fruit and vegetables from 540,000 tonnes in 1980, to 70,400 tonnes in 2011 and 76,500 tonnes in 2014; and salt from 5.4 mil. tonnes in 1987 to 2.6 mil. tonnes in 2006.

One thriving industries was the manufacture of *tobacco products*, which rose from 27,000 tonnes in 1990, to 49,000 tonnes in 2011 and to 56,800 tonnes in 2014.

Many of these developments were not the effect of innovative thinking or restructuring of the physical production in various industries; in fact, many of the products referred to above were outdated from the technical or quality points of view.

Some products died out either because of competition with similar, imported, goods—albeit these were of no better quality (for example, salt, in the case of which it is hard to claim a better quality standard, as if imported salt could be saltier than the domestic one); or they were ousted by imports of *second-hand* products, as was the case with clothing discarded by Western Europeans which invaded the Romanian market, thus causing the loss of more than two-thirds of the domestic production of textiles and ready-mades, together with the related jobs. All these disruptions and distortions are the result of the free circulation of goods on the Romanian market, which was left defenceless in the absence of an adequate regulatory framework regarding quality both ex-ante and ex-post; they were also caused by the very poor terms that were accepted by the Romanian pre-accession negotiators (e.g., in the case of milk, meat, sugar, steel, etc.).

Both the developments in real terms of the value of total industrial production in the three sub-sectors and those reflected by the specific indicators of the System of National Accounts and by the indicators of physical production reflect substantial changes in the hierarchy of industrial branches and sub-sectors, in their financial flows with the other sectors of the economy and also with the external environment.

Notes

1. See, for example, (Chatillon 2011)

References

Chatillon, Alain. 2011. *Rapport d'information sur la deindustrialisation des territories*, No. 403. Senat France. http://www.senat.fr/notice-rapport/2010/r10-403-1-notice.html

National Accounts 2012–2013. 2016. NIS, Bucharest.

Romania's Statistic Yearbook, n.d. NIS, Bucharest, various editions.

Tempo Online, n.d. NIS.

5

Impacts of Romania's Deindustrialization on Labour Market and Productivity

5.1 Deindustrialization's Effects on Employment and the Number of Employees in Industry

The phases of industrialization and deindustrialisation as reflected in the evolution of employment and the total number of employees in the economy, particularly in industry, reveal a significant gap between Romania and the other EU member states.

According to Eurostat data, the industrial employment in the old EU member countries started to decline in the 1960s; after 1970, and until 1990, employment in industry as a share of total employment in economy followed a rather accelerated downward slope: 43.3% to 28.7% in Belgium, 37.8% to 26.6% in Denmark, 49.3% to 40.6% in Germany, 37.2% to 33.4% in Spain, 39.2% to 30% in France, 39.5% to 32.7% in Italy and 40.5% to 37% in Austria.

Employment in the industry of the old EU member states was in the range of 20.2%–34.7% in 2010, more specifically: 25.8% in Belgium, 25.3% in Denmark, 33.5% in Germany, 22.6% in Greece, 30.8% in Spain, 26.3% in France, 28.5% in Ireland, 31.8% in Italy, 20.7% in Luxembourg, 20.2% in The Netherlands, 30.0% in Austria, 34.4% in

L. Chivu et al., *Deindustrialization and Reindustrialization in Romania*,
DOI 10.1007/978-3-319-65753-0_5

Portugal, 27.9% in Finland, 24.4% in Sweden and 25.1% in the United Kingdom.

In Romania, the employment in industry, after having grown fourfold during 1950–1990, plunged by 2000 to less than half of what it was in 1990, (only 10 years) accounting for 25.8% of the entire labour force.

In 2015, the employment in industry in some EU Member States was as follows: 13.5% in Belgium, 21.9% in Bulgaria, 29.0% in Czech Republic, 12.6% in Denmark, 20.3% in Germany, 20.5% in Estonia, 12.1% in Ireland, 10.3% in Greece, 13.2% in Spain, 13% in France, 18.1% in Croatia, 19% in Italy, 8.5% in Cyprus, 14.8% in Latvia, 22.5% in Hungary, 16.9% in Austria, 21.8% in Poland, 17.6% in Portugal, 20% in Romania, 24.9% in Slovenia, 26.2% in Slovakia, 14.3% in Finland, 11.2% in Sweden and 10.7% in the United Kingdom.

The ratio between the number of persons employed in industry and the number of persons employed in agriculture in Romania was approximately 0.5:1 in 1999, and 0.8:1 in 2015. In 2015, the UE28 average was 3.7:1, more specifically, 11.5:1 in Belgium, 3.2:1 in Bulgaria, 9.9:1 in Czech Republic, 5.1:1 in Denmark, 14.6:1 in Germany, 5.3:1 in Estonia, 3.2:1 in Spain, 4.8:1 in France, 5.1:1 in Italy, 4.6: 1 in Hungary and in the Netherlands, 1.9:1 in Poland, 8.3:1 in Slovakia, 3.7:1 in Austria and Slovenia, 2.3:1 in Portugal, 3.4:1 in Finland, 5.5:1 in Sweden and 9.4:1 in United Kingdom.

These *ratios and the developments in the past decade have widened the gap between Romania and the other member countries,* creating strong economic, technical and institutional divergencies and asymmetries, rather than the expected convergence. This structure is nowadays in Romania completely disarticulated, non-functional and uncompetitive. In 2015, Romania had 22% of the active farm labourers in all of the EU 28 and only 4.7% of the industrial workers.

In Romania, the magnitude of the industrialization and deindustrialisation processes is reflected in the evolution of the number of industry employees. According to National Institute of Statistics (NIS) data, if in 1960, in Romania, approximately 1.26 million employees were employed in industry, their number increased continuously to 3.86 million in 1990, decreasing since this year to 1.87 million employees in 2000, 1.24 million in 2010 and slightly increasing to 1.33 million in 2015 (Fig. 5.1). In

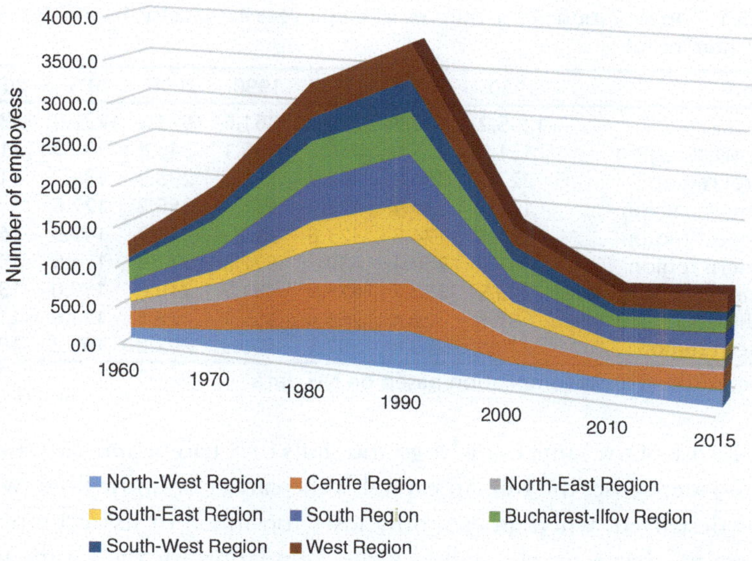

Fig. 5.1 The evolution of the number of employees in industry, in the period 1960–2015 (thou. pers.). Source: Authors' own compilation based on NIS data

2010, the number of employees in the Romanian industry was practically at the same level as in 1960.

These developments took place in the context of important changes in the architecture of the industrial sub-sectors and their repositioning in a territorial / regional profile (Table 5.1).

One of the consequences of industrial restructuring was that employers eliminated *a large number of jobs* as a means to achieve immediate growth in labour productivity.

Once the jobs were cut, the short-term benefits gained thereby were counterbalanced by long-term negative consequences in terms of know-how, skills, qualifications, dexterity and industrial culture in a very broad sense, which will render more difficult all future attempts at upgrading the economy.

It would be interesting to quote here the opinion of Gary S. Backer,[1] who made the observation that most often, the recovery of various peoples, in history, from wars or other disasters, was extremely fast. But, says John Stuart Mill, such recovery is fast only when those people are allowed

Table 5.1 The evolution of the number of employees in industry, by region, 1960–2015 (thou. pers.)

Region	1960	1970	1980	1990	2000	2010	2015
Total	1255.2	2066.0	3329.2	3861.6	1873.2	1237.3	1334.9
Northwest region	151.7	255.6	416.2	495.1	246.8	185.0	212.7
Central region	222.1	360.9	562.3	593.2	298.3	188.3	215.2
Northeast region	129.1	230.9	417.4	563.5	256.2	127.6	137.2
Southeast region	90.6	174.8	323.6	394.5	201.7	143.9	141.3
Southern region	147.9	250.2	480.5	572.3	272.6	174.9	186.6
Bucharest-Ilfov region	245.5	378.7	475.9	481.2	216.6	139.0	139.3
Southwest region	57.5	129.4	261.4	355.7	178.4	113.6	111.1
Western region	210.8	285.4	392.1	406.3	202.8	165.2	199.2

Source: Authors' own compilation based on NIS data

to make use of the same knowledge and skills they had before the disaster. In a broader sense, the human capital is the carrier of know-how. When this is destroyed, when an economy loses too much of its accumulated knowledge, that economy will lack the foundation for the future accumulation of knowledge—be it be it cultural or technological—because this is the essence of economic growth.[2]

The growth and development of any nation depends on how the nation valorises two basic and interdependent pillars: human capital and physical capital. Each of these two factors is capable of adjusting to the supply and demand of the particular market at hand. If we look at the evolution in history of these two pillars of society, we will notice that in the traditional economies they have brought about slow mutations, which generated a long process of adaptation and re-adaptation, both with regard to adopting the optimum response to technological changes, and with regard to allocation of resources. This process of adaptation was handed down from generation to generation.

In contrast to the traditional pattern, Romania's precipitous transition from one type of economy to another, from one political regime to another, caused a shock wave that entailed changes that were too sudden, deep and disruptive for the Romanian society, including its knowledge, values, mentalities, behavior as well as the management of the country's human resources and of its existing physical and natural capital.

In Romania, the need to adapt knowledge to the new economic and political context entailed huge costs, brought about a crisis of values and generated an enormous and immediate need for updated know-how, which requires slow evolution to thrive.

During 1990–2015, industry's share in Romania's overall employment declined from 36.9% to 22.4%. The share of industry in the total number of employees fell from 47.2% to 28.9%. The Romanian industry lost 2.5 million jobs, a number that is approximately equal to the number of Romanian citizens that had to look for employment in other labour markets, where they could not use their skills, training and versatility gained in an industrial environment. Instead they had to settle for menial jobs, such as fruit and vegetable pickers, unskilled labourers on building sites and cleaning and waste collection worker, and so on.

Practically speaking, Romanian workers who lost their jobs did not switch to positions yielding higher labour productivity compared to what they had been doing previously. Had this been so, it would have translated into a competitiveness gain for EU 28. Underusing human capital in this way resulted in a loss both for Romania and for the EU 28 as a whole; the competitive gains made from the low wages paid to Romanian workers are, in actual fact, much smaller than the potential loss of productivity.

In the extraction/mining industries, the number of jobs was reduced by 209,000 (from 267,000 in 1990 to 58,000 in 2015); the manufacturing industry released over 2.33 mil. workers; in the energy sector, the number of employees was diminished by 72,000, which was less than half of the previous number (from 127,000 to 55,000) (Tables 5.2 and 5.3).

In the period 1990–2008, the number of workers dropped by over 70% in the following sub-branches: extraction and processing of metal ores (98.6%), manufacture of textiles (87%), manufacture of machines and equipment (85.6%), manufacture of chemical products and substances (75.4%), manufacture of medical instruments (74%), coal mining and processing (73.7%) and metallurgy (72.3%).

The only activities where the number of employees increased during the period 1990–2008 were water distribution (by 9000 jobs); publishing houses, printing and reproduction of recorded media (6000 jobs); and waste recycling (2000 jobs).

Table 5.2 Average number of employees by industrial activities, 1990–2007 (thou. pers.)

	1990	2008	2008–1990	(2008–1990)/1990 (%)
Total—Industry	**3846**	**1570**	**−2276**	**−59.2**
Mining industry	**267**	**81**	**−186**	**−69.7**
Coal mining and processing	99	26	−73	−73.7
Extraction of hydrocarbons and related services	69	39	−30	−43.5
Extraction and processing of metallic ores	72	1	−71	−98.6
Other mining activities	27	12	−15	−55.6
Manufacturing industry	**3452**	**1368**	**−2084**	**−60.4**
Food and beverages	259	185	−74	−28.6
Tobacco products	6	2	−4	−66.7
Textile products	414	54	−360	−87.0
Clothing	258	193	−65	−25.2
Leatherwear and footwear	127	82	−45	−35.4
Wood processing and wood manufacturing (except for furniture)	94	70	−24	−25.5
Pulp, paper and paper products	43	13	−30	−69.8
Publishing, printing and registration on various media	26	32	6	23.1
Oil processing, coking of coal and treatment of nuclear fuels	33	11	−22	−66.7
Chemical substances and products	183	45	−138	−75.4
Products made of rubber and plastic materials	86	47	−39	−45.3
Manufacture of building materials, and of other products of non-metallic minerals	176	56	−120	−68.2
Metallurgy	173	48	−125	−72.3
Metal structures and metal products	189	98	−91	−48.1
Machines and equipment (except for electric and optical devices)	603	87	−516	−85.6
Office computing machines and equipment	4	4	0	0.00

(*continued*)

Table 5.2 (continued)

	1990	2008	2008–1990	(2008–1990)/1990 (%)
Electric machines and apparatuses	127	88	−39	−30.7
Radio, TV and communication equipment	40	11	−29	−72.5
Precision, optical and medical apparatuses and instruments, watchmaking	50	13	−37	−74.0
Road transport vehicles	163	65	−98	−60.1
Means of transport other than road vehicles	184	60	−124	−67.4
Furniture, and other industrial activities n.e.c.	204	92	−112	−54.9
Waste recycling	10	12	2	20.0
Electricity, heating, gas and water	**127**	**121**	**−6**	**−4.7**
Production, supply and distribution of electric power, heating, gas and hot water	96	83	−13	−13.5
Water catchment, treatment and supply	31	38	7	22.6

Note: n.e.c. - not elsewhere classified
Source: Authors' own calculations based on NIS and NBR data

Between 2008 and 2015, some 270,700 jobs were lost in industry as a whole (219,500 in the manufacturing industry, 229,000 in the extraction/mining industry and 281,000 thousand in the production and supply of electricity, heating, and so on). The sub-branches that suffered most during this period were manufacturing of clothing, metal structures and metal products; metallurgy; and furniture making (Table 5.3).

The changes in the workforce with respect to numbers and structure and in the number of salaried workers in Romania point to great gaps between Romania and the other EU member states, both with regard to the rate of employment per total population and per total population of fit-for-work persons, which is considered as a target indicator in the Europe 2020 strategy, and also with regard to the share of employees in total employment.

In the case of unemployment, Romania has constantly been under the EU 28 average (with an unemployment rate of 7.6% in Romania in 2000, compared to the EU average of 8.9%, and with 6.8% in 2015, as against

Table 5.3 Average number of employees by industrial activities 2008–2015 (thou. pers., %)

			2015/2008	
	2008	2015	thou pers.	%
Total—Industry	**1606**	**1335**	**–270.7**	**–16.9**
Mining industry	**81**	**58**	**–22.9**	**–28.4**
Mining of hard coal and light coal	26	17	–9.2	–34.8
Extraction of crude oil and natural gas	30	19	–10.9	–36.8
Mining of metallic ores	3	2	–0.8	–25.8
Other mining activities	12	11	–1.1	–8.9
Mining-related activities	10	9	–1.0	–10.1
Manufacturing industry	**1342**	**1122**	**–219.5**	**–16.4**
Food industry	156	147	–9.3	–6.0
Manufacture of beverages	29	19	–10.5	–36.1
Manufacture of tobacco products	2	2	0.0	2.4
Manufacture of textiles	35	35	–0.5	–1.4
Manufacture of clothing	211	140	–71.7	–33.9
Tanning and dressing of hides; manufacture of travelling bags and leatherwear, saddlery and harness and footwear; dressing and dyeing of furs	81	62	–18.7	–23.2
Processing of wood and cork, except for furniture; manufacture of products of straw and other vegetal plaiting materials	68	53	–15.5	–22.7
Manufacture of paper and paper products	13	12	–1.7	–13.0
Printing and reproduction of recorded media	20	15	–5.5	–26.6
Manufacture of coking products, and products obtained from the processing of crude oil	10	4	–6.1	–60.4
Manufacture of chemical substances and products	36	24	–11.7	–32.4
Manufacture of basic pharmaceuticals and pharmaceutical preparations	9	9	0.7	7.5
Manufacture of products of rubber and plastic materials	48	52	4.5	9.4
Manufacture of other products of non-metallic minerals	57	39	–17.4	–30.7
Metallurgical industry	50	29	–20.6	–41.4
Metal structures and metal products, except for machines, machinery and equipment	103	75	–27.4	–26.6
Manufacture of computers and electronic and optical products	26	29	3.3	12.6
Manufacture of electrical equipment	39	40	0.9	2.4

(*continued*)

Table 5.3 (continued)

	2008	2015	2015/2008 thou pers.	2015/2008 %
Manufacture of machines, machinery and equipment n.e.c.	68	48	−19.4	−28.6
Manufacture of transport motor-vehicles, trailers and semi-trailers	115	161	45.5	39.6
Manufacture of other means of transport	40	31	−9.4	−23.3
Manufacture of furniture	80	61	−19.2	−24
Other industrial activities n.e.c.	13	14	1	8.0
Repair and maintenance of machines and equipment	33	22	−10.6	−32.7
Production and supply of electric power, heating, gas and air conditioning	**84**	**55**	**−28.1**	**−33.6**
Water supply; sanitation, waste management, decontamination activities	**99**	**99**	**−0.1**	**−0.1**
Water catchment, treatment and supply	38	41	2.9	7.5
Collection and treatment of waste water	6	7	1.1	19.1
Collection, treatment and disposal of wastes; recycling of reusable materials; decontamination activities and services	55	51	−4.1	-7.5

Note: n.e.c. - not elsewhere classified
Source: Authors' own calculations based on NIS and NBR data

the EU average of 9.4% in the member states). In 2014, unemployment rates in Austria, the Czech Republic, Denmark, Luxembourg, Malta, United Kingdom, Estonia and Germany were higher than in Romania. Despite this, after 2002, the unemployment rate among young persons has always been higher than the EU 28 average (19.8% in Romania and 19.7% in the UE 28 in 2002; 19.3% and 15.9%, respectively, in 2007; 24.0% and 22.2% in 2014; and 21.7% and 20.4% in 2015).

One of the main factors that explain the lower rates of total unemployment in Romania has been the free circulation of labour force. Free circulation of labour, in conjunction with the much lower salaries paid to Romanians in Romania, caused the loss of more than 3 million persons from the active working population of Romania, who found better earning opportunities in other EU member states.

In 1990, a total of 40.2% of Romania's 23.2 mil. inhabitants were aged 0–24 years of age; in 2013, out of 19.98 mil. inhabitants, the age group under 24 years old accounted for only 27.2% of the a population; during the same reference period, the share of inhabitants aged 65 and over increased from 10.4% to 16.4%. Due to these changes in the demographics of Romania, the ratio between the two age groups changed from 3.9:1 in 1990 to 1.7:1 in 2013.

In the time period 1992–2014, out of the 103 cities of major importance, called *municipia*, 88 declined demographically, as follows: 6 of them by 15% - 20%, 14 by 10% - 15%, 42 by 5% - 10% and 26 by 0.1 - 5%. The same depopulation process took place in other *139 cities*: in 11 of them at rates of 20–45%, in 13 of them by 15–20%, in 30 by 10–15%, in 39 by 5–10% and in 46 by 0.1–5%.

The demographic depletion, and the social and economic decomposition of Romania, were triggered and fuelled by the decomposition of the industrial system. Romania's smallest administrative divisions, the 1995 *communes*, recorded the following population losses: 23 of them at rates between 60% and 70%; 60 of them at rates between 50% and 60%, 87 by 40–50%, 149 by 30–50%, 420 by 20–30%, 620 by 10–20%, and 592 by 0.1–10%.

These developments have a significant impact on demo-economic balances at the macroeconomic level. In 2015, for example, out of a total workforce of 8.3 million people, only 4.6 million were salaried employees. In the same year, 5.3 million retired people were registered in Romania, out of which 4.7 million persons under the state social insurance scheme received an average monthly pension of 190 euro; 464, 000 persons, former farmers, received an average monthly pension of about 77 euro; and the others were recipients of much lower social-assistance-type pensions. The support ratio (retired persons/number of employees) recorded by Romania (1.15) is worryingly low, with some of the consequences of this situation being reflected in the severe imbalances of the state social insurance and health insurance budgets.

The collective perception of the restructuring has been and is still a negative one, meaning in particular the loss of jobs and sources of income. Granting compensatory payments to about 1.5 million people, in addition to causing chronic budget deficits and dramatically diminishing the population's proactive attitude, has resulted in massive emigration, shortages of skilled labour and, in the absence of job supply, loss of the workforce's self-motivation for continuous vocational education and training.

In the period 1997–2005, in the context of privatisation, the compensatory payments for layoffs reached an amount, per person, ranging up to 20 gross average salaries.

In Romania, the loss of population by migration due to economic decomposition is reflected in the latest population census. The latest three of them (1992, 2002 and 2011) show that the population employed in industry decreased by 2.5 mil. persons.

According to NIS data, the official number of Romanian citizens who habitually resided abroad for more than 12 months increased from 1.48 million persons in 2007 to 2.56 million in 2014. According to the same source, 65% of Romanian emigrants are aged between 20 and 45 years and 14.5% between 46 and 59 years.

In terms of the size of non-resident Romanian communities abroad, in the EU countries, and their share in the foreign-born population of those countries, according to Eurostat data, in 2015, Italy recorded a presence of 1.15 million immigrants from Romania (first place, with 22% of the total number of immigrants in Italy), Spain recorded 595,100 Romania-born persons (first place with 15.6% of total immigrants in Spain), Germany recorded 444,200 immigrants from Romania (fourth place with 5,1% of total immigrants in Germany). Hungary had 29,700 Romania-born persons (first place with 19% of total immigrants in Hungary), Portugal recorded a number of 30,500 immigrants from Romania (8.5% of total immigrants in Portugal) and Slovakia 4,900 Romania-born persons (8.4% of total immigrants in Slovakia).[3] The picture is completed by the United Kingdom, which, in 2015, ranked Romania in fourth place among the countries of origin of immigrants, with a Romania-born population of 237,100 people.[4]

The NIS census data also reveal the drastic deterioration of the age group balance: the 15–24 age group's share of the total employed population dropped from 23.2% in 1992 to 8.6% in 2011 and that the share of employed population aged 25 to 34 years dropped from 30.4% to 24.5%; the share of persons aged 34 and over increased from 46.5% in 1992 to 66.9% in 2011. The state of things is much worse in the extraction industries, where the individuals aged 34 and over accounted for 83.3% of overall employment in 2011, and in the energy sector, where the share of the same age group had diminished from 49.4% of persons aged up to 34 years in 1992 to just one-third—17.6%—in 2011.

The reduction in the number of employees has had a severe impact on the social dialogue, its specific institutions and, last but not least, on the bargaining power of employees vis-a-vis employers.

The trade union density remains a delicate issue. While during the period 1990–1996 the inertia of the centralized economy may have been felt—in the sense that in the old political system where employees' trade union membership was mandatory membership density was 80–90%—the deindustrialization processes, accompanied by a substantial reduction in the size of companies and number of employees, led to a significant decrease in the trade union density. A slight increase in the number of trade union members was observed in the successive years after the civil servants obtained the right to organize themselves into trade unions in 2003. At present, based on the available information, it is possible to estimate that the trade union density remains around 30% nationwide (75–80% in the public sector).

Reforming the institutions of social dialogue according to the Law no. 40/2011, which radically changed the Labour Code and the new Law of Social Dialogue, has also led to a crisis of these institutions and actors, particularly the trade unions and employers associations, amplifying the negative effects on economic and financial issues, due to the lack of the social partner's participation and support.

5.2 Deindustrialization, Wages and Labour Costs

A first finding is the one coming from Romania's place among the EU member states in terms of minimum wage and average wage at European level. Since its accession into the EU in 2007, the only certainty for Romanian employees was the penultimate place in the EU member states ranking in terms of gross minimum wage, with the exception of the first semester of 2013, when Romania was last. According to Eurostat data, in 2015, the monthly minimum gross wage of approximately 218 euro in Romania was 7 times lower than in Belgium; about 6.7 times less than that in France, Germany, the Netherlands or Ireland; 3.6 times less than Slovenia's, and half of the minimum wage in Poland.

In Romania, the monthly average salary, expressed in current ecu/euro, has risen slowly from 123 ecu in 1990 to 418.2 euro in 2015. In 1997, the all-economy average wage earnings have dropped to 56.2% of the 1990 value, then rose to 97.4% in 2006, 111.8% in 2007 and to 131.3% in 2014. During the economic crisis, if we take 2008 as reference year, the *real wage index* in 2014 was 100.8%.

The Eurostat data (Eurostat 2016) show that the *hourly labour costs in companies with more than 10 employees* continued to make Romania attractive for investors, but less so for the Romanian workforce, particularly youths. This data places Romania in the penultimate position (27 out 28) in the among the EU member states, with an average rate of 5.0 euro, as against 41.3 euro in Denmark, 39.1 euro in Belgium, 37.4 euro in Sweden, 35.1 euro in France and so on.[5]

Another example for comparison purposes is the *annual average gross wage per capita in all member states,* which, in 2014, stood at approximately 10,377 euro, while in Romania, in the same year, the total annual gross wage per capita was 1941 euro, compared to 37,191 euro in Luxembourg, 22,269 euro in Denmark, 17,871 euro in Sweden, 4477 euro in the Czech Republic, 5384 euro in Estonia and 1974 euro in Bulgaria (Table 5.4).

In the period 2007–2014, the average gross salary per capita in Romania grew from 1853 euro to 1941 euro; however, this meagre growth was caused mainly by the loss of more than 1.6 mil. people; that is the population decreased from 21.565 mil. inhabitants to 19.947 mil. inhabitants (Chivu, Ciutacu, Georgescu L. 2015, 141–147).

As a matter of fact, the annual amount of gross salaries paid during the same period, in overall economy, diminished by 1.25 bn. euro (from 39.96 bn. euro to 38.72 bn. euro).

In 2014, while Romania's share of EU 28 total population was 3.9%, only 0.7% of the total amount of gross salaries earned in the member countries was paid to Romanian workers, a figure that speaks for itself about the potential demand for goods and services, which is one of the drivers of economic growth.

At the overall economy level, as shown, the average net monthly wage earnings expressed in ecu/euro increased from 123 ecu in 1990 to 418.2 euro in 2015 (Table 5.5).

The *monthly net average salaries*, expressed in current euro, for industry overall, followed an ascending curve: from 111 euro in 2000, to 347 euro

Table 5.4 Gross salaries paid as average per capita in EU 28

	2003			2004		
	Population (mil. pers.)	Total gross wages paid (bn. euro)	Gross wages paid/ inhabitant (euro)	Population (mil. pers.)	Total gross wages paid (bn. euro)	Gross wages paid/ inhabitant (euro)
EU 28[a]	**486.61**	**3966.4**	**8150**	**506.80**	**5259.4**	**10,377**
Belgium	10.36	105.8	10,220	11.20	147.7	13,178
Bulgaria	7.85	5.1	644	7.25	14.3	1974
Czech Rep,	10.20	26.5	2593	10.51	47.1	4477
Denmark	5.38	94.5	17,526	5.63	125.3	22,269
Germany	82.54	922.2	11,173	80.77	1208.3	14,960
Estonia	1.36	2.9	2160	1.31	7.1	5384
Ireland	3.96	50.5	12,746	4.61	70.6	15,330
Greece	11.00	46.7	4246	10.90	45.5	4177
Spain	41.66	295.2	7086	46.51	391.2	8411
France	61.86	616.4	9964	65.84	820.7	12,466
Italy	57.32	389.9	6802	60.78	468.3	7705
Cyprus	0.71	4.8	6703	0.86	5.5	6428
Latvia	2.33	3.3	1393	2.00	8.8	4393
Lithuania	3.46	5.2	1493	2.94	11.5	3904
Luxembourg	0.45	10.6	23,667	0.55	20.4	37,191
Hungary	10.14	26.5	2613	9.88	36.9	3735
Malta	0.40	1.9	4756	0.42	3.2	7562
Netherlands	16.19	193.8	11,968	16.83	253.9	15,091
Austria	8.10	90.9	11,223	8.51	130.6	15,350
Poland	38.22	63.3	1656	38.02	...	...
Portugal	10.41	56.5	5428	10.43	59.8	5733
Romania	**21.77**	**16.2**	**742**	**19.95**	**38.7**	**1941**
Slovenia	1.99	11.3	5651	2.06	15.7	7623
Slovakia	5.38	8.8	1639	5.42	22.5	4148
Finland	5.21	56.4	10,829	5.45	82.2	15,084
Sweden	8.94	113.3	12,673	9.64	172.4	17,871
United Kingdom	59.44	760.9	12,803	64.31	922.3	14,343

Source: Authors' own compilation based on Eurostat data
[a]2003, EU 27; ... = Not available data

in 2011, and to 411 euro in 2015; in extraction and mining, the monthly net average salary rose from 184 euro, to 608 euro and respectively 777 euro in 2015; in the production and supply of electricity, from 191 to 658 euro, and respectively 692 euro in 2015.

Table 5.5 Earnings and salary costs in the economy and industry

	1990	1995	2000	2005	2007	2010	2011	2014	2015
Net monthly wage earnings (total economy, current euro)	123.2	80.4	107.2	205.9	312.2	330.4	339.8	381.8	418.2
Net monthly wage earnings in industry (current euro)	121.5	86.5	111.7	202.8	292.2	329.7	346.9	387.0	411.1
Ratio between wage earnings in economy and wage earnings in industry (total economy = 1.0)	0.99	1.08	1.04	0.99	0.94	1.00	1.02	0.99	0.98
Average monthly wage cost (total economy, current euro)	...	146.4	217.8	361.5	549.5	588.4	606.2	672.2	717.5
Average monthly wage cost in industry (current euro)	...	158.4	224.8	362.6	522.9	602.9	632.9	697.2	723.1
Ratio between wage cost in economy and wage cost in industry (total economy = 1.0)	...	1.08	1.03	1.00	0.95	1.02	1.04	0.96	1.01

Source: Authors' own compilation based on NIS and NBR data
Note: ... = Not available data

The *monthly net average salary* in the manufacturing industry went up from 99 euro in 2000, to 312 euro in 2011 and to 383 euro in 2015 (Appendix A.22).

A comparison between industry, with its sub-branches, and the rise of the monthly net average salary expressed in euro shows that during 2000–2015, certain visible changes took place: in 2000, the monthly net average salary in industry was higher than the national economy average by 3.7%, while in 2015, the monthly net average salary in industry was lower by 1.7% than the national average (Ciutacu, Chivu, Dimitriu et al. 2013).

In 2015, oil and natural gas drilling were first in the classification of salaries in industrial branches and sub-branches, with a monthly net average salary of 1124 euro, which was 2.68 times higher than the national average; while in 2000, this sub-branch ranked third, with a monthly salary of 199 euro, which was 1.86 times higher than the national average (Table 5.6).

Ranking last in 2015 with respect to salaries were the food industry (281 euro and 67.2% of the national average), tanning and dressing of hides (278 euro and 66.5%), wood processing (276 euro and 66.1%) and the manufacture of clothing (265 euro and 63.3%).

The average net salaries in industry, manufacturing and the overall economy are higher in the state-owned companies than in the private sector (Appendix A.23).

In 2015, salaries in the private sector were higher than those in the public sector in the mining the oil and natural gas drilling sectors; the manufacture of clothing, paper and paper products; processing of crude oil, and manufacture of chemical products and substances.

5.3 Evolutions in Terms of Labour Productivity

As an effect of the drastic reduction of employment in industry, *labour productivity expressed as the average gross value added (GVA) per employed person* grew faster in Romania than the average for the EU 28 (Table 5.7).

Compared to 2005, the labour productivity per employed person in industry increased in Romania from 8600 euro to 12,900 euro in 2010, and to 21,100 euro in 2015; Romania was contributing 16% of the average labour productivity of the EU member states in 2005 and 29.7% in 2015.

It also should be noted that while in Romania *the share of the workers' pay in the GVA decreased* from 53.5% in 2005, to 34.2% in 2014 and to 35.2% in 2015, in the EU 28 the rate was 54.2% in 2005 and 52.9% in 2015.

In Romania, the ratio between some of the components of GVA, particularly between compensation of employees and gross operating sur-

Table 5.6 Ranking of industrial branches and sub-branches by the monthly net average salary (euro, % of the all-economy average)

	2000			2015		
	Sub-branch	euro	%	Sub-branch	euro	%
1	Manufacture of tobacco products	225	210.3	Drilling of crude oil and natural gas	1124	268.7
2	Mining of light coal and hard coal	206	192.1	Services related to mining	956	228.6
3	Drilling of crude oil and natural gas	199	186.0	Manufacture of tobacco products	943	225.5
4	Production and supply of electricity, heating, hot water and air conditioning	191	178.5	Manufacture of coking products and products obtained from crude processing	937	224.0
5	Manufacture of coking products and products obtained from crude processing	186	173.4	Mining industry	777	185.8
6	MINING INDUSTRY	184	172.0	Production and supply of electricity, heating, gas, and air conditioning	692	165.5
7	Manufacture of basic pharmaceuticals and pharmaceutical preparations	180	167.8	Manufacture of basic pharmaceuticals and pharmaceutical preparations	636	152.0
8	Services related to mining	163	151.9	Mining of light and hard coal	622	148.7
9	Mining of metal ores	151	141.1	Mining of metal ores	545	130.4
10	Metallurgical industry	147	137.4	Manufacture of other means of transport	545	130.2
11	Manufacture of other means of transport	143	133.6	Metallurgical industry	526	125.7
12	Manufacture of beverages	136	127.1	Manufacture of computers and electronic and optical devices	514	122.9
13	Manufacture of computers and electronic and optical devices	132	123.4	Manufacture of chemical products and substances	510	121.9

(*continued*)

Table 5.6 (continued)

	2000			2015		
	Sub-branch	euro	%	Sub-branch	euro	%
14	Other extraction activities	132	122.9	Manufacture of road transport vehicles, trailers, and semi-trailers	504	120.5
15	Manufacture of chemical products and substances	132	122.9	Manufacture of machines, machinery, and equipment	484	115.7
16	Repair, maintenance, and manufacture of machines and equipment	119	110.7	Manufacture of beverages	472	112.7
17	Catchment, treatment and distribution of water	114	106.1	Catchment, treatment, and distribution of water	425	101.7
18	Manufacture of machines, machinery and equipment n.e.c.	113	105.1	TOTAL ECONOMY	418	100.0
19	Manufacture of road transport vehicles, trailers and semi-trailers	112	104.7	Manufacture of other products from non-metallic ores	417	99.8
20	INDUSTRY—total	111	103.7	Manufacture of electrical equipment	414	99.1
21	Printing and reproduction of recorded media	111	103.7	INDUSTRY—total	411	98.3
22	Manufacture of other products from non-metallic ores	109	101.9	Manufacture of products from rubber and plastic materials	409	97.9
23	Manufacture of electrical equipment	108	100.5	Catchment and treatment of waste water	408	97.5
24	TOTAL ECONOMY	107	100.0	Manufacture of paper and paper products	406	97.0
25	Catchment and treatment of waste water	106	98.6	Repair, maintenance, and erection of machines and equipment	403	96.4

(*continued*)

Table 5.6 (continued)

	2000			2015		
	Sub-branch	euro	%	Sub-branch	euro	%
26	Manufacture of paper and paper products	104	97.2	Printing and reproduction of recorded media	398	95.2
27	Water supply, sanitation, waste management, decontamination services	102	95.3	Industry of metal structures, and metal products, except for machines, machinery and equipment	384	91.8
28	Manufacture of rubber products and plastic materials	100	93.0	Manufacturing industry	383	91.7
29	Manufacturing industry	99	92.1	Water supply, sanitation, waste management, decontamination services	354	84.7
30	Manufacture of metal structures, and metal products, except for machines, machinery and equipment	95	88.8	Other extraction activities	336	80.3
31	Collection, treatment, and disposal of waste; recycling and decontamination services	84	78.0	Manufacture of textile products	327	78.2
32	Other industrial activities, n.e.c.	78	72.4	Other industrial activities, n.e.c.	323	77.1
33	Food industry	77	72.0	Collection, treatment, and disposal of waste; recycling and decontamination services	291	69.5
34	Manufacture of textiles	77	71.5	Manufacture of furniture	289	69.0
35	Manufacture of furniture	76	71.0	Food industry	281	67.2

(continued)

Table 5.6 (continued)

	2000			2015		
	Sub-branch	euro	%	Sub-branch	euro	%
36	Manufacture of clothing	75	69.6	Tanning and dressing of hides; manufacture of travelling bags and luggage, leather items, saddlery and harness, and footwear; dressing and dyeing of furs	278	66.5
37	Wood processing, manufacture of wooden and cork products, except for furniture; manufacture of products of straw and other plaiting vegetal materials	69	64.5	Wood processing, manufacture of wooden and cork products, except for furniture; manufacture of products of straw and other plaiting vegetal materials	276	66.1
38	Tanning and dressing of hides; manufacture of travelling bags and luggage, leather items, saddlery and harness, and footwear; dressing and dyeing of furs	67	62.1	Manufacture of clothing	265	63.3

Source: Authors' own compilation based on NIS and NBR data, Bucharest, 2016

plus, with the latter getting higher with time, should have prompted shareholders to invest in upgrading industrial production.[6]

In 2013, for example, the all-economy expenses for compensation of employees (CE) accounted for 36% of the GVA; the gross operating surplus (GOS), the remaining 64%. Distributed by branches and groups of industrial products, the GOS represented 92.8% of the GVA in crude oil processing (with the CE consuming only 6.9% of the GVA); in the food industry, the ratio between the two indicators was GOS 86.6% and CE 12.9%; in the wood products branch, the GOS was 71% and CE 28.3%; in the electricity, heating, gas, steam and air conditioning sector, the

Table 5.7 Gross value added, labour productivity and compensation of employees in industry

		Gross value added (bn. euro)	Employed persons (thousand persons)	Productivity (thousand euro/ employed person)	Compensation of employees (bn. euro)	Share of workers' pay in the GVA (%)
EU 28	2005	2086.8	38,818.4	53.8	1130.1	54.2
	2007	2326.2	38,960.6	59.7	1224.1	52.6
	2010	2204.1	35,702.5	61.7	1175.3	53.3
	2014	2386.8	35,318.9	67.6	1282.8	53.7
	2015	2521.1	35,503.4	71.0	1332.7	52.9
Romania	2005	20.0	2328.6	8.6	10.7	53.5
	2007	29.0	2247.2	12.9	15.7	54.1
	2010	35.4	1931.6	18.3	12.1	34.2
	2014	37.4	1833.4	20.4	12.8	34.2
	2015	37.2	1762.9	21.1	13.1	35.2
Romania's share in the EU 28 (%)	2005	0.96	6.00	15.98	0.95	–
	2007	1.25	5.77	21.61	1.28	–
	2010	1.61	5.41	29.69	1.03	–
	2014	1.57	5.19	30.19	1.00	–
	2015	1.48	4.97	29.72	0.98	–

Source: Authors' own compilation based on Eurostat data
Note: – = Not the case

shares for the two indicators were 70% for GOS and 27.9% for CE (Table 5.8).

In 2003, the all-economy gross operating surplus represented 57.9% of the GVA, while the CE represented 42.2%; the highest share for the GOS was recorded in the food industry (71.8%), compared to a CE of only 27.2% (Appendix A.24).

Expressed in terms of gross value added *to 1 euro of salary costs,* labour productivity was higher in the processing industry of Romania than the average of the EU 28 by 6% in 2005, 25.5% in 2010 and 20.0% in 2013.

The highest upper differentials of labour productivity in Romania versus the EU 28 were recorded in 2010, in the manufacture of other, non-metallic, products (2.1 times); wood processing and manufacture of wooden products (1.73 times in 2010 and 1.7 times in 2013); manufacture of electrical equipment (1.44 times in 2010 and 2013); and manu-

Table 5.8 Shares held by the gross operating surplus and compensation of employees in the gross value added, in 2013 (%)

	Compensation of employees (CE)	Gross operating surplus (GOS)
Products of the extraction industry	68.1	27.1
Textile, clothing and leather products	53.9	45.9
Food, beverages and tobacco products	12.9	86.6
Wood and paper products, printing services	28.3	71.0
Coking products and products obtained from crude oil processing	6.9	92.8
Products of the chemical industry	36.7	62.3
Basic pharmaceuticals and pharmaceutical preparations	42.2	56.2
Products made of rubber, plastic materials and other, non-metallic, minerals	32.0	67.0
Processing of primary materials, metallurgical products (except for machines, machinery and equipment)	42.0	57.4
Computers, electronic and optical devices	37.9	61.8
Electrical equipment	33.0	66.6
Machines, machinery and equipment n.e.c.	44.8	54.2
Means of transport	57.3	42.0
Furniture; other industrial goods; and services for the repair, maintenance of machines, machinery and equipment	43.1	56.7
Electricity, heating, gas, steam and air conditioning	27.9	70.0
Water supply, sanitation, waste management and decontamination services	46.7	52.5
Total, by groups of products	34.1	65.0
Total, economy	36.0	64.5

Source: Authors' own compilation based on data from *National Accounts 2012–2013*, NIS, Bucharest, 2016

facture of machines, machinery and equipment (1.35 times in 2010 (Table 5.9).

The apparently higher competitiveness of Romanian industry was, in fact, the result of the low salaries paid to Romanians, which caught the immediate interest of foreign investors, rather than the result of investing in the upgrading the technical and technological level of the industrial infrastructure. In the manufacturing industry as a whole, the share held

Table 5.9 Ranking of certain industrial sectors in Romania compared to the EU27 average, 2005, 2010 and 2013

		Number of companies (thou.)	Number of employees (thou.)	Turnover (mil. euro)	Gross added value (mil. euro)	Employment costs (mil. euro)	GAV/1 euro salary cost	Employment costs as a share of GVA (%)	Investment/ employed person
Total manufacturing industry									
EU 27	2005	2183.5	34,185.0	6,894,818.9	1,667,642.9	1,055,738.8	1.60	63.3	...
	2010	2130.0	30,000.0	6,410,000.0	1,590,000.0	1,010,000.0	1.57	63.5	...
	2013	2080.0	29,700.0	6,980,000.0	1,630,000.0	1,070,000.0	1.5	65.6	7.4
Romania	2005	54.6	1593.2	39,940.7	8912.1	5327.0	1.7	59.8	2.7
	2010	48.9	1282.2	56,036.1	12,778.0	6488.7	1.97	50.8	...
	2013	46.8	1166.3	65,676.9	13,962.6	7710.3	1.8	55.2	4.1
% Romania in EU 27	2005	2.5	4.7	0.58	0.5	0.5	106.3	–	...
	2010	2.3	4.3	0.9	0.8	0.6	125.5	–	...
	2013	2.25	3.9	0.9	0.9	0.7	120.0	–	55.4
Manufacture of road transport motor-vehicles, trailers and semi-trailers									
EU 27	2005	21.0	2487.6	917,886.2	151,283.8	109,723.0	1.38	72.5	...
	2010	20.5	2178.8	740,587.0	141,063.0	95,269.0	1.48	67.5	...
	2013	19.3	2298.9	867,015.7	158,081.4	110,297.3	1.43	69.8	14.2
Romania	2005	0.48	106.8	3324.2	643.4	430.3	1.50	66.9	4.8
	2010	0.4	116.6	7767.7	1533.3	899.0	1.71	58.6	...
	2013	0.43	137.5	12,485.3	2247.4	1341.9	1.67	59.7	6.0
% Romania in EU 27	2005	2.3	4.3	0.36	0.43	0.39	108.7	–	...
	2010	2.0	5.4	1.0	1.1	0.9	115.5	–	...
	2013	2.2	6.0	1.44	1.42	1.22	111.3	–	42.3

(*continued*)

Table 5.9 (continued)

		Number of companies (thou.)	Number of employees (thou.)	Turnover (mil. euro)	Gross added value (mil. euro)	Employment costs (mil. euro)	GAV/1 euro salary cost	Employment costs as a share of GVA (%)	Investment/ employed person
Manufacture of computers, and electronic and optical devices									
EU 27	2005	49.6	1363.3	394,984.0	86,694.5	55,109.8	1.57	63.6	...
	2010	44.1	1141.1	290,000.0	77,679.0	50,651.0	1.53	65.2	...
	2013	41.8	1117.5	274,703.7	75,260.3	53,582.0	1.40	65.2	7.6
Romania	2005	1.04	23.3	881.8	254.4	116.4	0.46	45.8	4
	2010	1.0	25.0	2862.3	407.9	194.0	2.10	47.6	...
	2013	0.84	26.5	1582.6	411.1	248.9	0.60	60.5	4.7
% Romania in EU 27	2005	2.1	1.7	0.22	0.29	0.21	29.3	–	...
	2010	2.3	2.2	1.0	0.5	0.4	137.3	–	...
	2013	2.	2.37	0.58	0.55	0.46	43.0	–	61.8
Manufacture of electrical equipment									
EU 27	2005	53.1	1548.7	310,000.0	81,394.2	60,000.0	1.36	73.7	...
	2010	52.0	1458.5	279,411.0	84,937.0	58,832.0	1.44	69.3	...
	2013	49.0	1450.0	289,507.2	84,608.9	62,900.0	1.35	74.6	5.5
Romania	2005	0.8	44.0	1318.9	301.7	168.0	1.80	55.7	2.2
	2010	0.7	36.3	2418.7	512.6	246.1	2.08	48.0	...
	2013	0.6	37.0	2893.8	546.4	282.1	1.94	51.6	7.6
% Romania in EU 27	2005	1.5	2.8	0.4	0.37	0.28	132.0	–	...
	2010	1.3	2.5	0.9	0.6	0.4	144.4	–	...
	2013	1.2	2.6	1.0	0.65	0.45	143.7	–	28.9

(continued)

Table 5.9 (continued)

		Number of companies (thou.)	Number of employees (thou.)	Turnover (mil. euro)	Gross added value (mil. euro)	Employment costs (mil. euro)	GAV/1 euro salary cost	Employment costs as a share of GVA (%)	Investment/ employed person
Manufacture of machines, machinery and equipment n.e.c.									
EU 27	2005	105.7	3079.6	549,433.1	170,351.7	120,756.4	1.41	709	…
	2010	98.1	1835.6	545,931.2	172,695.7	121,011.1	1.43	70.1	…
	2013	92.0	2920.0	622,000.0	191,000.0	136,000.0	1.40	71.2	5.5
Romania	2005	1.3	87.5	1329.2	448.6	366.0	1.23	81.6	1.6
	2010	1.4	51.2	1948.3	706.2	365.4	1.93	51.7	…
	2013	1.27	54.3	2776.2	892.2	461.2	1.93	51.7	7.2
% Romania in EU 27	2005	1.2	2.8	0.24	0.26	0.3	…	–	…
	2010	1.4	2.8	0.4	0.4	0.3	135.0	–	…
	2013	1.4	1.9	0.45	0.47	0.34	…	–	130.9
Manufacture of textiles									
EU 27	2005	70.0	…	…	…	20,000.0	…	…	…
	2010	62.0	662.5	80,000.0	22,000.0	15,000.0	1.47	68.2	…
	2013	59.3	604.5	75,000.0	21,000.0	15,000.0	1.40	71.4	3.7
Romania	2005	1.9	50.7	686.8	200.2	130.4	1.54	65.1	2.2
	2010	1.5	28.1	841.6	227.0	125.6	1.81	55.3	…
	2013	1.3	29.9	1120.2	276.5	155.0	1.78	56.1	2.8
% Romania in EU 27	2005	2 .71	…	…	…	0.65	…	–	…
	2010	2.4	4.2	1.1	1.0	0.8	123.1	–	…
	2013	2.19	4.95	1.49	1.32	1.03	127.1	–	75.7

(continued)

Table 5.9 (continued)

		Number of companies (thou.)	Number of employees (thou.)	Turnover (mil. euro)	Gross added value (mil. euro)	Employment costs (mil. euro)	GAV/1 euro salary cost	Employment costs as a share of GVA (%)	Investment/ employed person
Manufacture of clothing									
EU 27	2005	...	1600.0	...	30,000.0	...	...	...	...
	2010	129.4	1059.8	73,000.0	19,400.0	13,800.0	1.41	71.1	...
	2013	122.9	975.9	68,341.3	18,763.0	13,250.0	1.42	70.6	1.2
Romania	2005	6.4	316.0	2217.5	967.1	756.7	1.28	78.2	0.6
	2010	4.5	155.5	1897.1	822.2	584.5	1.41	71.1	...
	2013	4.4	159.1	2086.3	971.1	682.3	0.70	70.3	0.6
% Romania in EU 27	2005	...	19.8	...	3.2	...	...	–	...
	2010	3.5	14.7	2.6	4.2	4.2	100.0	–	...
	2013	3.58	16.3	3.06	5.18	5.15	49.3	–	50
Tanning and dressing of hides, manufacture of leatherwear, footwear and travelling bags									
EU 27	2005	45.0	550.7	57,845.2	14,660.3	10,082.9	1.45	68.8	...
	2010	36.5	414.1	43,471.0	11,730.0	7283.0	1.61	62.1	...
	2013	36.2	434.5	51,378.6	13,386.6	8202.2	1.63	61.3	2.6
Romania	2005	2.1	101.2	814.0	315.9	249.0	1.27	78.8	0.8
	2010	1.6	57.8	895.5	325.2	226.6	1.40	69.7	...
	2013	1.5	61.6	1085.7	378.1	292.6	0.77	77.4	0.7
% Romania in EU 27	2005	4.67	18.3	1.41	2.15	2.47	87.6	–	...
	2010	4.4	14.0	2.1	2.8	3.1	87.0	–	...
	2013	4.14	14.18	1.74	2.82	0.36	86.0	–	26.9

(*continued*)

Table 5.9 (continued)

		Number of companies (thou.)	Number of employees (thou.)	Turnover (mil. euro)	Gross added value (mil. euro)	Employment costs (mil. euro)	GAV/1 euro salary cost	Employment costs as a share of GVA (%)	Investment/ employed person
Wood processing, manufacture of wood products, except for furniture									
EU 27	2005	187.8	1291.9	137,796.1	36,172.0	23,876.4	1.80	66.0	…
	2010	184.0	1050.0	117,000.0	31,200.0	20,500.0	1.51	65.7	…
	2013	171.8	967.1	118,449.8	29,584.8	20,100.0	1.47	68.0	4.9
Romania	2005	7.4	84.6	1629.6	318.9	176.4	1.81	55.3	3.2
	2010	5.8	34.6	2157.2	522.3	200.2	2.61	38.3	…
	2013	5.3	58.6	2968.5	610.3	244.1	2.50	40.0	5.8
% Romania in EU 27	2005	3.94	6.55	1.18	0.88	0.74	100.6	–	…
	2010	3.2	3.3	1.8	1.7	1.0	172.8	–	…
	2013	3.08	6.06	2.51	2.06	1.21	170.1	–	118.4
Manufacture of furniture									
EU 27	2005	130.0	1284.0	…	36,362.7	25,079.0	0.69	69.0	…
	2010	136.0	1040.0	95,000.0	30,000.0	22,310.0	1.36	74.4	…
	2013	119.9	971.6	91,655.9	28,281.7	20,740.7	0.73	73.3	2.9
Romania	2005	3.8	96.9	1345.3	358.1	244.4	0.68	68.2	1.7
	2010	3.7	60.5	1475.1	388.3	243.6	1.59	62.7	…
	2013	3.3	61.2	1655.6	453.8	284.7	0.63	62.7	1.7
% Romania in EU 27	2005	2.9	7.55	…	0.98	0.97	100.0	–	…
	2010	2.7	5.8	1.6	1.3	1.1	116.9	–	…
	2013	2.75	6.3	1.81	1.60	1.37	86.3	–	58.6

(*continued*)

Table 5.9 (continued)

		Number of companies (thou.)	Number of employees (thou.)	Turnover (mil. euro)	Gross added value (mil. euro)	Employment costs (mil. euro)	GAV/1 euro salary cost	Employment costs as a share of GVA (%)	Investment/ employed person
Manufacture of paper and paper products									
EU 27	2005	21.3	757.0	185,000.0	45,636.6	27,000.0	1.69	57.0	...
	2010	21.0	645.8	170,000.0	41,000.0	24,988.0	1.64	60.9	...
	2013	20.1	639.5	178,695.2	41,281.5	25,766.9	1.60	62.4	11.3
Romania	2005	0.8	17.3	516.4	94.5	56.9	1.66	60.2	3.0
	2010	0.7	12.1	670.8	143.3	66.0	2.17	46.1	...
	2013	0.7	12.5	822.0	173.2	78.4	2.21	45.3	7.4
% Romania in EU 27	2005	3.76	2.29	0.28	0.21	0.21	98.2	–	...
	2010	3.3	1.9	0.4	0.3	0.3	132.3	–	...
	2013	3.48	1.95	0.46	0.42	0.30	138.1	–	65.5
Manufacture of food									
EU 27	2005	...	...	...	...	...	...	...	...
	2010	264.1	7173.9	813,589.6	166,871.9	99,604.6	1.68	59.7	...
	2013	263.4	4059.0	940,000.0	174,000.0	105,000.0	1.66	60.3	6.7
Romania	2005	9.8	174.0	5329.1	879.0	460.0	1.91	52.3	3.9
	2010	7.9	162.9	7434.2	1480.2	747.8	1.98	50.5	...
	2013	7.9	163.9	9050.3	1401.1	794.1	1.76	56.7	3.0
% Romania in EU 27	2005	...	...	...	...	...	...	–	...
	2010	3.0	0.2	0.9	0.9	0.8	118.1	–	...
	2013	3.0	4.04	0.96	0.85	0.76	106.0	–	44.8

(*continued*)

Table 5.9 (continued)

		Number of companies (thou.)	Number of employees (thou.)	Turnover (mil. euro)	Gross added value (mil. euro)	Employment costs (mil. euro)	GAV/1 euro salary cost	Employment costs as a share of GVA (%)	Investment/ employed person
Manufacture of chemical products									
EU 27	2005	29.1	1300.0	460,836.2	…	58,242.0	…	…	…
	2010	28.6	1180.0	490,000.0	111,000.0	60,000.0	1.85	54.1	…
	2013	28.3	…	…	110,000.0	60,000.0	1.83	54.5	17.7
Romania	2005	1.1	43.6	2240.0	388.9	212.8	1.83	54.7	6.1
	2010	0.9	30.9	2337.1	545.7	257.1	2.12	47.1	…
	2013	0.86	28.9	2261.5	566.6	284.5	1.99	50.2	8.6
% Romania in EU 27	2005	3.8	3.35	0.49	…	0.36	…	–	…
	2010	3.1	2.62	0.5	0.5	0.4	114.7	–	…
	2013	3.04	…	…	0.52	0.47	108.7	–	48.6
Manufacture of pharmaceuticals									
EU 27	2005	4.2	549.8	170,187.6	59,044.0	28,624.5	2.06	48.5	…
	2010	4.0	535.3	231,191.3	85,872.1	32,279.5	2.66	37.6	…
	2013	4.2	557.7	229,432.4	79,545.0	34,288.2	2.32	43.1	14.3
Romania	2005	0.13	8.9	377.4	164.7	58.8	2.80	35.7	7.5
	2010	0.1	8.87	704.6	298.0	94.7	3.15	31.8	…
	2013	0.14	9.1	777.8	284.8	116.3	2.45	40.9	6.2
% Romania in EU 27	2005	3.1	1.62	0.22	0.28	0.21	135.9	…	…
	2010	3.2	1.66	0.3	0.3	0.3	118.3	…	…
	2013	3.33	1.63	0.34	0.36	0.34	105.6	…	43.4

(continued)

Table 5.9 (continued)

		Number of companies (thou.)	Number of employees (thou.)	Turnover (mil. euro)	Gross added value (mil. euro)	Employment costs (mil. euro)	GAV/1 euro salary cost	Employment costs as a share of GVA (%)	Investment/ employed person
Manufacture of rubber products									
UE 27	2005	...	333.6	...	...	...	...	...	...
	2010	8.5	340.0	70,000.0		12,000.0	...	...	...
	2013	7.6	...	...	20,000.0	...	...	...	9.0
Romania	2005	...	...	...	...	...	...	...	...
	2010	0.3	12.5	1336.3	327.1	96.2	...	...	...
	2013	0.28	14.5	1873.3	466.9	135.0	...	...	11.5
% Romania	2005	...	...	...	...	...	...	...	...
in EU 27	2010	3.5	0.4	1.9	...	0.8	...	...	...
	2013	3.7	...	...	...	...	...	...	...
Manufacture of other products of non-metallic minerals									
UE 27	2005	105.7	1604.9	249,603.9	81,496.8	47,754.1	...	...	...
	2010	102.3	1400.0	207,827.4	64,256.4	42,269.7	1.52	65.8	...
	2013	95.5	1231.6	201,205.6	59,166.0	41,030.4	...	...	7.9
Romania	2005	2.6	65.4	1874.5	589.1	252.3	...	...	4.4
	2010	2.6	41.1	2457.7	881.2	277.0	3.18	31.4	...
	2013	2.4	39.1	2472.2	665.5	285.0	...	...	6.4
% Romania	2005	2.46	4.08	0.63	0.72	0.53	...	...	...
in EU 27	2010	2.5	2.9	1.2	1.4	0.7	209.3	–	...
	2013	2.5	3.2	1.2	1.12	0.69	...	...	81.0

(continued)

Table 5.9 (continued)

		Number of companies (thou.)	Number of employees (thou.)	Turnover (mil. euro)	Gross added value (mil. euro)	Employment costs (mil. euro)	GAV/1 euro salary cost	Employment costs as a share of GVA (%)	Investment/ employed person
Metallurgy									
EU 27	2005	18.1	1173.7	448,416.9	102,274.9	52,823.2	1.94	89.1	...
	2010	18.0	1030.0	337,061.3	60,681.7	41,274.3	1.47	68.0	...
	2013	17.1	1000.0	340,000.0	57,000.0	43,000.0	1.33	75.4	11.6
Romania	2005	0.44	66.9	4275.5	654.8	378.3	1.73	57.8	5.0
	2010	0.5	37.9	4027.2	562.1	351.1	1.60	62.5	...
	2013	0.41	31.6	3768.2	496.8	331.4	1.50	66.7	7.3
% Romania in EU 27	2005	2.43	5.7	0.95	0.64	0.72	...	–	...
	2010	2.5	3.68	1.2	0.9	0.9	108.9	–	...
	2013	2.40	3.16	1.1	0.87	0.77	...	–	62.9
Manufacture of metal products, except for machines and equipment									
EU 27	2005	370.0	3842.8	...	152,634.1	104,125.7	1.47	68.2	...
	2010	388.2	3632.3	433,000.0	149,000.0	104,000.0	1.43	69.8	...
	2013	373.9	3568.9	460,202.6	159,513.4	111,543.6	1.43	69.9	4.8
Romania	2005	5.9	109.9	2029.2	546.7	388.9	1.41	71.1	2.1
	2010	5.8	83.3	2899.4	777.6	455.7	1.71	58.6	...
	2013	5.6	86.6	3559.9	957.2	542.9	1.76	56.7	3.8
% Romania in EU 27	2005	1.59	2.86	...	0.36	0.37	95.9	–	...
	2010	1.5	2.29	0.7	0.5	0.4	119.1	–	...
	2013	1.5	2.43	0.77	0.60	0.49	123.1	–	79.2

Source: Authors' own compilation based on Eurostat data

Note: ... = Not available data; – = Not the case case; n.e.c. = not elsewhere classified

by Romania in the overall gross value added created in the member states grew from 0.5% in 2005, to 0.8% in 2010 and 0.9% in 2013.

In 2013, Romania contributed 1.4% to the GVA of the EU 28 in the manufacture of motor vehicles (as against only 0.43% in 2005), 5.2% to the GVA in the manufacture of apparel, 2.18% to the manufacture of footwear and 2.1% and1.60%, respectively, to the GVA in the wood processing and manufacture of furniture sectors.

Notes

1. See Backer (1997, 381).
2. See also Rodrik (2015).
3. *Migration and migrant population statistics*, Eurostat, 2017 (http://ec.europa.eu/eurostat/statistics-explained/index.php/Migration_and_migrant_population_statistics).
4. See Rienzo and Vargas-Silva (2015).
5. Eurostat, *Estimated Hourly Labour Costs*, 2016. http://ec.europa.eu/eurostat/statistics-explained/index.php/File:Estimated_hourly_labour_costs,_2016_(EUR)_YB17.png
6. On capital-income ratio, see the model and analysis of Thomas Piketty 2013: *Le Capital au XXI siècle*, Seuil, Paris.

References

Backer, Gary. 1997. *Human Capital—A Theoretical and Empirical Analysis, with a Focus on Education [Capitalul uman—o analiză teoretică şi empirică cu referire specială la educaţie]*. Bucharest: Editura ALL [Publishing House].

Chivu, Luminiţa, Constantin Ciutacu, and Laurenţiu Georgescu. 2015. Consequences of Wage Gaps in the EU. *Procedia Economics and Finance* 22: 141–147. https://doi.org/10.1016/S2212-5671(15)00244-0.

Ciutacu, Constantin, Luminiţa Chivu, Raluca Dimitriu, and Tiberiu Ţiclea. 2013. *The Impact of Legislative Reforms on Industrial Relations in Romania*. International Labour Office, Industrial and Employment Relations Department; ILO DWT and Country Office for Central and Eastern Europe.

Eurostat. 2016. *Estimated Hourly Labour Costs.* http://ec.europa.eu/eurostat/statistics-explained/index.php/File:Estimated_hourly_labour_costs,_2016_(EUR)_YB17.png

Migration and Migrant Population Statistics. 2015. Eurostat. http://ec.europa.eu/eurostat/statistics-explained/index.php/Migration_and_migrant_population_statistics

Piketty, Thomas. 2013. *Le Capital au XXI siècle.* Paris: Seuil.

Rienzo, Cinzia, and Carlos Vargas-Silva. 2015. *Migrants in UK: An Overview.* The Migration Observatory at the University of Oxford, 2015 Edition. http://www.migrationobservatory.ox.ac.uk/sites/files/migobs/Migrants%20in%20the%20UK-Overview.pdf

Rodrik, D. 2015. *Premature Deindustrialization.* NBER Working Paper, No. 20935, Cambridge.

6

Industry and Industrial Policies in the European Union

6.1 Current and Future Framework for Industrial Development in Europe

In the past three decades in Europe, not just the advanced economies, but also the emerging economies, have been developed under the influence of increasingly faster, and therefore often disturbing, effects of the new information and communication technologies, and, no less, of the findings in other areas, such as new sources of energy and new materials.

All these developments bring deep changes in the architecture and structure—from concept to construction, institutions, functionality, organisation, dimensions—of the existing companies and industrial platforms. They also bring changes in trade mechanisms and policies.

In addition to this pressure, in parallel, the issues of resources prone to depletion, climate change and the protection of the environment, accelerated migration rates—including migration of brains (brain drain)—the flight of highly trained engineering and technical professionals, the ageing of population and so on all require a new approach to ensure that the economy becomes smart, sustainable and attractive in order to retain a young and well-trained workforce, as support, to narrow the existing

L. Chivu et al., *Deindustrialization and Reindustrialization in Romania*,
DOI 10.1007/978-3-319-65753-0_6

productivity gap and avoid the creation of new one and to maintain economic and social cohesion at the national and European level.

The rapid changes in the industrial landscape in Europe and in every EU member state are taking place in a climate of distrust, uncertainty in the markets, difficulty accessing finance and skill shortage—all of which make an active and constructive partnership between the EU and its member states more necessary than ever.

In general terms, the new industrial revolution (NIR) that is often referred to in academic and political speeches and, in practice, marks its sharp presence every day, must be understood as follows: energy should increasingly come from renewable sources, and new manufacturing methods should be designed as well as innovative materials and intelligent communication systems.

With this in mind, the priorities of Europe 2020 Strategy are, inevitably, linked to intelligent, sustainable, efficient and competitive socially inclusive economic growth.

For the purposes of European 2020 Strategy, the EC proposed five objectives and concrete targets: improving the employment rate, increasing investment in research and development, implementing 20/20/20 targets for climatic changes and energy, keeping students in school till graduation and reducing the number of the citizens at risk of poverty.

Progress in achieving the objectives is sustained by initiatives aiming to address issues like capitalising on the information and communication technology (ICT), youth in motion, innovation, an integrated industrial policy for the globalisation era, employment based on new skills, fighting poverty through social and territorial cohesion and the efficient use of resources.

There are voices saying that Europe needs an industrial policy to function in an integrated context suitable to the globalisation era. The need for this is explained by the fact that one out of four jobs in the private sector of the EU is in the manufacturing industry; and at least one other job out of four is in related services that depend on industry in the upstream or downstream chain.

In other words, 50% of the jobs in the private sector are dependent on industry, and 80% of the private sector research activities sustains, as an innovative engine the industrial development further and provides solutions for achieving industrial competitiveness.

Industry plays the most important role in the new development model of the EU and in the health and viability of the EU's economy. The recent financial crisis brought to the fore the critical importance of the competitive and diversified value-added chains of industrial processing, for which information and communication technologies and skills are the foundation of international competitiveness.

With a continuously stronger competition for sources of energy and raw materials, it is necessary to develop an industry based on low carbon emissions and better use of resources, supported by new horizontal and vertical policies.

These policies must provide a positive impact on costs, prices and competitiveness through innovation and sectorial standardisation. Also, a careful analysis must be carried out on policies governing energy, transportation, the environment, social issues, competition and consumer protection to see what effects these have on competitiveness.

There are proposals using a differentiated approach and transitional strategies adapted to the specifics of each sector for the promotion of industrial excellence and coordination with the EU policies (where national sectors or industries with a lower interaction with other sectors or with the rest of the world become less relevant), These proposal must consider the entire value chain of production and supply, from raw materials accession up to post-sales services and recycling reusable materials.

Improving the conditions in which industry operates, will require, first of all, an intelligent basis for all levels of government intervention in political domains that have the potential to influence industrial competitiveness.

Achieving such a policy framework will require a thorough analysis of the impact these policies will have on competitiveness (internal market, access to financial markets, climate change), investment, costs, prices, innovation and consumer satisfaction, with the due development of public roadmaps to ensure transparency and with opinion polling of enterprises and of the parties interested in drafting legislative initiatives and designing policies.

The ex-post assessment of the effects of legislation on competitiveness is necessary as well; regular evaluations must become an integral part of *smart regulations*, enabling the creation of reactive policies based on evidence and transparency, in order to identify opportunities to improve quality of the EU laws and simplify the dispensation of justice.

In addition to the strengthening of the single market, by way of observing industrial property rights, *through non-discriminatory and equitable competition policy for all EU member states* and through standardisation, a new industrial innovation policy is necessary.

The EC proposed that investment in innovation should focus on six strategic areas: Key Enabling; Technologies; Essential Products; Constructions and Raw Materials, Clean Vehicles and Smart Grids, with the commitment not to encourage new investment in products that are marketable.

Innovation, alongside with more profitable market conditions and access to financial and human capital must be one of the pillars of a consolidated industrial policy.

The decisive factor in innovation will always be research and development, materialised into industrial advantages. The drivers of innovation for the industrial revolution shall be the new technologies emerging in energy, information, and production (intelligent materials, 3D printing, smart grids, bioplastic materials, creative industries, medical technologies and devices), with the priority lines of action focused on—

- advanced technologies for organic production—the basic component of the NIR (3D printing, recycling of reusable materials, energy saving). For this purpose, a proposal was made to set up a working group to coordinate national policies regarding advanced technologies (guidance, coordination, dissemination, commercialization, partnerships, supply and demand for innovative technologies, public procurement in innovation, partnerships for low carbon emissions, trans-border cooperation for promotion and use of advanced technologies);
- key enabling technologies (micro-electronics, nano-electronics, advanced materials, industrial biotechnology, photonics, nanotechnology and advanced manufacturing methods);
- bio-based products (bio-plastic materials, biodegradable lubricants, bio- solvents, chemical food, bio-fuels, bio-refineries);
- sustainability in industry, construction, enduring raw materials (environmental friendly design, recycling reusable materials, closed-circuit economy, urban mining for wastes);

- clean vehicles and boats, and a trans-European transport network (interoperability, connectivity, infrastructures for alternative fuels, reloading, refueling networks);
- smart grids (integration of energy from renewable sources into power grids, smart metering systems, interoperability of smart grids at the trans-border level through compatible standards).

With special stress placed on innovation, it is important to support pilot projects demonstrating the advantages of developing marketable technologies—to create a market for innovative goods and services; to stop the widening gap between national performance in research and development among the member countries; to use the ICT for purposes of industrial competitiveness; to optimise the use of resources and innovation; *to stop the further drain of ICT experts to other markets; and to increase the number of graduates in the sciences, technology, engineering and mathematics and recruit them for fast-growing industries* (environmental protection, energy).

These are only some of the lines of action for the new innovation policy.

Another set of drivers are those devoted to the upgrading of industry and to sectoral configuration of policies.

In principal, these drivers have to do with the transition to a low-carbon emission economy, capable of using resources and energy in an efficient way, through structural changes of the industrial, energy and transport systems; investment in energy efficiency; and incentives for the companies that undertake such measures. They also have to do with the need for research and development in both the private and the public sector, and the need to stop the relocation of industries outside the EU.

And, finally, the sectoral dimension requires an approach focused on issues like climate change, health and safety (and the development of environmentally friendly technologies designed to improve them) and the important value chains (chemistry, transport equipment, agro-food industries, services to companies), tailored to the specifics of the high-energy-consuming sectors (with a broad understanding of innovation that considers not only technology, but also new models of doing and organising business). The approach should be focused, also, on the industrial side of other policies that may influence competitiveness (such as improving the business environment, streamlining public administration, enhancing the capacity for innovation, energy efficiency); on climate change, energy, demographic ageing, competencies/knowledge, interaction and coordination of policies that affect competitiveness (ensuring that the new policy proposals have enhanced competitiveness at their core).

To follow such lines of action, which will be the backbone of the new industrial policy, the internal market needs to function flawlessly, as well as valorise the opportunities offered by the emerging economies.

The current trend of automation and data exchange in manufacturing technologies, generically called "Industry 4.0", provides the background upon which environmental accounting tools could be enhanced, incorporating, at the company level or at the level of the national economy, more accurate and higher-quality data on the costs of environmental impact. As shown by Burritt and Christ, at European or global levels, the networking of computer systems channelling financial information and data to a common base, such as a cloud, providing a platform for potential inquiries by managers, external stakeholders and larger or smaller companies, across multiple countries, could make a major contribution to making more efficient use of resources and, long-term, securing the prerequisites for smart economic growth—that is, growth that is environmentally and socially sustainable (Burrit and Christ 2016).

At the same time, turning the new strategic approaches into reality will not be possible without equal and non-discriminatory access to finance both for strategic major investors and the small and medium-sized enterprises (SMEs). More public funds will be needed, but also an easier access to the capital market.

In other words, the state, through its *public authorities,* must take action towards creating adequate market conditions and offer solutions to smooth out market-related deficiencies, even if the companies themselves are ultimately responsible for their own success or failure in the market.

Using these ideas, EU industry should be able to increase its share of contribution to the EU's GDP from a current 15.5% to 20% in 2020; and the investment in equipment should grow to 9% of the GDP in 2020.

6.2 European Commission's New Industrial Policy: Towards an Industrial Renaissance

Statement of facts: The role played by industry in the EU exceeds by far that of the manufacturing industry. Industry's role starts with the energy sector and raw materials; and it goes all the way to business (logistic) services, consumer services (including post-sale services for durable goods) and tourism. Industry accounts for 75% of the EU's exports (the trade balance for manufactured goods has a surplus of 365 bn. euro), which demonstrates that its importance is much greater than would be expected from its share in the GDP (15.5% in 2015). Approximately 80% of the R&D expenditures in the private sector come from industry.

One-quarter of the jobs for highly skilled personnel in the private sector are in industry. Every new job in industry spawns other 0.5–2 jobs in other sectors. Despite this replication capacity, in the post-crisis period, the EU manufacturing industry lost 3.5 million jobs, and its performance in terms of competitiveness did not keep the pace with other rivals.

While recognizing the importance and vital role of industry in the sustainable recovery of economic growth and creation of jobs in the post-crisis period, the EC has set a target of 20% for the contribution of industry to GDP by 2020; and for that purpose, it laid down new coordinates for an EU industrial policy, with priority objectives and actions to be taken, as follows:

Key priorities:

I. Integrating industrial competitiveness with all the other areas of economic policies, considering the contribution of industry to competitiveness and economic performance for the entire EU;
II. Maximizing the potential of the internal market;
III. Making effective use of the instruments for regional development so to help boost innovation, skills and entrepreneurship;
IV. Promoting access to resources and encouraging investment;
V. Facilitating the integration of EU companies into global value chains.

The following actions aim to upgrade a broad platform of industries: manufacturing industry, constructions, raw materials, tourism, creative industries, and the related business services, such as—

- putting in place a stable, simplified and predictable legal framework for the business environment;
- creating the conditions for internal market services;
- integrating the capital markets;
- ensuring access to energy and raw materials at affordable prices, with terms similar to those of the world market;
- implementing European financing instruments based on the optimum mix of the programmes COSME, HORIZON 2020, Structural Funds and of the national innovation, investment and reindustrialisation funds;
- recreating normal conditions for the financing of the real economy, for which purpose the European Investment Bank will have to play the strategic role of monitoring financing, particularly that which is targeted at supporting innovation and industrial projects. Similarly, the EU will supervise the development of the necessary framework for the development of alternative sources of finance, including measures to eliminate bottlenecks resulting from the fragmentation of the financial markets;
- supporting the progressive integration of EU companies, particularly SMEs, in international added value chains of, by helping them to operate beyond EU borders (Box 6.1).

6.3 Experiences From Other Countries' Efforts to Support the Industry Development, Innovation and Competitiveness

On the global scale, all countries have strategies and programmes to support—in one way or another and more or less, depending on the available financial resources— industrial development, innovation and competitiveness.

Box 6.1. Objectives and Actions to Encourage Industrial Renaissance in the EU

Objectives	Actions
Supporting industrial competitiveness	The Communication *For a European Industrial Renaissance*, adopted on 22 January 2014, focuses on supporting industrial competitiveness, and the EC invites the European Council and the Parliament to take action for the reindustrialisation of Europe and for the encouragement of growth and competitiveness.
Regulation and policy initiatives	The Commission strives to maximise the efficiency of the regulatory policies and legislation governing the industrial sectors and to promote the integration of the EU's priorities into the national regulatory policies of the member states. DG internal market is preparing a road map on industrial competitiveness, accompanied by adequate policies, including aspects related to the competitiveness, as part of the European Semester. The Commission is monitoring the progress made by the EU member states towards improving competitiveness through the *EU Competitiveness Report* and the member states' reports on competitiveness.
Functional Internal Market	In order to support the functionality of the Internal Market, the Commission shall— – develop adequate infrastructure; – improve public administration and simplify the business environment; – act towards the liberalisation and integration of the internal energy market; – promote market surveillance and product safety; – set standards to accelerate innovation and observe intellectual property rights; – make sure that the services related to the internal market contribute to industrial competitiveness.
Access to resources	Actions

Objectives	Actions
Energy and raw materials	Access to critical inputs, especially energy and raw materials, at affordable prices aligned with international costs, will be a key factor in encouraging investment in the EU's industry. The main element that keeps the price distortion between the EU and the US, to the detriment of the EU (where the price of electricity is twice as higher as it is in US, and natural gas three- to fourfold higher) is the high level of taxation, including the excise tax. The Commission will act towards the drafting and enforcement of the economic policy instruments both for the UE, and for its member states, which might cause distortions of prices into disproportionately higher prices for inputs. In order to secure access to critical inputs, the Commission has put in place, in addition to the Communication of 22 January 2014, a package of measures regarding climate and energy until 2030.
Skilled labour	In order to make possible the development of human capital, the EU initiatives focus on— – Ensuring mobility of learning (Erasmus + student practice and exchanges); – Making the most of the green economy and the ICT sector to generate new jobs and skills; – Easing industrial exchanges at the regional level, in order to support EU regions to upgrade their industrial base.
Finance	Provide an increasingly greater share of the EU funds allocated for the member states to regions and to the industrial sector, in order to stimulate investments in innovation (COSME Programme, ESIF funds, Horizon 2020); Improve SMEs access to finance, as SMEs provide some two-thirds of the jobs in EU 28; Develop the public sector's capacity to provide financing, by diversifying and taking over some of the risks through EU guarantees; render more functional the pan-European risk capital market and the use of alternative sources of financing.

Objectives	Actions
Promoting investment in innovation	Six strategic areas of innovation have been identified where investment is encouraged: advanced key-enabling technologies (KETs)," clean" vehicles, bio-based products and construction, raw materials and smart grids; promoting industrial clusters ("innovative ecosystems") and support services for SMEs' innovations. Encourage the commercialization of innovative products and services on the demand side, for example, through measures such as public procurement in innovation.
Developing key technologies	Stimulate the development of key technologies to shape the future of the EU industry, including European large-scale projects like development of batteries for electric mobility, intelligent materials, highly efficient production and industrial bio-processes.
Access to international markets	Render support to companies operating outside EU borders, thereby helping them integrate into global value chains, as a complement to the companies' own effort to go international and to access world markets. This can be done through various instruments, such as Free Trade Agreements, Economic Missions for Growth and Market Access Strategies, subject to the observance of the agreements signed under the WTO. At the forthcoming negotiations, with the help of diplomatic missions, special attention should be devoted to improving the access of EU companies to the raw materials available in various parts of the globe.
Supporting strategic sectors	Monitoring sectors: put in place the requisite conditions to boost competitiveness; review regularly the adequacy of the existing background through polling all the interested parties, verify the results of such polls and the evaluate of the cumulative costs. Space: ensure the marketability of the services provided by key strategic sectors where investment has "spillover" effects, such as the global satellite navigation system (Galileo) and Earth monitoring (Copernicus).

Source: Authors' own compilation based on data from European documents, DG Internal Market, Industry, Entrepreneurship and SMEs

In the US for instance, industry, academia and federal partners have been gathered through a network of advanced manufacturing and innovation strategy under the public name *Manufacturing USA*, enacted into law in 2014 (US Government 2016).[1] Beside this strategy, in order to support businesses and R&D infrastructure, there are programs and initiatives such as SelectUSA, for the attraction and retention of business investment; Investing in Manufacturing Communities Partnership, designed to revolutionize the way federal agencies leverage economic development funds; AMTech, to strengthen existing or establish new industry-driven consortia that address high-priority research challenges; Hollings Manufacturing Extension Partnership to commit services and partnerships strengthening the US manufacturing; MForesight, a mechanism to provide coordinated private-sector input on national advanced manufacturing technology research and development priorities; National Export Initiative, to help more American companies reach more overseas markets and expand opportunities to sell their goods and services abroad; National Robotics Initiative, to develop the next generation of robotics; and National Nanotechnology Initiative and Materials Genome Initiative, to discover, manufacture and deploy advanced materials.

To support reindustrialization and the increase national competitiveness, the US federal government has made efforts to find the best ways to create new jobs in manufacturing, optimise tax incentives and structure and stimulate investments and R&D spending. With regard to targeting industries with highest value added, the state of California state has been a success story, concentrating the manufacturing of the most advanced computer and electronic products, to the point that it has become an innovation hub and US innovation incubator (Subran 2013, 32).

At the EU level, a number of funding possibilities related to programmes and instruments that support, directly or indirectly, business internationalization and better framework conditions, amounting to tens of billions of euros in the financial exercise of 2014–2020, have been set, among others, COSME (Competitiveness of Enterprises and Small and Medium-sized Enterprises); ICI (Industrialised Countries Instrument); PI (Partnership Instrument); ENI (European Neighbourhood Instrument); DCI (Development Cooperation Instrument) and EDF (European Development Fund); HORIZON 2020; ESIF (European

Structural Investment Fund) to which, more recently, the European EPI (External Investment Plan) has been added. As noted by an official document of the EC, the potential interested stakeholders and SMEs in particular are not sufficiently aware of these significant EU funding possibilities (European Commission 2017).[2]

With regard to specific national policies and instruments to support competitiveness, the internationalization of companies and the increase in exports of goods and services, although there are some limitations on the government's ability to manoeuver imposed by international rules and/or agreements, the operationalization of measures in this area can be better focused, which ensures a higher consistency of their applicability and, implicitly, the achievement of the expected effects. Table 6.1 presents the human and financial resources of selected countries for sustaining competitiveness, exports and internationalization of companies, including SMEs.

If we analyse some European experiences, we find that the most notable results have been obtained by countries that have designed and implemented a coherent system with a quasi-unitary administration and a clear objective to maximize the competitiveness of companies in external markets, directly from that country but also indirectly, using the process of internationalization throughout the global value-added chains and using the third countries as exporting platforms.

An example of a success story is Italy, which may seem less significant, given that it is not a leading economic power. But from the viewpoint of

Table 6.1 Human and financial resources mobilised by some of EU and non-EU countries to promote competitiveness, exports and internationalization of companies in 2013

Agency (country)	Number of employees[a]	Expenditures (mil. euro)
US Commercial Service (USA)	1700	230
JETRO (Japan)	1600	240
KOTRA (South Korea)	1100	250
UKTI (United Kingdom)	1600	440
UBIFRANCE (France)	1400	360
ICEX (Spain)	600	100
ICE (Italy)	900	110

Source: Based on data from Graph 2 of *Piano della Performance 2015-2017*, ICE, p. 19,

[a]In both domestic and foreign–based offices

international exchanges its case is remarkable: until 2011, Italy recorded trade deficits between 10 and 30 bn. euro; since then, the trade balance has become positive with the surplus growing steadily and reaching more than 45 bn. euro in 2015 (414 bn. euro compared to 369 bn. euro in imports). The performance is noteworthy given that only nine of the EU member states managed to achieve trade surpluses, with Italy ranked third in this respect, being exceeded only by Germany (252 bn. euro) and the Netherlands (55 bn. euro).

Among the EU's emerging countries, the Czech Republic seems to be a good example from the point of view of export support capabilities, having managed to achieve more and more consistent trade surpluses throughout the post-accession period, reaching over 16 bn. euro in 2015 (143 bn. euro exports vs. 127 bn. euro imports). Both the Czech Republic and Romanian exports are characterized by a high degree of concentration in the composition of product groups (dominated by several industrial sectors, namely, cars and electronics) and also as geographic destinations (around 70% on EU markets), with around two-thirds of total exports being provided by companies with foreign capital.

Below, the system, mechanisms and instruments that have led to such performances in the cases of Italy and Czech Republic, two of the most important economic partners of Romania are presented, as lessons which can be learned.

Italy's System for the Support of Industry, Investments, Exports and Internationalisation of Italian Companies

I. *Cassa Depositi e Prestiti (CDP), a joint venture with majority public shareholding* (Capital: 3.5 bn. euro; Shareholders: 80.1% Ministero dell' Economia e delle Finanze; 18.4% various banking foundations; 1.5% its own shares)

CDP ha 165 years of history, having been founded in 1850 by King Vittorio Emanuele II, financed by the state and various public entities.

In 2003 CDP was converted into a joint stock company, and since 2009 its scope of business has expanded to the direct funding of public interest projects, financing exports, social housing and SME support.

The Parliament of Italy and the EU assigned in 2015 to the CDP the status of National Promotion Institute (*Istituto Nazionale di Promozione*), which gives the CDP the prerogatives to—

- represent the only channel for accessing the resources of the Junker Plan for Italy;
- act as financial advisor to the public administration bodies, for a better use of national and European funds;
- stimulate the development of new activities with a view to contributing to the country's economic growth, starting from design; cooperating in the identification of resources; co-investing its own resources; and attracting the private investors as well.

The CDP Mission and purpose of business is promote the development of the economic and industrial system of Italy, through providing finance from postal savings guaranteed by the state and from the issuance bonds, in order to contribute to—

- financing public investments, sustaining international cooperation and developing the country's infrastructure;
- supporting Italian companies during their entire life cycle, encouraging start-ups and innovation, investing in companies of national importance;
- promoting exports and internationalisation, improving competitiveness of the national productive system and supporting the growth factors of the national economy;
- developing the Italian real estate market, acting as a main operator of social housing at affordable prices and reviving the areas of activity that carry a strategic interest for the country.

The total resources of CDP at 31 December 2015 were 323 bn. euro, of which 252 bn. euro came from postal savings derived from selling state-guaranteed Postal Savings PassBooks and Postal Savings Bonds through the approximately 13,000 post offices in Italy. Over 20 million Italians have invested in these saving instruments.

In 2015, the CDP Group attracted and managed financial resources of more than 30 bn. euro that have been invested in sustaining the Italian companies businesses and supporting their internationalisation (22 bn. euro), the public and local entities (6 bn. euro) and infrastructures (2 bn. euro).

The *2016–2020 Industrial Plan (Piano Industriale Gruppo CDP 2020)*[3] enables the CDP to make available to Italy 160 bn. euro, supplemented with another 105 bn. euro of internal and external public and private funding attracted to the system in order to develop four strategic domains:

- services of general economic interest for governance and public Administration (supporting public investment and international cooperation);
- infrastructure, environmental protection and energy efficiency (including PPP and access to capital markets);
- supporting companies throughout their entire life cycle and sustaining exporting activities, for which some three-quarters of the allocated financial resources are earmarked;
- real estate sector (social housing and tourism).

II. *SACE—Mission and scope of business*

- insurance services and products;
- access to finance for investments in innovation;
- providing financing and guarantees for the internationalisation of Italian companies, SMEs included;
- protection of Italian investment projects abroad against political risks;
- providing guarantees for the participation of Italian companies in international tenders;
- granting foreign clients payment concessions of up to 12 months;
- consultancy for export (maps and country risk profile for 189 countries, export forecasts).

SACE, with net assets of 4.7 bn. euro and over 80 bn. euro insurance operations in 189 countries, sustains the competitiveness of 25,000 companies in Italy and abroad, turning risks into opportunities for development.

SACE uses the Sviluppo Export Fund and Trade Finance as instruments to boost exports and internationalisation.

III. *Simest—Mission and scope of business*

- support Italian companies' efforts to expand internationally through equity investment up to a 49% stake of the nominal capital of business ventures established by Italian companies abroad, through direct investment in EU countries or through the Venture Capital Fund, in EU and non-EU countries;
- support loans for exports of investment goods produced in Italy;
- provide financial instruments to support exporting SMEs;
- finance participation of Italian companies in international fairs and exhibitions outside the EU;
- subsidise feasibility studies and technical assistance programmes.

In 2015 *Simest* attracted and managed financial resources of 5.4 bn. euro (up from 2.6 bn. euro in 2014), of which 5.3 bn. euro were allocated to encourage exports and internationalization of some 1300 Italian companies in over 100 countries. In 2015 alone, Simest invested 107 mil. euro in the social capital of the companies set up by Italian companies abroad.

IV. *Istituto per il Commercio con l'Estero (ICE)*

Mission and scope of business: promote internationalisation of Italian companies, and the image of Italian products in the world (initiatives like *Made in Italy, Sistema Italia*), with the help of—

- first guidance services (general information, market information, export opportunities, statistics, virtual showcases), free of charge;
- personalised services (market studies, client searching, business meetings, consultancy/assistance to penetrate/operate in a market, organisation of promotional events), for a moderate fee.

ICE has offices both in every region of Italy and outside the country (79 representative offices in 64 countries), and closely cooperates with the diplomatic missions and the foreign-based offices of the Italian Chamber of Commerce. In order to achieve its objectives, ICE has put in place cooperation arrangements with other institutional structures: regions,

Table 6.2 The public system for supporting Italian companies' exports and internationalisation (2015)

System entities	Number of users	Funds expended (mil. euro)
Promotion services		
Ministry of Economic Development (Ministero dello Sviluppo Economico)	152	30
Regions	–	106
ICE	39,784	110
Chambers of Commerce	43,033	40
Financial services	**Number of assisted companies**	**New insurance commitments (mil. euro)**
SACE	24,443	9.750
	Number of assisted companies	**Equity/worth of assisted transactions (mil. euro)**
Simest	27	1389/3075
Simest	269	509/5281

Source: Authors' own compilation based on data from *Il sostegno publico all'internalizazzione delle imprese*, ICE, 2016, p. 307

provinces, ministries, universities and business organisations (Confindustria, Unioncamere, company networks, professional associations). In 2015, ICE had over 500 employees in Italy and some 400 others in its offices abroad, plus a number of domestic staff in each such country (Italian Trade Agency 2016)[4] (Table 6.2).

The Czech Republic's System for Supporting Industry, Investments and Exports

The Czech Republic's system for supporting industry and investments includes the Ministry of Industry and Trade and its Agency for Business and Investment Development (CzechInvest), the Ministry of Foreign Affairs and its external network of economic advisers attached to the foreign embassies, Czech Export Promotion Agency (CzechTrade).

CzechInvest has as its main objectives to develop domestic companies through its services and financial support programmes and to attract foreign investors, being authorised to grant investment incentives. CzechInvest focuses on increasing the Czech economy's competitiveness and the country's business infrastructure and innovation. The agency also promotes the interests of Czech companies abroad and helps SMEs in implementing the EU structural funds in the Czech Republic. CzechInvest has 260 employees, eight of which are in offices abroad (such as in the US, China and UK), plus 22 foreign centres promoting the image of the country worldwide. In 2014 and 2015, the investments managed by CzechInvest had an aggregate value of nearly 5 bn. euro, creating more than 30,000 new jobs, most of them in electronics and vehicle manufacturing.

The Czech Republic's *Strategy for Competitiveness 2016: Industry for the 21st Century* focuses on ten industrial sectors that are seen as having a significant potential for development and which are then targeted by CzechInvest support, among them nanotechnology and advanced materials, automotive industry, aerospace, high-tech mechanical engineering, ICT, electronics and electrical engineering, energy and environment.

CzechTrade is offering comprehensive support to Czech exporters through a variety of services, by establishing business contacts for them, finding valuable business partners, providing marketing assistance and long-term assistance in the territories they operate in and helping companies to participate in international fairs and business missions. The agency has 120 employees in 45 external offices in 48 countries (Wnukowski 2016). In 2014, CzechTrade managed more than 3200 export opportunities, and its foreign offices were involved in nearly 1300 contracts. The agency helps the implement the Czech Republic's *Export Strategy 2012-2020*, which is built on three pillars and provides support for exporters in order to diversify the structure of exports and to expand on external markets outside the EU (12 priority countries and 25 countries of interest have been defined), as well as to gain a more advantageous position in international value chains through the production of goods and services with high added value.

This system is completed by two financial support structures, namely, the Czech Export Bank (CEB), which has granted export credits worth about 15 bn. euro in the last 10 years (of which about 80% are generated by the SME segment), and Export Insurance and Export Guarantees (EGAP), which secured new export credits, bank guarantees and foreign investment worth about 2 bn. euro in 2015 (accounting for 54% of total export insurance).

Notes

1. US Government, *National Network for Manufacturing Innovation Program. Strategic Plan*, Executive Office of the President National Science and Technology Council, Advanced Manufacturing National Program Office, https://www.manufacturingusa.com/sites/prod/files/docs/resource/2015-NNMI-Strategic-Plan.pdf, February, 2016.
2. European Commission, *Overview of EU Instruments contributing to the internationalization of European Business*, DG for Internal Market, Industry, Entrepreneurship and SMEs, EC, 2 March 2017.
3. *Piano Industriale Gruppo CDP 2020. Linee guida strategiche*, Press Conference, Rome, 17 December, 2015.
4. Italian Trade Agency, *Piano della Performance 2015-2017*, ICE, Rome, 2016.

References

Burritt, Roger, and Katherine Christ. 2016. Industry 4.0 and Environmental Accounting: A New Revolution? *Asian Journal of Sustainability ans Social Responsibility*, December. doi:https://doi.org/10.1186/s41180-016-0007-y.

European Commission. 2017. *Overview of EU Instruments Contributing to the Internationalization of European Business*. DG for Internal Market, Industry, Entrepreneurship and SMEs, EC, 2 March 2017.

Italian Trade Agency. 2016. *Piano della Performance 2015–2017*. Rome: ICE.

Piano Industriale Gruppo CDP 2020. 2015. *Linee guida strategiche*. Press Conference, Rome, 17 December 2015.

Subran, L. 2013. *The Reindustrialization of the United States*. Special Report No. 1187, Euler Hermes Economic Outlook, 25 January 2013. http://www.eulerhermes.dk/oekonomisk-analyse/Documents/Outlook_no.1187.pdf

US Government. 2016. *National Network for Manufacturing Innovation Program. Strategic Plan*. Executive Office of the President National Science and Technology Council, Advanced Manufacturing National Program Office, February 2016. https://www.manufacturingusa.com/sites/prod/files/docs/resource/2015-NNMI-Strategic-Plan.pdf

Wnukowski, Damian. 2016 (February 24). Export Promotion Agency: The Experience of Selected European Countries. *PISM Bulletin* 18: 868.

7

Conclusions on How the Industrial Economy in Romania Should Be Supported

The economic development of a country relies, in principle, on three factors of prime importance: the government, the local administration bodies and the business environment, that is, the companies in business.

In a world of economic and financial globalisation, each component of this trio must contribute, by consensus, coherence and coordination to targeting the specific objectives, building up the required capacity to carry them out, monitoring the progress made and deciding on the corrections that may need to be undertaken due to the changes occurring in the local, regional and global business environment.

7.1 Government Policies and Interventions

The latest economic and financial recession created an enormous pressure on the governments of all the countries in the world to find solutions aimed at preserving, relaunching and/or accelerating economic growth.

Many actions were directed towards the sustaining of the financial and banking sector, industrial production, and exports, which sharpened the competition between governments and companies.

L. Chivu et al., *Deindustrialization and Reindustrialization in Romania*,
DOI 10.1007/978-3-319-65753-0_7

The basic reasons for resorting to such interventions through industrial policies undertaken by central administrations were the use of the local/national resources, infrastructures, and labour force; with the additional motivation that the health of industry is founded on innovation, competitiveness/productivity and trade, and that the measures taken would not impair the competition rules.

Good economic and industrial policies are based on facts and on comparative analyses of data and information as well as on assessment of the probable future evolution of facts.

Ex-ante and ex-post evaluations have as purpose—to find the comparative advantages derived from the natural resources, capital and fixed assets endowments, the size and quality of the labour force, transport infrastructures, energy and possible sources of finance for the industrial systems.

With the labour force no longer creating the same advantage for investors, either in terms of numbers or low cost, that it had during the past 20–25 years (a tendency that is also felt in Romania as well as a consequence of the continuous emigration of young workers and the increasing cost of the remaining domestic labour, irrespective of the latter's level of competence), a growing need will arise for additional capital and for the development of capital-based industries, which heavily depend on research, development, and innovation, an area where Romania has no advantage.

Public economic and industrial policies promoted by the government must comply with the concrete tendencies and realities as reflected in the demand in the national, regional and global markets.

With regard to the national market, it is true that the demand for industrial goods by an ageing population seems to be different from the demands of a young population, particularly in relation to the current supply, which comes mainly from imports of industrial goods.

The creation of value chains is required according to the market demand, including innovation, acquisitions, processing and sales supply, locally, regionally and globally, enabling Romania to direct its economic activities mainly towards the national and regional markets, but in cooperation with its neighbours, not alone.

Actions and measures are needed, including *state aid schemes*, in order to support and finance business, through the banking system, and to facilitate exports to developing countries and export/import banks.

Similarly, *incentives* should be granted to encourage the progress of *technical know-how (in microelectronics, robotics, nano- and bio- technologies among others), but also to help Romanian products penetrate new markets* (market surveys, anticipation of market requirements and potential demand); *trade diplomacy should be stimulated, because its purpose cannot be limited to initiatives designed to attract only foreign investors;* and, to do this, market data need to be collected and made available to Romanian producers, including SMEs, which cannot undertake such logistic services on their own.

Productivity acquired through research and innovation—and competitiveness—are of an utmost interest not only for companies themselves, but also for the government (especially research in new technologies, new materials, and so on).

It is of critical importance to manage how much of the expenditure for science is allocated to research as such, and how much of it is channelled towards the commercial development of new technologies and intelligent products.

The RDI sector can be helped to grow through grants, tax exemptions for energy-saving products and so forth, that is, through measures that do not violate competition rules.

The government's actions could focus on two areas of critical importance for the future of companies: the safe supply of energy at fair prices and the access to qualified labour.

The immediate future will present companies with the *human capital challenge*: the need for highly skilled workers and the deficit of labour in technical and analytical professions have generated manpower shortages in all branches, including the key sectors of the Romanian industry in its current configuration (motor vehicles, and aerospace industries); access to talent is an essential driver of future development.

Romania, through its neglectful policies of the past 27 years, has offered, free of any charge, both human capital and the fixed assets of its industry, under the rationale that Romania did not have the necessary money to operate its own economy, and that, therefore, foreign investors were welcome.

Securing human capital by various means, such as government co-financing of early hiring of students, has become a must, which explains why education and vocational training have to be treated as national priority. As shown by Hoareau, Ritzen and Marconi (2013), the use of European structural and cohesion funds could improve the performance of higher education in less developed regions, as in the case of Poland, with a multi-billion euro investment.[1]

To conclude, the government is responsible for four intervention pillars, through public policies aimed at economic development, including economy and industrial policies, as follows:

- Setting the development horizon, with road maps and basic rules; by this, we mean priorities and general regulations on how business should be conducted, rules governing the human capital (training, employment), and the capital market *et cetera*;
- Building and empowering facilitation entities (in education—training, in supporting research, development and innovation, in building infrastructures, such as roads, highways, ports, energy distribution networks *et cetera*);
- Coordinating interventions (support should be convergent and coherent with the lines of development at national, regional, local and sectoral levels; procurement, environment, consumer and natural resources should be protected by adequate legislation *et cetera*);
- Act as a main actor for the survival, subsidising and restructuring, both active and creative, of companies and the business environment.

For all these policy areas, planning, monitoring, control and execution will be more important than the choice of how to implement the policies themselves.

The responsibilities of local administrative bodies are added to those of central authorities. There is a network of administrative entities that play the role of local government. Their duty is to put in effect and supervise compliance with the government's regulations and policies and to put in place development programmes, measures, actions and strategies, in accordance with the principle of subsidiarity, and with the actual needs of their communities.

Their commitments should rely, in general, on the four pillars of central government policy and intervention, which means that they should: determine the development horizon, identify the best value chains for the processing of local resources, support industrial clusters and parks, set up and operate local development poles and a network of facilitator entities to help the growth of the local business environment and the local infrastructures, coordinate locally and ensure the coherence of interventions, secure access to utilities for individual and corporate consumers, promote and sustain development projects with European funding, encourage intra-regional and regional cooperation between local entities and identify best practices among other things.

7.2 Building an Effective RDI System for the Increase of Romania's Competitiveness

The industrial decomposition of Romania during the transition period had a domino effect for the entire research, development and technological design sector. Dozens of research and development institutes were rendered useless, some of them surviving with just subsistence funding, or no funding at all, or having to shut down or being left with just a once celebrated logo. The number of researchers decreased from 38,600 in 1993 to 19,000 in 2014; the number of researchers in the business enterprise sector decreased from 27,400 in 1993 to 5200 in 2014. In the context of a roundtable on research, development and innovation, professor Gheorghe Zaman has mentioned that, while in the developed countries the private sector is the main source of funding the R&D expenditures, in Romania's case, the private sector is largely held by subsidiaries, which receive research results from their foreign parent companies, and thus are no longer interested in developing research in their own country (National Institute of Statistics 2016).[2]

Romania's budget allocation for research ranks it last in Europe with only 0.4% of the GDP in 2015. Due to Romanian business's shortage of funds for research, because more than 90% of them are SMEs and another 200,000 of them are sole-proprietorships, it is hard to believe that they will be able to support the research and development expenditures from their own resources.

Emphasising the weak performance of the Romanian manufacturing sector compared to other EU member countries, due in part to a significant lack of innovation and skills, the EC has pointed out that Romania should recognize competitiveness as a transversal issue and integrate measures aimed at increasing competitiveness increase into policies in other areas (European Commission 2014).[3] According to the European Innovation Scoreboard, Romania is rated as a modest innovator, performing well below the EU average with regard to most of the 25 indicators composing the innovation index, with the relative performance (EU = 100) dropping from almost 50% in 2008 to 34.4% in 2015, last among the EU member states (European Commission 2016).[4]

The Global Competitiveness Report 2016–2017 also puts Romania in a modest position (62 in 2016–2017 among 140 countries, ten places lower than the previous period); within the composite index GCI, Romania scores poorly on the sub-indexes of innovation (ranked 94) and business sophistication (ranked 100), the most problematic factors for doing business consisting of difficult access to financing and an inefficient government bureaucracy (World Economic Forum 2016).[5]

In terms of doing business, the WB, however, places Romania in the first quarter of the global ranking (36 out of 190 countries) but cautions about some weaknesses concerning starting businesses, longer times needed to register for VAT and resolving insolvency cases (World Bank 2017).[6]

Increasing Romania's competitiveness, promoting the public research sector, and increasing the allocation of funds to develop research and technological innovation will need the support of the government, whose financial commitment for this purpose is by no means in violation of the competition rules.

The new industrial policies in Romania should address the challenges of its competitiveness level, especially in terms of the RDI sector, and its underfunded and underdeveloped infrastructures, thus positioning itself as a actor generating horizontal interventions in the economy and society, capable of enhancing growth and sustainability.

The theoretical and analytical support of the new-built innovation system should be based on the "triple helix" concept (Ranga and Etzkowitz 2013, 237–262), in a systematized interaction of a university–industry–government relationship.

The analysis of Fitjar et al. showed that companies exploiting internal triple-helix networks with a wider range of partners succeeded in capturing a significantly higher share of their income from new products and product innovation, and even more, by engaging in international triple-helix-type networks (Fitjar, Gjelsvik and Rodrigues-Pose 2014).

In the case of Romania, which faced industrial destructuring during the transition period, the economic innovation potential of the "creative destruction" can be even greater in terms of upgrading the manufacturing sector and increasing the research intensity.

However, given the circumstances of new technologies and their worldwide externalities, a better estimation of creative and destructive components of innovations and their contribution to welfare and employment is needed, according to Professor John Komlos.[7]

Under these circumstances, with the main general objective of increasing Romania's competitiveness through innovation, the National Strategy for Research, Development and Innovation for the period 2014–2020 was created based on three pillars—

Pillar 1. Regional and global affirmation: the companies become key operators of innovation. The Romanian economy moves towards mobilizing innovative SMEs with global orientation and perspectives that have the interest and ability to enter the regional and global added value chains.

Pillar 2. Excellence through internationalization: RDI sector as a place of opportunity. The Romanian RDI sector develops around strategic areas, internationally integrated and providing an attractive environment for the global scientific community members, including predictable flow of projects by national and European research infrastructures.

Pillar 3. Regional "leadership" at the frontier of science and technology: breakthroughs in strategic areas. Romania positions itself through RDI alongside major European and international initiatives, either through participation or by taking a leading role (in cases such as the science-driven cluster *Extreme Light Infrastructure*—Nuclear Physics in Magurele, Romania).

The RDI strategy identified four smart specialization areas in Romania (bio-economics; information and communication technology, space and security; energy, environment and climate change; eco-nanotechnologies and advanced materials) which will be financially supported, by—in addition to domestic public and private sources— European funds (ERDF) through the Competitiveness Operational Program 2014–2020 (1580 mil. euro allocated to Romania) and also, under Innovation Union strategy, through EU Horizon 2020 and the European Research Area partnership.

7.3 Improving the Business Environment

The basic actors for general economic development, industry, construction, agriculture and services are the companies themselves and their related associations.

The vital feature of any successful company, and particularly so for the yet-to-be-born ones, is intelligence. One cannot even think of intelligent products and smart development without their being intelligent companies.

The key words in outlining the performance criteria for the existing companies, and all the more so for the future ones, are intelligence, agility, anticipation, flexibility, modularity, speed, environment-friendliness, viability, endurance, skilfulness, talent, quality, innovation, and personalisation of the products/services.

Each of the features enumerated above could be expanded upon in a separate treatise. What matters is that each company should be able to create an original print for the products or services it offers to its clients; to recruit the best partners to work with in its network; to recognise and motivate its talents, to stimulate a fidelity bond among them; and to set up its own database to aid in making prompt decisions.

A company's future and life expectancy depend, to an increasingly larger extent, on actions and concepts like networking, cooperation, segmentation/fragmentation, vertical integration (at control and functions levels, not necessarily ownership wise), recycling and circular economy, productivity of input resources and research/innovation.

Every company dreams of growing big; nowadays, this means to creating products and services, but setting up their production in Asia; there are voices that claim that in Europe there has little room left to grow.

Investing in research and development will become mandatory for all businesses, including the very small ones, representing something between 0.1 and 0.5% of the turnover; this will be possible through an association for the creation of a national RDI fund.

Companies and their associations cannot expect to grow without having their own strategy and without very strict development, action and business plans designed to make their own products, services and budgets sustainable.

Below is a conceptual framework for actions to support the competitiveness and internationalisation of Romanian companies, especially SMEs:

I. *Basic prerequisite:* competitiveness, defined as a company's capability to sell its products/services in a competitive market, relying on the efficient use of resources (capital, labour, technology), which is now playing out in a globalised market; as such, it will have to be evaluated as a transversal issue in terms of internationalisation.
II. *Objective*: create a coherent and functional system to support the competitiveness of Romanian companies, with a stress on the companies operating with local capital, and on SMEs, similar to the systems existing in other EU countries (Germany Trade&Invest, Business France, Sistema Italy, UK Trade and Investment) or non-EU countries (US National Export Initiative).
III. *Strategic aims*:

- diversify exports of goods and services to the EU and non-EU countries;
- raise the national value chain to as high a level as possible in processing, particularly in areas where Romania has the necessary raw materials and energy;
- penetrate, in the best possible terms, the international value chains run by MNC;
- promote sale of goods and services carrying the highest possible added value;

- expand to new markets, or broaden the supply of new products in areas of higher risk, but be capable of a higher rate of absorption of Romanian products and services;
- assist Romanian companies to bid in international tenders (procurement, acquisitions, complex projects).

IV. *Main system institutional components that require reconfiguration/restructuring*:

- export council (harmonisation of strategies, coordination and monitoring prerogatives);
- territorial/local structures (public/private);
- foreign trade and international relations department;
- employers' organisations (unified for the whole industry);
- professional associations (unified by main branches of industry);
- Chambers of Commerce and Industry (unified for the entire territory);
- foreign representative offices network (economic diplomacy, PPP offices abroad);
- structures to provide state financial support (financing, shareholding, insurance, guarantees);
- policies to redefine the scope of business acting for and on behalf of the Romanian Savings Bank (CEC) and the Export-Import Bank (EXIMBANK), including EximAsig; Inter-institutional cooperation agreements with similar EU and non-EU structures.

V. *Review/harmonise the strategic implementation and government monitoring instruments*:

- National Strategy for Competitiveness 2015–2020;
- National Export Strategy 2014–2020;
- National Strategy for Research, Development and Innovation 2014–2020 (Government Decision—HG No. 929/2014);
- Government Strategy for the development of the small and medium enterprise sector, and the improvement of the business environment in Romania—Horizon 2020 (Government Decision—HG No. 859/2014);

- export promotion system based on finance from the state budget (Government Emergency Ordinance—OUG No. 120/2002);
- programme to increase the competitiveness of industrial products;
- programme to support the small and medium enterprises to increase exports.

Considering the fact that all the strategies heretofore have remained simple declarative documents, without practical relevance and implementation, used for electoral or political impression, we propose that, in the future, strategies and policies should be converted into plans (for example, France and Italy are only two of the many countries that do this), with the stipulation, for managers and all decision-makers at all levels, that such a plan shall be one of the performance criteria for their activities.

7.4 Economic Strategy Challenges: Measures and Actions Which Could Boost the Reindustrialisation of Romania

Under the circumstances of the new international and European context of industrial policies and development, a series of measures and actions should be undertaken in order to boost the reindustrialisation of Romania: the legal and institutional framework, the tax regime, the business environment, overall investment and investments in innovation, the financial background, the workforce's skills and competencies, transparency in information. Among these, the more important would be the following:

A. *Amendment of the legal framework to the effect of enabling*:

- access for Romanian companies, especially SMEs, to energy and raw material resources, at affordable and steady prices, in terms similar to those enjoyed by their competitors on the global market (for example, this could be accomplished by setting ceilings of prices for energy and some raw materials, and/or entering into long-term contracts for their supply);

- protection and rational harvesting of natural resources, based on temporary restrictions to exports of scrap iron and unprocessed wood;
- central and local authorities should commit themselves to provide the necessary infrastructure to investors (roads, utilities, indemnification for property condemned for public utility reasons *et cetera*), particularly to Romanian capital investors, and especially in disfavoured regions;
- analysis of the efficiency of results, and, based thereon, the correction of the legislation regarding distressed areas, industrial and/or technological parks, industrial clusters, centres for excellence, urban/rural development poles and so on;
- settlement of arrears and financial blockages caused by delayed payment of bills by public entities, by various means, including a state aid scheme to serve this purpose;
- observance of public consultation procedures for all legislative initiatives, and the obligation to assess their impact;
- evaluation of whether the legislative background continues to serve the purpose for which it was put in place, with special attention to the legislation governing the SMEs.

B. *Broaden the institutional framework, as follows*:

- reorganise the Department of Industrial Policies and Competitiveness of the Ministry of Economy by adding responsibilities for the drafting of strategies/policies for industrial and territorial development;
- reorganise the Foreign Trade Department of the Ministry of the Business Environment and establish a single structure, similar to those existing in other countries, charged with the responsibility to promote exports, competitiveness and internationalisation of the Romanian companies;
- harmonise government strategies with one another, and with the companies' business plans;
- develop a uniform methodology for impact studies;
- draft the economic profile of each development region, and define priority sectors;

- create a methodology to evaluate the impact of industrial branches on the economic grow and the development of each development region;
- make the most of the opportunities permitted by EU legislation regarding state aid, including concessions based on regional criteria aimed at local development for the purpose of minimising territorial disparities.

C. *Improve the tax legislation, by—*

- reducing the number of charges, taxes, contributions to the budget, and the taxation of labour;
- bringing the VAT rate to a level permitting competitiveness in the EU, and particularly in the relations with the neighbouring countries;
- scaling the VAT rates in accordance with Romania's economic interests;
- introducing incentives for the use of products and services generated by the Romanian economy, specifically targeting those furnished by the local SMEs running on domestic capital;
- granting tax and non-tax incentives for the efficient use of energy and non-polluting technologies;
- identifying alternatives to stimulate, tax-wise, the micro-enterprises, and the SMEs, by methods already in place in other EU countries.

D. *Improve the business environment, through—*

- providing access to financing, especially for the SMEs, by reducing the cost of capital from the banking institutions, relax the conditions for loan and collaterals, give priority to projects involving new technologies, using European funds as well;
- reducing administrative obligations, simplify taxation, reporting, licensing, and permit issuance procedures (for construction, connection to electricity, among others);
- developing and rendering more efficient the de minimis status for the SMEs;

- respecting the market competition rules, and severely detect/punish unfair competition practices, including, but not limited to, transfer prices, intra-group export prices;
- addressing, in an efficient and speedy manner, insolvency cases.

E. *Ensure the financial background, by—*

- recapitalising the CEC Bank and EXIMBANK, or converting these two state-owned banks into development/investment banks, to support local companies, with a priority for innovative SMEs, and/or companies oriented to exports of high added value products and services (loans, guarantees, insurance); the two banks should also make available working capital, associated with the assumption by the banks of a higher share of risks and affordable costs;
- learning from the experience of the past 27 years, which shows that we cannot expect capital finance and the funding of local industry as long as the Romanian state-owned banks currently hold only 5% of the total banking system assets;
- creating a Romanian-capital bank and/or a Sovereign Investment Fund, for the economic development of Romania, a step that is not only imperative, but it is also a matter of common sense;
- broadening the venture capital market, setting up venture capital funds, or creating the conditions for their creation, primarily for innovation purposes, innovation being known to carrying a higher degree of risk;
- encouraging banks to take a greater part in financing (including pre-finance, and co-finance) European projects from the European Structural and Investment (ESI) funds allocated to Romania, primarily those designed to help the SMEs enhance their competitiveness, and to cover certain risks from a special fund made available to the Operational Programmes management authorities;
- analysing the activities of the state-capital guarantee fund for SMEs (FNGCIMM), to assess how and whether it fulfils its mission (improve access of SMEs to financing, including for the inception of new activities); taking measures to stimulate the fund

to support private initiative (raising the loan guarantee ceilings, relaxing prudential and risk coverage policies and so on);

- setting up a Technological Development Fund with a view to integrating value chains in the territory of Romania. Its mission would be to provide financing to joint projects that require horizontal and vertical integration of technological products through technology transfers, the amplification of the research and development resources along a value chain fully responsive to the Romanian economy. Such projects could be partly financed through ESIF or Junker Plan;
- create a fund for financial and technological restructuring of enterprises, for the purpose of granting financial aid for restructuring to the SMEs that comply with a number of requirements; the initial sources of finance may come from the government's reserve; after the first results, the amount can be supplemented with bank capital from the distress funds abroad, and the fund's revenues may accrue from capital gains and interests;
- creating a National Industrial Development Fund with the voluntary contributions of Romanian population and Romanians based abroad; the contributions made by employees, sole proprietors, and pensioners to this fund should be exempted from the taxes ordinarily levied on salaries, revenues and pensions.

F. *Promote innovation and investment in innovation, as follows*:

- finance the development and marketing of new, innovative products;
- stimulate innovation through personalised services offered to SMEs;
- support start-ups that bring to the market innovative products or processes;
- stimulate cooperation among innovative SMEs, the big companies and universities;
- increase co-finance for the research&development projects with public/EU funds support;
- introduce multi-annual state aid schemes for the SMEs.

G. *Counteract the deficit of human resources and competences/qualifications, by—*

- adapting academic curricula to the current needs of Romanian industry, according to industrial development policies and strategies;
- introducing new concepts in the academic curricula related to entrepreneurship, innovation, marketing and management;
- attracting the private sector/entrepreneurs to teaching activities;
- encouraging framework agreements among universities and employer organisations/professional associations/companies, enabling students to take up practice stages, do internships and work on pilot projects that reflect the real market demand;
- introducing a probation period for the young graduates, against pay from the state budget;
- designing an initial vocational training and a dual apprenticeship system;
- stopping the "brain drain" by granting scholarships to young talents; providing them employment opportunities, including youths working abroad that wish to return to their home country;
- putting to the best use the knowledge acquired, by subcontracting some of the activities to foreign partners (know-how, management, foreign market demand), in order to valorise them in export activities undertaken for an on behalf of themselves.

H. *Increase transparency of information, by—*

- providing statistical data of critical importance for the local capital; a special department should be created in the NIS for this purpose;
- strengthening the communication between public institutions and the business environment, especially SMEs, with regard to the latest developments on the EU and global markets;
- smoothing the access of companies dealing with R&D and SMEs operating in specific industries to the specialised international databases that are subject to restrictions; encouraging their participation in debates and dissemination activities (international con-

ferences, work-shops et cetera) at EU level, by earmarking dedicated funds;
- creating a clerical structure in charge of collecting proposals or observations emerging from the debates on EU draft directives or amendments thereto, and transmitting them to the Romanian members of the EU Parliament, for submission;
- creating conditions for a closer interaction between the business environment and Romania's missions abroad, including the EU, for the purpose of identifying tendencies, and making the best of the market opportunities.

* * *

During the transition to the market economy, while undergoing major institutional and legislative changes, Romania suffered a process of deindustrialization and repositioning of all economic structures in terms of ownership, employment, sector contribution to the GDP and resource-use effectiveness.

Romania's EU membership is a major opportunity for achieving beneficial reindustrialization, and the Europe 2020 Strategy reaffirms the crucial importance of industry as a key element of the new European development model.

The economic and financial crisis has brought to the forefront the industrial processing value chain as a lever for enhancing competitiveness potential. Globalization and international competitiveness require specializations and industrial policies geared towards high value-added products. The EU industries must take the lead in the transition to a low-carbon economy and efficient use of resources.

The new approach of EU industrial policy, based primarily on the innovative competitiveness of the industrial sectors, implies, for the less developed countries in the EU, such as Romania, a reindustrialization based not only on technological transfer from the advanced EU states, but also the support, through its own policies and government actions, of appropriate changes in the institutional framework, and the development of an effective RDI system as well as business environment improvements.

As shown in Romania's Development Strategy for the next 20 years, elaborated under the aegis of the Romanian Academy, the target in this area is the structural remodelling of industry by supporting high-technology sectors and developing good export prospects so that Romania's contribution to GDP creation remains relatively the same (Vlad 2016).[8]

According to various development scenarios, by 2040, the GDP per capita in Romania (expressed in Purchasing Power Standard - PPS) will be aligned with the European average. Romania is expected to see an improvement in its position in the ranking of EU 27 countries; and it prospects will be sustained by large investment initiatives, based on foreign direct investments and domestic companies' capital and government funds, especially in the field of infrastructure and advanced industrial sectors, leading the economy to enter the trajectory of a "virtuous circle" of investments–economic growth–investments.

Notes

1. See (Hoareau, Ritzen and Marconi 2013, 2–24)
2. *Trends in research, development and innovation in Romania and the requirements of the EU 2020 strategy*, Joint roundtable: Institute of National Economy—National Institute of Statistics, Information Bulletin, no. 3 (24), NIS, March, 2016.
3. European Commission, *Reindustrialising Europe. Member States' Competitiveness Report 2014*, SWD (2014) 278, European Union, Luxembourg, 2014, p. 222.
4. European Commission, *European Innovation Scoreboard*, Country Profile Romania, 2016.
5. World Economic Forum, *The Global Competitiveness Report 2016–2017*, WEF, Geneva, 2016, pp. 304–305.
6. WB, *Doing Business 2017. Equal Opportunity for All*, WB, Washington, 2017, p. 234.
7. See Komlos (2014).
8. *Strategia de dezvoltare a României în următorii 20 de ani* (coordinator acad. Ionel-Valentin Vlad), Volume II, Editura Academiei Române, București, 2016, pp. 236–238. http://academiaromana.ro/bdar/strategiaAR/doc12/StrategiaII.pdf

References

European Commission. 2014. *Reindustrialising Europe. Member States' Competitiveness Report 2014*. SWD (2014) 278, European Union, Luxembourg, p. 222.

———. 2016. *European Innovation Scoreboard*. Country Profile Romania.

Fitjar, Rune Dahl, Martin Gjelsvik, and Andres Rodrigues-Pose. 2014. Organizing Product Innovation: Hierarchy, Market or Triple-Helix Networks? *Triple Helix* 1: 3. https://doi.org/10.1186/s40604-014-0003-0.

Hoareau, Cecile, Jo Ritzen, and Gabriele Marconi. 2013. Higher Education and Economic Innovation, a Comparison of European Countries. *IZA Journal of European Labour Studies* 2: 24.

Komlos, John. 2014. *Has Creative Destruction Become More Destructive?* NBER Working Papers No. 20379, August. http://www.nber.org/papers/w20379.pdf. doi:https://doi.org/10.3386/w20379.

Ranga, M., and H. Etzkowitz. 2013. Triple Helix Systems: An Analytical Framework for Innovation Policy and Practice in the Knowledge Society. *Industry and Higher Education* 27 (4): 237–262.

Trends in Research, Development and Innovation in Romania and the Requirements of the EU 2020 Strategy. 2016. Joint Roundtable: Institute of National Economy—National Institute of Statistics, Information Bulletin, no. 3 (24), NIS, March 2016.

Vlad, Ionel-Valentin (coordinator). 2016. *Strategia de dezvoltare a României în următorii 20 de ani*. Vol. II, București, Editura Academiei Române (publisher house). http://academiaromana.ro/bdar/strategiaAR/doc12/StrategiaII.pdf

World Bank. 2017. *Doing Business 2017. Equal Opportunity for All*. Washington: World Bank, p. 234.

World Economic Forum. 2016. *The Global Competitiveness Report 2016–2017*. Geneva: WEF, pp. 304–305.

Appendix A.1: Gross production, intermediate consumption and gross value added, by economic branches (current bn. euro)

L. Chivu et al., *Deindustrialization and Reindustrialization in Romania*,
DOI 10.1007/978-3-319-65753-0

Branch	Indicator	1990	1995	2000	2005	2007	2008	2009	2010	2011	2012	2013	2014
Total national economy	Gross production	76.22	60.86	78.63	151.21	234.92	267.65	230.57	246.80	266.87	268.62	288.73	302.79
	Intermediate consumption	47.50	33.45	42.18	80.77	124.55	143.14	124.14	133.50	149.87	151.02	162.42	167.77
	Gross added value	28.72	27.42	36.45	70.44	110.38	124.51	106.43	113.30	117.00	117.60	126.31	133.02
Agriculture, forestry, fishing	Gross production	11.14	9.62	8.53	13.70	15.86	19.90	15.92	15.29	17.22	13.38	16.46	15.67
	Intermediate consumption	4.32	4.37	4.14	6.99	8.68	10.63	8.30	8.14	8.64	7.13	8.72	8.56
	Gross added value	6.82	5.25	4.39	6.70	7.18	9.27	7.62	7.10	8.58	6.25	7.75	7.10
Total industry	Gross production	45.38	27.81	32.78	59.32	87.88	93.34	81.47	84.38	95.15	93.54	102.39	106.47
	Intermediate consumption	32.72	19.05	22.20	39.53	57.57	61.88	53.77	50.70	59.10	62.12	67.65	69.59
	Gross added value	12.67	8.75	10.58	19.80	30.31	31.47	27.70	33.68	36.04	31.42	34.74	36.88
Constructions	Gross production	4.59	4.21	4.56	11.42	24.28	31.81	27.17	31.51	30.90	30.86	28.03	23.56
	Intermediate consumption	2.92	2.42	2.61	6.21	12.91	16.98	14.71	20.12	20.30	19.54	17.93	14.19
	Gross added value	1.68	1.79	1.95	5.21	11.36	14.83	12.46	11.39	10.60	11.32	10.10	9.37
Trade	Gross production	2.23	3.12	6.17	12.87	21.15	24.88	18.58	24.10	25.05	31.20	28.48	30.89
	Intermediate consumption	0.71	1.03	2.17	5.10	8.26	10.07	7.50	17.26	19.04	19.50	20.36	21.05
	Gross added value	1.52	2.09	4.00	7.76	12.89	14.81	11.08	6.84	6.01	11.70	8.13	9.84

(*continued*)

(continued)

Branch	Indicator	1990	1995	2000	2005	2007	2008	2009	2010	2011	2012	2013	2014
Hotels and restaurants	Gross production	2.50	1.41	1.60	3.12	5.36	5.57	4.80	3.36	3.60	3.46	4.75	4.73
	Intermediate consumption	2.08	0.76	0.75	1.72	3.01	3.20	2.80	2.13	2.16	1.69	2.29	2.79
	Gross added value	0.42	0.65	0.85	1.40	2.34	2.37	2.00	1.23	1.44	1.77	2.46	1.93
Transport, ware-housing and communications	Gross production	3.39	3.82	7.13	14.23	22.51	24.36	24.86	29.96	30.37	32.14	36.42	36.89
	Intermediate consumption	1.59	1.99	3.32	6.14	9.47	10.38	11.06	15.18	16.90	16.36	18.89	20.48
	Gross added value	1.80	1.83	3.81	8.10	13.04	13.98	13.80	14.78	13.47	15.78	17.52	16.42
Other services	Gross production	6.99	10.88	17.86	36.55	57.88	67.79	57.77	58.20	64.59	64.04	72.19	84.58
	Intermediate consumption	3.17	3.82	7.00	15.08	24.64	30.01	26.00	19.92	23.73	24.68	26.58	33.10
	Gross added value	3.82	7.05	10.87	21.47	33.24	37.78	31.77	38.28	40.86	39.36	45.61	51.48

Source: Authors' own compilation based on data from *Romania's Statistic Yearbook*, NIS, Bucharest, various editions, and NBR data regarding the Leu/euro annual average exchange rates

Appendix A.2: Indices of gross production, intermediate consumption and gross added value, by economic branches (1990 = 100.0)

L. Chivu et al., *Deindustrialization and Reindustrialization in Romania*,
DOI 10.1007/978-3-319-65753-0

Branch	Indicator	1990	1995	2000	2005	2007	2008	2009	2010	2011	2012	2013	2014
Total national economy	Gross production	100.00	91.53	94.49	131.92	154.72	168.18	159.94	160.90	167.01	167.18	172.86	213.48
	Intermediate consumption	100.00	91.52	101.70	149.54	182.78	200.69	192.66	197.87	210.93	210.72	216.62	279.87
	Gross added value	100.00	92.36	86.94	114.21	131.61	141.48	133.28	130.88	131.40	131.93	137.34	153.35
Agriculture, forestry and fishing[a]	Gross production	100.00	100.36	85.63	110.09	96.71	115.66	112.08	99.52	107.88	83.61	106.69	111.81
	Intermediate consumption	100.00	112.06	117.30	171.44	151.02	179.26	174.06	145.51	150.89	122.37	149.66	157.44
	Gross added value	100.00	93.37	66.23	81.58	71.45	86.24	83.39	78.81	89.76	66.34	88.70	92.51
Extraction industries	Gross production	100.00	82.94	65.01	70.84	72.98	58.75	61.51	68.15	83.00	66.16	53.52	46.46
	Intermediate consumption	100.00	99.34	77.63	91.96	95.21	75.02	78.10	83.33	133.33	105.06	95.50	100.66
	Gross added value	100.00	64.46	50.34	48.91	49.85	41.67	44.05	51.90	42.77	34.98	24.59	15.98
Processing industries	Gross production	100.00	79.93	84.11	119.71	138.72	143.57	135.68	137.71	142.53	141.53	151.44	164.01
	Intermediate consumption	100.00	81.84	88.49	129.58	151.01	157.35	147.12	148.15	158.96	162.14	172.84	188.91
	Gross added value	100.00	75.89	74.94	100.86	115.58	118.35	113.97	117.28	114.58	108.74	117.33	124.96
Electricity, heating, gas and water	Gross production	100.00	95.40	75.30	80.70	84.50	96.60	110.40	93.20	109.23	108.14	96.24	91.14
	Intermediate consumption	100.00	77.90	65.30	72.00	75.50	87.40	99.50	83.20	95.10	98.05	84.91	75.82
	Gross added value	100.00	420.30	281.00	275.60	286.00	311.50	361.60	316.40	387.59	356.58	342.32	371.42
Construction	Gross production	100.00	137.19	122.37	197.95	329.69	415.41	378.44	424.99	383.77	373.79	357.34	341.62
	Intermediate consumption	100.00	144.66	137.85	225.70	378.59	476.64	438.99	555.32	531.44	513.37	468.71	427.93
	Gross added value	100.00	128.98	104.93	165.40	273.30	344.90	310.76	296.77	240.09	237.40	247.85	258.76

(*continued*)

(continued)

Branch	Indicator	1990	1995	2000	2005	2007	2008	2009	2010	2011	2012	2013	2014
Trade	Gross production	100.00	85.40	115.86	184.53	251.94	287.72	248.30	292.00	310.10	390.11	344.86	383.69
	Intermediate consumption	100.00	111.50	184.16	314.28	432.39	508.92	435.63	551.51	571.36	648.50	649.15	733.54
	Gross added value	100.00	76.92	93.73	152.83	207.95	232.70	201.98	225.21	254.04	418.40	281.58	314.24
Hotels and restaurants	Gross production	100.00	59.57	51.66	73.41	95.41	102.38	95.11	64.86	68.95	68.67	85.91	85.65
	Intermediate consumption	100.00	62.31	56.74	90.18	122.14	133.14	124.62	92.71	91.78	85.27	109.15	109.04
	Gross added value	100.00	59.22	49.38	62.40	76.99	80.84	74.29	44.20	52.55	57.65	70.56	70.21
Transport, warehousing and communications	Gross production	100.00	88.39	95.75	145.73	167.43	177.48	169.67	156.27	153.77	159.00	170.45	182.72
	Intermediate consumption	100.00	82.87	95.02	157.39	181.51	194.40	194.20	185.27	197.87	191.93	210.55	230.97
	Gross added value	100.00	92.18	94.80	136.98	156.79	164.95	151.75	135.51	120.60	136.40	141.99	147.81

Source: Authors' own compilation based on data from *Romania's Statistic Yearbook*, NIS, Bucharest, various editions
[a]1990–2008, excluding fishing

Appendix A.3: The main trade deficits and surpluses by industrial product groups between Romania and the EU member states during the period 2000–2014 (mil. euro)

L. Chivu et al., *Deindustrialization and Reindustrialization in Romania*,
DOI 10.1007/978-3-319-65753-0

		2000–2006			2007–2014		
		Import	Export	Balance	Import	Export	Balance
Total EU	Total	104,078.7	82,616.9	−21,461.8	305,001.1	229,259.0	−75,742.1
	Total groups of industrial products	97,144.4	79,441.9	−17,702.5	282,956.9	225,255.7	−57,701.2
	Chemical products	9602.6	1447.3	−8155.3	32,584.1	10,644.1	−21,940.1
	Electric machines, apparatuses and equipment; machines to record or render sound and images	26,683.9	16,465.6	−10,218.3	88,317.2	67,007.2	−21,310.0
	Ordinary metals and products made of such	8941.7	7802.0	−1139.7	33,237.4	22,888.9	−10,348.5
	Footwear, hats, umbrellas and other similar products	1785.6	8169.9	6384.3	3609.5	10,275.1	6665.6
	Various goods and products	2306.6	5238.8	2932.2	5774.0	11,670.8	5896.7
	Textiles and products made of such	17,309.1	24,435.5	7126.4	22,682.4	26,563.4	3881.0
Austria	**Total**	**5890.4**	**3570.0**	**−2320.4**	**17,924.5**	**7529.7**	**−10,394.8**
	Total groups of industrial products	**5527.7**	**3511.6**	**−2016.0**	**17,055.5**	**7284.3**	**−9771.2**
	Electric machines, apparatuses and equipment; machines to record or render sound and images	1943.8	1465.7	−478.1	6346.3	2197.0	−4149.3
	Chemical products	357.8	51.6	−306.3	2182.2	208.1	−1974.1
	Means and materials for transport	383.1	272.5	−110.6	1817.0	725.7	−1091.3
	Footwear, hats, umbrellas and similar products	14.4	210.5	196.0	81.9	819.6	737.7
	Products made of wood, except for furniture	143.2	164.7	21.5	274.1	580.6	306.5
	Fats and animal or vegetal oils	7.2	1.3	−5.8	12.0	35.9	23.9
Belgium	**Total**	**2602.0**	**2075.8**	**−526.2**	**8654.2**	**5791.1**	**−2863.1**
	Total groups of industrial products	**2473.8**	**1997.1**	**−476.7**	**8172.1**	**5166.5**	**−3005.6**
	Chemical products	465.9	51.9	−414.0	1936.4	184.2	−1752.2
	Plastic materials, rubber and products made of such	269.8	113.0	−156.8	881.1	394.1	−487.0
	Ordinary metals and products made of such	231.6	187.3	−44.3	907.0	432.9	−474.1
	Means and materials for transport	355.3	112.1	−243.3	855.9	1.168.3	312.4
	Various goods and products	46.5	175.2	128.7	137.2	467.4	330.2
	Products made of wood, except for furniture	9.3	59.6	50.3	40.6	91.0	50.4

(continued)

(continued)

		2000–2006			2007–2014		
		Import	Export	Balance	Import	Export	Balance
Bulgaria	**Total**	**0.0**	**0.0**	**0.0**	**10,409.4**	**11,626.3**	**1216.9**
	Total groups of industrial products	**0.0**	**0.0**	**0.0**	**8587.7**	**10,617.3**	**2029.5**
	Electric machines, apparatuses and equipment; machines to record or render sound and images	0.0	0.0	0.0	1536.3	1030.6	−505.8
	Products made of stone, gypsum, ceramic, glass and other, similar materials	0.0	0.0	0.0	541.3	181.2	−360.2
	Means and materials for transport	0.0	0.0	0.0	741.4	401.2	−340.2
	Mineral products	0.0	0.0	0.0	559.7	2789.3	2229.6
	Chemical products	0.0	0.0	0.0	905.5	1245.6	340.1
	Plastic materials, rubber and products made of such	0.0	0.0	0.0	601.4	834.6	233.2
Czech Rep.	**Total**	**2323.5**	**642.6**	**−1680.9**	**10,498.7**	**5719.7**	**−4779.0**
	Total groups of industrial products	**2267.7**	**634.2**	**−1633.5**	**10,082.6**	**5606.5**	**−4476.0**
	Means and materials for transport	648.4	76.7	−571.7	2064.2	867.4	−1196.8
	Electric machines, apparatuses and equipment; machines to record or render sound and images	542.3	228.9	−313.3	3263.1	2296.5	−966.6
	Plastic materials, rubber and products made of such	157.0	63.2	−93.9	979.3	450.3	−529.0
	Various goods and products	41.8	18.2	−23.6	201.9	383.7	181.8
	Fats and animal or vegetal oils	0.7	0.0	−0.6	14.1	14.7	0.6

(continued)

(continued)

		2000–2006			2007–2014		
		Import	Export	Balance	Import	Export	Balance
Cyprus	**Total**	**35.0**	**193.9**	**159.0**	**481.1**	**649.2**	**168.1**
	Total groups of industrial products	**32.9**	**181.8**	**148.9**	**397.2**	**468.8**	**71.6**
	Chemical products	21.6	2.1	−19.4	125.4	31.6	−93.8
	Electric machines, apparatuses and equipment; machines to record or render sound and images	6.2	2.8	−3.4	102.4	54.0	−48.4
	Paper and products made of such	0.9	0.1	−0.8	13.1	0.4	−12.8
	Mineral products	0.0	53.5	53.5	17.8	119.8	101.9
	Products of the food industry, beverages and tobacco products	1.0	0.2	−0.8	13.5	46.4	32.9
	Means and materials for transport	0.4	106.2	105.8	39.7	67.0	27.3
Croatia	**Total**	**0.0**	**0.0**	**0.0**	**168.7**	**246.3**	**77.6**
	Total groups of industrial products	**0.0**	**0.0**	**0.0**	**157.7**	**181.9**	**24.2**
	Electric machines, apparatuses and equipment; machines to record or render sound and images	0.0	0.0	0.0	49.3	16.0	−33.3
	Chemical products	0.0	0.0	0.0	38.7	17.9	−20.7
	Products made of stone, gypsum, ceramic, glass and other, similar materials	0.0	0.0	0.0	8.9	4.0	−4.9
	Textiles and textile products	0.0	0.0	0.0	11.6	21.9	10.4
	Means and materials for transport	0.0	0.0	0.0	6.0	15.3	9.2
	Paper and products made of such	0.0	0.0	0.0	0.7	9.6	9.0

(continued)

(continued)

		2000–2006			2007–2014		
		Import	Export	Balance	Import	Export	Balance
Denmark	**Total**	**683.2**	**271.0**	**–412.2**	**2321.1**	**1114.4**	**–1206.7**
	Total groups of industrial products	**619.3**	**266.0**	**–353.4**	**2012.4**	**1083.3**	**–929.1**
	Electric machines, apparatuses and equipment; machines to record or render sound and images	228.5	42.1	–186.5	788.2	254.3	–533.9
	Chemical products	175.8	0.3	–175.5	538.8	221.6	–317.2
	Optical instruments and devices	57.7	2.2	–55.6	85.3	3.2	–82.1
	Textiles and textile products	12.3	86.8	74.5	33.1	159.2	126.1
	Ordinary metals and products made of such	28.3	31.6	3.3	163.9	180.5	16.5
	Footwear, hats, umbrellas and similar products	0.1	10.2	10.1	12.9	19.9	7.0
Estonia	**Total**	**14.5**	**14.4**	**–0.1**	**97.4**	**282.0**	**184.6**
	Total groups of industrial products	**13.6**	**14.2**	**0.6**	**79.6**	**276.6**	**197.1**
	Plastic materials, rubber and products made of such	4.1	1.1	–2.9	18.8	9.3	–9.6
	Chemical products	0.4	0.0	–0.4	6.2	3.2	–3.0
	Mineral products	0.2	0.0	–0.2	3.0	0.4	–2.6
	Electric machines, apparatuses and equipment; machines to record or render sound and images	4.3	2.5	–1.8	14.7	133.6	118.9
	Textiles and textile products	0.5	2.2	1.6	0.7	23.1	22.4
	Ordinary metals and products made of such	0.1	2.7	2.6	4.3	23.5	19.2

(continued)

(continued)

		2000–2006			2007–2014		
		Import	Export	Balance	Import	Export	Balance
Finland	**Total**	**635.0**	**93.9**	**–541.1**	**1.323.5**	**726.3**	**–597.1**
	Total groups of industrial products	**632.9**	**92.5**	**–540.4**	**1.318.5**	**723.5**	**–595.1**
	Paper and products made of such	128.9	0.0	–128.8	211.7	0.3	–211.4
	Electric machines, apparatuses and equipment; machines to record or render sound and images	273.7	35.4	–238.3	618.1	423.6	–194.5
	Ordinary metals and products made of such	89.1	17.3	–71.8	271.5	92.0	–179.5
	Products made of wood, except for furniture	4.2	2.1	–2.1	15.2	52.1	36.8
	Means and materials for transport	17.1	2.2	–14.9	31.0	41.4	10.4
	Products of the food industry, beverages and tobacco products	5.4	2.4	–3.0	13.7	9.4	–4.3
	Mineral products	0.5	2.9	2.3	1.1	4.4	3.4
	Chemical products	45.7	0.9	–44.8	39.1	4.2	–34.9
	Plastic materials, rubber and products made of such	23.6	11.8	–11.8	59.7	36.2	–23.5
	Textiles and textile products	5.2	9.8	4.6	5.5	19.0	13.4
France	**Total**	**11,440.7**	**9285.4**	**–2155.4**	**24,427.8**	**23,668.6**	**–759.2**
	Total groups of industrial products	**11,036.8**	**9124.0**	**–1912.8**	**23,464.1**	**22,647.0**	**–817.1**
	Chemical products	1770.7	135.9	–1634.8	3460.9	618.1	–2842.8
	Electric machines, apparatuses and equipment; machines to record or render sound and images	3275.2	2496.8	–778.4	7310.4	5863.5	–1447.0
	Ordinary metals and products made of such	715.0	439.9	–275.1	2452.1	1547.6	–904.5
	Various goods and products	180.8	1256.1	1075.4	353.4	2177.8	1824.4
	Means and materials for transport	1615.9	555.5	–1060.4	4345.6	6066.0	1720.4
	Textiles and textile products	1812.4	2831.6	1019.2	1878.8	3064.7	1185.9

(continued)

(continued)

		2000–2006			2007–2014		
		Import	Export	Balance	Import	Export	Balance
Germany	**Total**	**25,331.9**	**18,518.7**	**−6813.1**	**73,254.9**	**58,877.4**	**−14,377.4**
	Total groups of industrial products	**24,615.0**	**18,170.8**	**−6444.2**	**70,186.7**	**57,704.8**	**−12,482.0**
	Chemical products	2132.6	193.3	−1939.3	6384.5	1584.8	−4799.7
	Plastic materials, rubber and products made of such	1853.1	600.8	−1252.3	6814.7	3059.0	−3755.7
	Ordinary metals and products made of such	1869.7	1426.8	−442.9	6869.2	4311.3	−2558.0
	Means and materials for transport	4977.8	2659.1	−2318.7	10,906.5	12,152.8	1246.3
	Textiles and textile products	3189.4	6130.3	2940.9	4790.9	5671.5	880.6
	Footwear, hats, umbrellas and similar products	34.8	582.6	547.8	327.5	777.4	449.9
Greece	**Total**	**2551.5**	**2986.9**	**435.4**	**5239.9**	**4724.2**	**−515.8**
	Total groups of industrial products	**2390.3**	**2665.5**	**275.1**	**4653.8**	**3950.1**	**−703.7**
	Plastic materials, rubber and products made of such	261.2	73.4	−187.8	693.6	299.3	−394.3
	Chemical products	251.0	93.4	−157.6	498.5	259.8	−238.7
	Textiles and textile products	216.5	142.8	−73.7	343.7	127.8	−215.8
	Products made of wood, except for furniture	3.9	208.2	204.3	14.3	243.8	229.6
	Mineral products	212.3	677.9	465.6	332.3	453.3	121.0
	Electric machines, apparatuses and equipment; machines to record or render sound and images	640.0	487.2	−152.9	660.8	777.7	116.9
Ireland	**Total**	**866.7**	**262.3**	**−604.4**	**2255.2**	**717.3**	**−1538.0**
	Total groups of industrial products	**832.4**	**262.0**	**−570.5**	**2228.5**	**672.3**	**−1556.3**
	Chemical products	343.2	3.5	−339.7	1320.1	16.7	−1303.5
	Electric machines, apparatuses and equipment; machines to record or render sound and images	333.5	115.5	−218.0	696.1	318.9	−377.2
	Products of the food industry, beverages and tobacco products	29.8	1.0	−28.8	42.6	7.3	−35.3
	Means and materials for transport	0.2	27.4	27.2	20.6	160.9	140.3
	Textiles and textile products	73.6	52.7	−20.9	44.2	79.5	35.4
	Various goods and products	3.0	46.5	43.5	2.6	27.2	24.6

(continued)

(continued)

		2000–2006			2007–2014		
		Import	Export	Balance	Import	Export	Balance
Italy	**Total**	**29,680.0**	**26,054.8**	**–3625.2**	**47,767.7**	**43,143.6**	**–4624.2**
	Total groups of industrial products	**25,895.7**	**24,557.8**	**–1337.9**	**42,585.9**	**39,746.1**	**–2839.7**
	Electric machines, apparatuses and equipment; machines to record or render sound and images	5993.6	2964.8	–3028.8	11,154.0	7739.8	–3414.2
	Ordinary metals and products made of such	2778.6	2538.3	–240.3	7486.0	4165.0	–3321.0
	Chemical products	1177.0	385.6	–791.4	2612.3	695.7	–1916.6
	Footwear, hats, umbrellas and similar products	1530.2	6119.5	4589.4	1910.6	6116.8	4206.2
	Textiles and textile products	8662.8	8763.5	100.7	8216.6	9946.5	1729.8
	Products of the food industry, beverages and tobacco products	177.6	41.3	–136.3	771.0	2495.8	1724.8
Latvia	**Total**	**11.0**	**18.0**	**6.9**	**180.7**	**168.4**	**–12.2**
	Total groups of industrial products	**11.0**	**17.5**	**6.5**	**174.4**	**166.5**	**–7.9**
	Various goods and products	0.6	0.3	–0.3	61.2	5.4	–55.8
	Products made of wood, except for furniture	0.7	0.7	0.0	16.3	4.2	–12.1
	Mineral products	0.3	0.0	–0.3	3.4	0.6	–2.8
	Textiles and textile products	0.4	0.8	0.4	10.4	48.3	37.9
	Electric machines, apparatuses and equipment; machines to record or render sound and images	5.6	5.6	0.0	40.6	53.6	12.9
	Products of the food industry, beverages and tobacco products	1.3	0.4	–0.9	10.0	22.6	12.6

(*continued*)

(continued)

		2000–2006			2007–2014		
		Import	Export	Balance	Import	Export	Balance
Lithuania	**Total**	**56.0**	**32.9**	**–23.2**	**358.9**	**295.4**	**–63.5**
	Total groups of industrial products	**55.7**	**32.6**	**–23.1**	**335.6**	**290.3**	**–45.3**
	Chemical products	11.7	2.5	–9.2	66.5	34.9	–31.6
	Means and materials for transport	3.3	0.2	–3.1	30.6	8.4	–22.3
	Plastic materials, rubber and products made of such	3.9	5.8	1.9	58.1	38.4	–19.7
	Textiles and textile products	13.5	10.2	–3.3	12.3	37.5	25.2
	Products of the food industry, beverages and tobacco products	1.3	0.1	–1.1	18.3	39.0	20.8
	Products made of wood, except for furniture	0.2	0.8	0.6	4.4	24.7	20.3
Luxembourg	**Total**	**96.0**	**31.1**	**–64.9**	**554.6**	**120.3**	**–434.2**
	Total groups of industrial products	**95.9**	**31.0**	**–64.9**	**549.1**	**116.1**	**–433.0**
	Electric machines, apparatuses and equipment; machines to record or render sound and images	18.9	8.0	–10.9	158.0	13.6	–144.4
	Ordinary metals and products made of such	29.3	2.3	–27.0	146.4	3.4	–143.0
	Chemical products	2.3	6.5	4.3	91.4	1.0	–90.4
	Means and materials for transport	2.6	5.7	3.2	13.1	35.6	22.6
	Mineral products	0.0	0.4	0.4	1.2	17.7	16.5
	Products made of wood, except for furniture	0.2	2.2	2.0	1.4	12.9	11.5
Malta	**Total**	**17.8**	**199.8**	**182.0**	**205.0**	**264.8**	**59.8**
	Total groups of industrial products	**17.8**	**199.5**	**181.7**	**197.1**	**237.1**	**40.0**
	Chemical products	0.0	0.2	0.1	146.9	29.3	–117.7
	Electric machines, apparatuses and equipment; machines to record or render sound and images	14.9	1.1	–13.8	24.1	10.8	–13.2
	Various goods and products	0.1	0.2	0.1	3.6	1.2	–2.4
	Mineral products	0.0	142.2	142.2	4.2	154.4	150.2
	Means and materials for transport	0.0	51.9	51.9	8.4	29.3	20.9
	Ordinary metals and products made of such	0.1	0.4	0.3	0.6	6.4	5.8

(continued)

(continued)

		2000–2006			2007–2014		
		Import	Export	Balance	Import	Export	Balance
Netherlands	**Total**	**3298.1**	**3644.4**	**346.3**	**15,051.7**	**9156.4**	**–5895.4**
	Total groups of industrial products	**2837.0**	**3481.4**	**644.5**	**13,156.3**	**7708.7**	**–5447.5**
	Electric machines, apparatuses and equipment; machines to record or render sound and images	644.6	551.8	–92.8	5208.5	2812.4	–2396.1
	Chemical products	563.8	59.2	–504.6	2586.8	212.7	–2374.1
	Products of the food industry, beverages and tobacco products	166.4	70.2	–96.2	715.4	245.5	–469.9
	Plastic materials, rubber and products made of such	247.9	93.8	–154.1	859.1	366.1	493.0
	Various goods and products	50.1	542.1	492.0	187.2	654.7	467.5
	Footwear, hats, umbrellas and similar products	7.8	333.5	325.7	47.2	306.4	259.2
Poland	**Total**	**2726.9**	**1043.8**	**–1683.1**	**16,496.9**	**7574.5**	**–8922.5**
	Total groups of industrial products	**2578.8**	**1035.6**	**–1543.3**	**15,498.8**	**7428.7**	**–8070.1**
	Mineral products	307.4	8.6	–298.9	1899.0	40.5	–1858.4
	Chemical products	243.4	46.9	–196.5	1479.2	357.1	–1122.1
	Products of the food industry, beverages and tobacco products	181.3	24.0	–157.3	1398.0	198.5	–1199.5
	Optical instruments and devices	11.2	22.1	10.9	105.9	354.8	248.8
	Means and materials for transport	190.5	76.8	–113.7	997.5	1110.6	113.0
Portugal	**Total**	**495.4**	**233.6**	**–261.7**	**1578.5**	**1206.2**	**–372.2**
	Total groups of industrial products	**482.9**	**169.3**	**–313.6**	**1507.9**	**847.2**	**–660.7**
	Electric machines, apparatuses and equipment; machines to record or render sound and images	168.7	12.1	–156.6	536.5	223.5	–313.1
	Textiles and textile products	169.6	21.0	–148.5	251.3	52.1	–199.1
	Means and materials for transport	24.5	7.6	–16.9	325.5	188.1	–137.4
	Various goods and products	6.0	2.8	–3.2	22.3	116.1	93.8
	Ordinary metals and products made of such	20.6	50.9	30.3	52.1	78.8	26.7
	Fats and animal or vegetal oils	0.7	0.0	–0.7	4.9	11.8	6.9

(continued)

(continued)

		2000–2006			2007–2014		
		Import	Export	Balance	Import	Export	Balance
United Kingdom	**Total**	**5413.2**	**6830.1**	**1416.9**	**9190.0**	**11,900.8**	**2710.8**
	Total groups of industrial products	**5349.9**	**6701.9**	**1352.0**	**9025.3**	**11,605.4**	**2580.2**
	Chemical products	858.9	25.8	−833.2	1400.0	578.5	−821.5
	Optical instruments and devices	151.3	13.5	−137.7	225.9	65.6	−160.3
	Paper and products made of such	92.7	9.8	−82.9	143.6	36.3	−107.3
	Textiles and textile products	1425.6	3577.0	2151.4	1728.8	3081.7	1352.9
	Electric machines, apparatuses and equipment; machines to record or render sound and images	1456.0	1631.4	175.4	2779.7	3569.5	789.8
	Various goods and products	101.2	362.3	261.2	149.3	830.8	681.6
Slovakia	**Total**	**1086.4**	**336.8**	**−749.5**	**7381.6**	**4788.1**	**−2593.5**
	Total groups of industrial products	**1048.8**	**324.6**	**−724.1**	**7081.8**	**4637.8**	**−2443.9**
	Electric machines, apparatuses and equipment; machines to record or render sound and images	204.3	105.3	−98.9	2615.3	1706.3	−909.0
	Ordinary metals and products made of such	328.9	95.0	−234.0	1412.1	624.7	−787.4
	Plastic materials, rubber and products made of such	96.4	12.5	−83.9	510.5	168.7	−341.9
	Mineral products	9.7	3.5	−6.2	64.1	225.1	161.0
	Various goods and products	9.6	10.7	1.2	115.6	206.4	90.8
	Footwear, hats, umbrellas and similar products	4.2	9.6	5.4	361.3	429.5	68.3

(continued)

(continued)

		2000–2006			2007–2014		
		Import	Export	Balance	Import	Export	Balance
Slovenia	**Total**	**477.1**	**291.8**	**−185.3**	**2959.4**	**1501.1**	**−1.,458.3**
	Total groups of industrial products	**469.3**	**280.1**	**−189.2**	**2.907.3**	**1.458.6**	**−1.448.7**
	Chemical products	150.8	3.4	−147.4	835.0	49.6	−785.4
	Electric machines, apparatuses and equipment; machines to record or render sound and images	111.0	15.2	−95.8	822.0	335.3	−486.7
	Means and materials for transport	16.3	6.8	−9.6	417.1	285.3	−131.8
	Mineral products	0.3	95.7	95.4	27.6	97.2	69.6
	Ordinary metals and products made of such	56.2	89.6	33.4	212.4	278.7	66.3
	Various goods and products	16.4	5.3	−11.1	62.3	119.7	57.4
Spain	**Total**	**3334.4**	**2340.0**	**−994.4**	**9342.9**	**8252.0**	**−1090.9**
	Total groups of industrial products	**3113.4**	**2131.8**	**−981.7**	**8578.4**	**6845.2**	**−1733.2**
	Electric machines, apparatuses and equipment; machines to record or render sound and images	878.7	395.3	−483.4	3194.6	1524.6	−1669.9
	Products made of stone, gypsum, ceramic, glass and other, similar materials	336.0	39.5	−296.5	399.0	40.1	−358.9
	Chemical products	323.0	175.1	−147.9	653.7	336.5	−317.1
	Various goods and products	81.8	71.1	−10.8	135.0	442.3	307.3
	Means and materials for transport	552.7	87.5	−465.2	1413.8	1657.5	243.7
	Plastic materials, rubber and products made of such	170.5	99.5	−71.0	412.2	634.9	222.8

(continued)

(continued)

		2000–2006			2007–2014		
		Import	Export	Balance	Import	Export	Balance
Sweden	**Total**	**1771.2**	**708.0**	**−1063.2**	**2805.4**	**2600.9**	**−204.5**
	Total groups of industrial products	**1764.2**	**702.1**	**−1062.0**	**2725.9**	**2580.7**	**−145.2**
	Electric machines, apparatuses and equipment; machines to record or render sound and images	750.7	169.1	−581.6	1073.6	917.5	−156.1
	Paper and products made of such	108.3	2.8	−105.5	147.7	3.4	−144.3
	Ordinary metals and products made of such	209.4	58.7	−150.6	460.1	316.4	−143.7
	Various goods and products	12.6	172.2	159.6	39.4	279.8	240.4
	Textiles and textile products	39.0	178.8	139.8	66.7	162.0	95.2
	Products made of wood, except for furniture	3.8	30.2	26.4	29.4	111.8	82.4
Hungary	**Total**	**3241.0**	**2922.8**	**−318.2**	**34,071.2**	**16,573.8**	**−17,497.4**
	Total groups of industrial products	**2982.4**	**2860.2**	**−122.3**	**30,232.4**	**15,254.9**	**−14,977.5**
	Electric machines, apparatuses and equipment; machines to record or render sound and images	778.7	856.5	77.8	9355.1	5649.2	−3705.9
	Chemical products	272.3	149.0	−123.3	4263.3	744.3	−3519.0
	Means and materials for transport	91.1	95.4	4.3	2437.7	553.4	−1884.3
	Footwear, hats, umbrellas and similar products	10.6	96.1	85.4	257.5	348.0	90.5

Source: Authors' own compilation of data from *Tempo online*, NIS

Appendix A.4: Companies operating in the manufacture of road transport motor vehicles in 2012

L. Chivu et al., *Deindustrialization and Reindustrialization in Romania*,
DOI 10.1007/978-3-319-65753-0

(continued)

Multinational companies	Turn-over (mil. euro)	Number of employees (pers.)	Romanian companies	Turn-over (mil. euro)	Number of employees (pers.)
Takata Petri Romania	346.92	4168	Raal	43.07	494
Leoni Wiring Systems Arad	127.46	3618	Rombat	67.11	641
EKR Elektrokontakt Romania	71.54	819	Turdeana	5.16	230
Nexans România	1.47	9	UAMT	18.87	370
Yazaki Component Technology	123.81	862	Superplast International	0.89	42
Coindu România	39.41	827	Gerom International	2.92	162
Delphi Packard Romania	382.22	9129	Compa	113.13	1804
Coficab Eastern Europe	273.40	381	Altur	25.17	668
Ert Group Automotive	0.54	2	Pulsor	0.83	38
Jurgen Armaturen	1.07	42	Fermit	4.01	201
Huff Romania	21.02	25	Romradiatoare	4.22	206
Continental Automotive Products	318.83	3942	Asam	11.68	188
Kromberg & Schubert Romania	93.10	2056	Comefin	9.04	273
Hella Lightining Romania	162.32	1023	Subansamable Auto Piteşti	9.55	234
Conti Tech Romania	154.65	1556	Musa Piteşti 96	1.65	70
Dura Automotive Romania	31.83	614	Presate Dacia	4.50	323
DPR Draxlmaier	17.72	467	Romautopart	0.65	13
Mahle Componente de Motor	38.68	317	Policolor	31.01	236
MGI Coutier Romania	22.59	281	Elba Romania	27.75	793
TRW Automotive Safety Systems	198.91	2648	Interpart Automotive	3.75	99
Plastique Forme Romania	2.48	36	Bega Tehnomet	5.11	142
Iorom Industry	0.00	1	G P& Company	1.46	87
Leman Industrie	9.81	182	Neferprod Impex	3.68	87
UCM Resita	27.62	2264	Spumotim	9.01	266
Sews Romania	200.73	7653	**Total**	**404.23**	**7667**

(*continued*)

(continued)

Multinational companies	Turn-over (mil. euro)	Number of employees (pers.)	Romanian companies	Turn-over (mil. euro)	Number of employees (pers.)
Lisa Draxlmaier	57.88	3408			
Thyssenkrupp Bilstein Compa	27.96	432			
Kuhnke Production Romania	40.31	571			
Faurecia Seating Talmaciu	33.10	720			
Brandl Ro	26.51	587			
SNR Rulmenti	16.91	496			
Takata Petri Sibiu	96.97	2178			
Kromberg & Schubert Sibiu	55.33	2064			
Continental Automotive Systems	342.52	1762			
Star Transmission Cugir	27.94	751			
Autoflex (Bosal)	0.96	16			
DRM Draxlmaier Sisteme Electrice	38.57	4547			
Schlemmer Romania	8.72	55			
Eckerle Romania	32.46	747			
Trelleborg Romania	32.29	205			
Leoni Wiring Systems BN	171.23	3142			
Parat Romania	1.08	107			
Autoliv Romania	425.21	3713			
Ina Schaeffler Brasov	320.43	3498			
Stabilus Romania	31.19	412			
DTR Draxlmaier Sisteme Tehnice	13.93	685			
Victoria (Michelin)	477.29	2666			
Yazaki Romania	166.79	3898			
Honeywell Garrett	35.98	646			
Lisa Draxlmaier Autopart Romania	57.88	3408			
Johnson Controls Romania	290.72	3.359			
Lear Corporation Romania	61.50	1760			
Valeo Cablaje	53.15	99			
Euro Auto Plastic Systems	93.97	628			

(*continued*)

(continued)

Multinational companies	Turn-over (mil. euro)	Number of employees (pers.)	Romanian companies	Turn-over (mil. euro)	Number of employees (pers.)
Borla Romcat	4.03	115			
Ronera Rubber	6.58	214			
Automotive Complete Systems	3.81	742			
Inergy Automotive System	33.89	139			
Koyo Romania	55.77	1378			
Cord Romania	80.70	490			
Pirelli Tyres Romania	341.47	2100			
Total components	**6233.16**	**94,660**			
Automobile Dacia	2859.55	13,640			
Ford Romania	556.36	3745			
Total motor vehicles	**3415.91**	**17,385**			
TOTAL	**9649.07**	**112,045**			

Source: Authors' own compilation based on data in the Ministry of Public Finance, balance report for 2013

Appendix A.5: Indices of industrial production (1990 = 100.0)

L. Chivu et al., *Deindustrialization and Reindustrialization in Romania*,
DOI 10.1007/978-3-319-65753-0

Activity (NACE headings Rev.1)	1995	2000	2005	2007	2008	2010	2011	2012	2013	2014
Total	**65.4**	**58.1**	**72.7**	**82.1**	**82.8**	**89.7**	**94.7**	**98.8**	**106.5**	**112.9**
Crude oil extraction	**83**	**65.1**	**65.7**	**67.1**	**66.8**	**81.1**	**56.7**	**92.1**	**94.2**	**95.0**
Coal mining and processing	102.1	69.0	70.8	76.1	75.0	…	…	…	…	…
Extraction of hydrocarbons and related services	77.8	68.2	66	64.4	62.4	…	…	…	…	…
Mining and processing of metal ores	74.9	52.7	42.4	6.4	1.5	…	…	…	…	…
Other extraction activities	52.9	38.8	54.5	80.1	90.8	…	…	…	…	…
Manufacturing industry	**62.7**	**57.9**	**76.4**	**87.7**	**88.3**	**98.5**	**104.0**	**108.7**	**118.7**	**127.6**
Food and beverages industry[a]	52.9	52.5	73.4	92.8	98.8	92.1	96.3	96.4	103.2	107.7
Tobacco products	83.7	99.6	108.3	124.7	157.5	123.8	162.1	177.2	162.5	192.8
Textile products	55.2	35.0	47.3	43.3	33.6	37.0	36.9	41.7	46.1	47.1
Clothing	89.0	137.6	137.3	98.1	96.5	72.7	71.6	72.3	78.0	78.2
Leatherwear and footwear	71.4	80.8	78.3	77.7	79.5	53.2	51.9	51.8	53.8	56.6
Wood processing and wooden products (except for furniture)	50.4	49.5	73.2	92.7	92.6	119.4	134.7	145.2	163.0	158.6

(continued)

(continued)

Activity (NACE headings Rev.1)	1995	2000	2005	2007	2008	2010	2011	2012	2013	2014
Pulp, paper and paper products	62.6	56.5	70.2	82.8	74.0	71.7	74.9	82.8	92.8	117.8
Oil processing, coal coking and treatment of nuclear fuels	70.9	54.6	74.7	69.6	66.6	55.1	54.6	51.9	54.7	61.6
Chemical substances and products	49.3	32.4	44.5	55.1	55.5	49.7	54.1	51.2	55.3	56.5
Products of rubber and plastic materials	39.1	24.4	40.6	46.7	47.3	72.7	76.9	86.4	92.2	97.1
Manufacture of building materials and other products of non-metallic minerals	52.3	45.6	54.6	69.8	74.3	59.7	67.2	69.3	77.1	80.6
Metallurgy	58.9	47.7	61.5	64.3	54.5	43.7	46.9	43.8	40.4	42.1
Metal structures and other metal products	58.3	31.9	31.1	38.3	37.4	42.3	41.7	43.9	45.5	46.1
Machines and equipment (except for electrical equipment and optic devices)	62.4	36.1	40.9	42.0	43.4	…	…	…	…	…
Electric machines and apparatuses	102.5	120.6	183.8	192.5	161.1	97.4	109.6	112.0	134.4	152.9

(continued)

(continued)

Activity (NACE headings Rev.1)	1995	2000	2005	2007	2008	2010	2011	2012	2013	2014
Equipment for radio, television and communications	182.2	92.1	75.1	80.4	86.3	…	…	…	…	…
Medical, precision and optic instruments, watchmaking	73.5	71.9	86.5	83.6	89.1	…	…	…	…	…
Vehicles for road transport	61.3	86.6	173.8	250.2	256.5	354.8	387.3	410.5	467.3	485.0
Means of transport, not included in road vehicles	42.4	57.8	62.0	84.5	88.9	43.7	39.8	50.4	59.0	70.1
Furniture and other industrial activities n.e.c.	113.0	141.1	194.9	240.3	220.0	…	…	…	…	…
Electricity, heating, gas and water	79.2	58.5	53.2	55.0	58.4	59.4	63.2	63.1	62.3	59.3

Source: Authors' own compilation based on NIS data
[a]except beverages, since 2010; … = Not available data

Appendix A.6: Indices of production in the mining industries (2005 = 100.0)

	2006	2007	2008	2009	2010	2011	2012	2013	2014	2015
Belgium	106.1	113.2	117.8	105.5	117.6	122.4	119.6	120.6	121.5	121.8
Bulgaria	106.0	116.2	117.0	95.6	97.6	103.2	102.9	102.7	104.6	107.6
Czech Rep.	108.3	119.9	117.7	101.7	110.4	116.9	115.9	115.8	121.5	127.2
Denmark	103.3	100.7	99.1	84.4	86.0	87.5	87.7	88.0	88.8	89.9
Germany	105.3	111.4	112.1	93.6	104.2	111.5	110.6	110.5	112.0	113.6
Estonia	109.9	117.0	110.9	84.4	104.2	124.9	126.3	131.5	136.6	133.5
Greece	100.9	103.2	98.8	89.3	83.8	79.0	77.3	74.8	73.3	74.1
Spain	103.7	106.1	98.6	82.6	83.3	81.6	76.2	74.8	75.9	78.4
France	100.9	102.1	99.0	85.8	89.6	91.9	89.7	89.0	88.2	89.8
Croatia	104.2	109.3	110.7	100.4	99.0	97.8	92.4	90.7	91.8	94.3
Italy	103.1	105.7	102.3	83.2	89.0	89.3	84.0	81.4	80.5	81.9
Latvia	106.5	107.6	104.2	85.3	97.9	106.8	113.4	112.3	111.2	115.2
Lithuania	105.5	107.0	112.3	96.8	102.9	109.5	113.5	117.3	117.3	122.9
Hungary	109.9	118.6	118.6	97.6	107.9	113.9	111.9	113.1	121.8	130.7
Netherlands	102.0	106.3	106.9	98.8	106.5	105.8	105.1	105.8	102.7	99.3
Austria	107.0	113.2	115.9	102.2	109.4	116.2	116.1	117.0	117.9	120.5
Poland	112.1	122.7	126.0	121.1	134.6	143.6	145.5	148.9	154.0	161.4
Portugal	103.0	103.4	99.2	90.6	92.2	91.0	85.7	86.4	87.8	89.5
Romania	**109.2**	**120.5**	**123.7**	**116.9**	**123.3**	**132.6**	**135.8**	**146.4**	**155.2**	**159.6**
Slovenia	105.7	113.3	116.0	95.9	102.8	104.1	103.0	102.0	104.2	110.1
Slovakia	115.7	135.3	155.1	130.9	141.6	149.0	160.9	167.0	181.3	194.1
Finland	110.1	115.2	116.4	95.5	100.9	102.6	100.4	97.3	95.6	94.8
Sweden	103.1	106.6	103.8	85.2	93.2	95.7	93.7	89.3	87.6	90.6
United Kingdom	100.6	100.9	98.2	89.8	92.7	92.1	89.6	89.0	90.4	91.6

Source: Authors' own compilation of Eurostat data

L. Chivu et al., *Deindustrialization and Reindustrialization in Romania*,
DOI 10.1007/978-3-319-65753-0

Appendix A.7: Indices of production in the manufacturing industry (2005 = 100.0)

	2006	2007	2008	2009	2010	2011	2012	2013	2014	2015
Belgium	106.9	114.7	120.3	104.8	118.2	124.9	122.3	123.2	126.7	127.3
Bulgaria	108.7	119.1	119.9	93.1	96.7	101.7	101.7	102.2	106.1	110.6
Czech Rep	109.5	123.1	121.2	102.7	113.0	121.5	120.7	121.6	129.7	137.5
Denmark	105.3	105.9	105.1	86.9	89.5	93.7	95.6	98.0	101.1	103.6
Germany	105.8	112.3	113.5	93.9	105.2	114.1	112.8	112.7	114.9	116.2
Estonia	110.5	117.1	111.9	83.4	102.7	125.9	128.0	132.9	139.4	138.7
Greece	102.0	104.2	99.3	88.3	83.8	76.2	73.6	72.7	74.1	75.4
Spain	103.9	106.6	98.3	81.5	82.0	80.7	74.7	73.6	75.2	78.3
France	101.0	102.4	98.8	84.4	88.0	91.3	88.6	87.7	87.5	89.0
Croatia	103.9	110.0	111.1	99.4	97.3	97.2	92.0	88.3	91.1	94.5
Italy	103.3	106.2	102.8	82.9	88.9	89.5	83.7	81.3	80.9	82.4
Latvia	106.3	106.6	103.0	82.1	95.7	106.9	116.8	116.9	116.6	121.5
Lithuania	106.6	108.3	115.1	97.8	105.2	115.8	121.6	127.2	128.2	135.6
Hungary	110.9	120.2	119.4	97.5	109.1	115.6	113.7	115.4	125.4	135.3
Netherlands	103.6	109.7	108.1	98.8	105.7	109.2	108.5	107.3	108.5	109.1
Austria	107.0	113.7	116.0	100.6	108.1	114.8	114.6	115.8	117.1	119.7
Poland	114.3	126.8	130.7	126.3	142.0	153.0	155.3	159.2	166.5	176.1
Portugal	102.9	104.4	100.3	90.0	92.0	90.9	89.1	90.2	91.6	93.2
Romania	**112.5**	**126.2**	**130.0**	**121.6**	**128.9**	**139.2**	**142.3**	**155.3**	**166.9**	**172.8**
Slovenia	106.2	115.2	118.2	96.2	103.4	104.6	102.1	100.5	104.9	111.2
Slovakia	120.9	146.7	171.0	139.1	152.7	163.4	182.0	190.8	211.1	227.0
Finland	108.6	115.0	117.3	93.3	98.0	101.0	99.1	95.4	94.0	93.2
Sweden	104.8	108.3	104.7	84.3	92.1	94.8	90.3	86.4	84.3	87.0
United Kingdom	102.2	102.8	99.9	90.6	94.7	96.8	95.4	94.4	97.2	97.2

Source: Authors' own compilation of Eurostat data

L. Chivu et al., *Deindustrialization and Reindustrialization in Romania*,
DOI 10.1007/978-3-319-65753-0

Appendix A.8: Indices of production in the electricity, heating, gas and water sector (2005 = 100.0)

	2006	2007	2008	2009	2010	2011	2012	2013	2014	2015
Belgium	99.4	102.3	100.1	107.5	110.0	100.8	97.9	99.4	86.0	83.6
Bulgaria	98.8	117.5	120.2	112.5	110.0	118.8	118.2	119.4	116.6	115.8
Czech Rep.	103.1	104.7	100.0	96.1	100.5	99.0	98.4	97.0	94.1	91.6
Denmark	113.2	98.1	89.5	88.3	96.4	90.6	85.8	98.8	94.8	89.2
Germany	101.4	97.8	96.3	91.6	95.6	90.6	93.4	93.7	89.5	95.3
Estonia	96.2	111.5	98.7	86.7	114.3	111.4	108.0	113.7	108.3	94.2
Greece	98.3	101.7	98.9	94.7	86.0	89.4	91.1	84.8	73.2	73.6
Spain	100.7	102.7	103.8	96.0	98.7	95.1	95.2	91.4	89.2	89.4
France	99.6	98.9	101.1	97.3	103.6	97.9	99.4	100.9	95.2	97.6
Croatia	102.0	102.7	106.6	109.0	116.0	107.9	105.8	116.8	110.8	104.5
Italy	102.1	101.8	102.5	93.3	95.6	93.6	90.9	86.9	82.2	84.0
Latvia	106.8	111.4	106.9	99.2	107.4	108.5	105.4	100.4	95.7	95.7
Lithuania	100.2	101.7	100.4	94.8	95.1	82.3	78.5	72.9	67.8	66.5
Hungary	100.5	104.1	109.2	96.5	97.4	95.8	92.6	88.2	84.0	89.2
Netherlands	97.4	95.4	98.8	98.7	104.7	91.5	91.3	91.3	87.1	94.7
Austria	107.9	109.4	120.4	116.3	122.2	124.7	143.6	136.7	120.5	114.9
Poland	100.3	102.5	101.9	96.8	97.4	98.9	100.4	99.3	96.3	94.0
Portugal	106.9	98.5	91.4	95.7	96.2	95.0	73.2	73.4	76.4	79.0
Romania	**92.4**	**96.3**	**96.6**	**103.5**	**111.9**	**117.0**	**118.9**	**117.2**	**111.7**	**113.2**
Slovenia	99.1	88.0	89.8	83.9	85.5	89.7	99.1	103.0	88.4	90.6
Slovakia	97.2	92.7	97.7	97.4	99.5	96.7	87.9	85.4	81.7	84.2
Finland	116.1	114.5	105.2	104.7	116.6	106.2	101.3	102.4	97.7	98.3
Sweden	91.0	94.0	95.5	86.9	94.3	95.2	105.0	96.9	98.0	102.9
United Kingdom	99.7	100.4	102.2	99.8	104.0	97.6	96.8	96.6	90.7	91.2

Source: Authors' own compilation of Eurostat data

L. Chivu et al., *Deindustrialization and Reindustrialization in Romania*,
DOI 10.1007/978-3-319-65753-0

Appendix A.9: Gross production, intermediate consumption and the gross value added in industry (bn. euro)

L. Chivu et al., *Deindustrialization and Reindustrialization in Romania*,
DOI 10.1007/978-3-319-65753-0

Branch	Indicator	1990	1995	2000	2005	2007	2008	2009	2010	2011	2012	2013
Total industry	Gross production	45.38	27.81	32.78	59.32	87.88	93.34	81.47	84.37	95.16	97.19	102.98
	Intermediate consumption	32.72	19.05	22.20	39.53	57.57	61.88	53.77	50.83	59.10	64.98	68.05
	Gross added value	12.67	8.75	10.58	19.80	30.31	31.47	27.70	33.55	36.03	32.21	34.94
Mining industry	Gross production	2.18	1.75	1.89	2.93	4.71	3.73	3.71	4.21	5.22	3.89	3.26
	Intermediate consumption	1.16	0.99	1.04	1.89	3.02	2.32	2.31	2.15	3.54	2.00	1.76
	Gross added value	1.01	0.76	0.84	1.05	1.70	1.41	1.40	2.06	1.68	1.89	1.50
Manufacturing industry	Gross production	39.18	22.63	26.07	47.46	70.99	76.08	63.08	67.30	74.50	78.08	84.97
	Intermediate consumption	27.70	15.62	17.54	30.56	44.93	48.66	39.67	40.42	45.84	51.58	55.70
	Gross added value	11.48	7.01	8.53	16.90	26.05	27.42	23.41	26.88	28.63	26.50	29.27
Electricity, heating, gas and water	Gross production	4.03	3.43	4.82	8.93	12.18	13.54	14.68	12.87	15.44	15.22	14.75
	Intermediate consumption	3.86	2.44	3.62	7.08	9.62	10.90	11.79	8.26	9.72	11.40	10.59
	Gross added value	0.17	0.99	1.20	1.85	2.56	2.64	2.89	4.61	5.72	3.82	4.17

Source: Authors' own compilation based on data from *Romania's Statistic Yearbook*, NIS, Bucharest, various editions, and NBR data regarding the Leu/euro annual average exchange rates

Appendix A.10: Gross production, intermediate consumption and gross value added in the manufacturing industry (bn. euro)

L. Chivu et al., *Deindustrialization and Reindustrialization in Romania*,
DOI 10.1007/978-3-319-65753-0

Branch	Indicator	1990	1995	2000	2005	2007	2008	2009	2010	2011	2012	2013
Manufacturing industry	Gross production	39.2	22.6	26.1	47.5	71.0	76.1	63.1	67.3	74.50	78.08	84.97
	Intermediate consumption	27.7	15.6	17.5	30.6	44.9	48.7	39.7	40.4	45.84	51.58	55.70
	Gross added value	11.5	7.0	8.5	16.9	26.1	27.4	23.4	26.9	28.63	26.50	29.27
Food industry, beverages and tobacco	Gross production	7.6	6.0	8.0	12.7	18.4	19.9	16.8	16.8	17.71	17.98	20.03
	Intermediate consumption	5.8	4.2	5.4	7.9	11.5	12.5	10.5	9.9	10.59	10.97	12.64
	Gross added value	1.9	1.8	2.6	4.8	6.9	7.4	6.3	6.9	7.12	7.00	7.39
Textiles, clothing, leatherwear, footwear	Gross production	5.0	2.2	2.5	4.4	5.8	5.6	4.5	4.6	5.43	6.05	6.48
	Intermediate consumption	2.9	1.4	1.5	2.6	3.4	3.3	2.6	2.0	2.27	3.16	3.35
	Gross added value	2.1	0.8	1.0	1.8	2.4	2.3	1.8	2.6	3.16	2.90	3.13
Wood, furniture	Gross production	1.7	1.3	1.9	3.6	5.4	6.2	5.6	6.5	6.37	6.75	7.70
	Intermediate consumption	1.0	0.7	1.1	2.1	3.1	3.8	3.6	3.1	3.43	4.42	4.96
	Gross added value	0.7	0.6	0.9	1.5	2.3	2.4	2.1	3.4	2.94	2.33	2.74
Crude oil processing, coking of coal et cetera	Gross production	2.9	1.8	2.2	3.9	3.7	5.0	3.3	2.8	4.35	5.19	7.37
	Intermediate consumption	3.0	1.6	1.8	2.9	2.8	3.8	2.5	2.5	3.50	4.60	5.11
	Gross added value	−0.1	0.3	0.4	1.0	0.9	1.3	0.8	0.4	0.86	0.59	2.26
Chemical substances and products	Gross production	2.7	2.0	1.9	2.6	3.8	3.6	2.6	2.7	2.87	2.97	2.61
	Intermediate consumption	2.2	1.4	1.4	1.9	2.8	2.8	2.0	2.3	2.35	2.00	1.83
	Gross added value	0.5	0.5	0.5	0.7	1.1	0.8	0.6	0.4	0.52	0.96	0.78

(continued)

(continued)

Branch	Indicator	1990	1995	2000	2005	2007	2008	2009	2010	2011	2012	2013
Metallurgy, metal structures and metal products	Gross production	5.4	4.0	4.0	8.3	13.6	10.4	6.3	8.9	9.97	9.86	9.13
	Intermediate consumption	4.1	2.9	2.9	6.0	9.3	7.6	4.4	6.1	7.21	6.83	6.27
	Gross added value	1.3	1.1	1.1	2.3	4.3	2.8	1.9	2.8	2.76	3.04	2.86
Machines and equipment (except for electrical and optic devices)	Gross production	4.8	1.6	1.2	2.2	3.3	2.5	2.2	2.6	2.98	3.10	3.18
	Intermediate consumption	2.9	1.0	0.7	1.4	2.0	1.5	1.4	1.5	2.05	1.94	2.06
	Gross added value	1.9	0.6	0.5	0.9	1.3	1.0	0.9	1.1	0.93	1.16	1.12
Means of transport	Gross production	2.1	1.2	1.4	3.9	6.7	7.8	8.9	8.9	10.29	10.57	12.63
	Intermediate consumption	1.5	0.8	1.0	2.3	3.8	4.4	5.1	4.9	5.60	8.10	9.80
	Gross added value	0.6	0.4	0.4	1.7	2.9	3.4	3.9	4.0	4.68	2.47	2.83
Electric equipment, computers, electronic and optical devices	Gross production	2.6	1.2	1.2	2.6	4.8	5.0	4.6	5.7	2.60	1.76	2.34
	Intermediate consumption	1.5	0.7	0.7	1.5	2.8	2.8	2.6	2.4	0.95	1.16	1.20
	Gross added value	1.1	0.5	0.5	1.1	2.1	2.2	2.0	3.3	1.65	0.59	1.14
Other sub-branches	Gross production	4.3	1.3	1.7	3.2	5.4	10.0	8.3	7.7	11.93	13.85	13.50
	Intermediate consumption	2.7	0.9	1.1	2.1	3.5	6.2	5.1	5.7	7.89	8.4	8.48
	Gross added value	1.6	0.5	0.6	1.1	1.9	3.9	3.2	2.0	4.01	5.46	5.02

Source: Authors' own compilation based on data from *Romania's Statistic Yearbook*, NIS, Bucharest, various editions, and NBR data regarding the Leu/euro annual average exchange rates

Appendix A.11: Ratio between resources and use, per product, in 1991 (%, current prices)

L. Chivu et al., *Deindustrialization and Reindustrialization in Romania*,
DOI 10.1007/978-3-319-65753-0

	Resources						Resource uses				
	Production of goods and services	Import	Product taxes	Commercial and transport margins	Product subsidies	Total	Intermediate consumption	Final consumption	Gross fixed capital formation	Export	Stock change
Products of the mining industries (coal, coking coal, crude oil, petroleum products, natural gas, ferrous and non-ferrous ores, ores for constructions and other ores)	80.6	14.1	2.2	3.6	−0.5	100.0	66.5	19.5	0.8	4.2	9.0
Textile products, clothing and leatherwear	78.5	5.1	6.7	10.9	−1.1	100.0	44.5	39.1	0.0	8.0	8.4
Products of the food industry, beverages and tobacco products	80.0	5.4	10.4	7.4	−3.2	100.0	35.4	60.2	0.0	1.5	2.9
Products of wood, paper and printing services	79.8	3.5	2.5	14.3	0.0	100.0	56.3	18.2	0.4	18.1	6.9
Products of the chemical industry	80.8	13.6	2.0	3.5	0.0	100.0	88.1	1.4	0.0	12.9	−2.3

(*continued*)

(continued)

	Resources					Resource uses					
	Production of goods and services	Import	Product taxes	Commercial and transport margins	Product subsidies	Total	Intermediate consumption	Final consumption	Gross fixed capital formation	Export	Stock change
Products of rubber, plastic materials and other non-metallic, minerals	88.4	3.1	2.1	6.3	0.0	100.0	85.7	5.5	0.0	5.4	3.4
Products of the metallurgical and steel industries	85.4	4.7	0.9	8.9	0.0	100.0	89.5	0.0	0.0	15.2	−4.7
Machine building, manufacture of household appliances, electric and electronic products	77.6	10.5	2.4	9.5	0.0	100.0	59.6	7.5	14.7	8.8	9.4
Means of transport	89.6	5.1	2.6	2.7	0.0	100.0	42.9	9.2	14.2	15.7	17.9
Electricity, heating, gas and water	98.2	6.1	5.4	0.3	−10.0	100.0	95.7	4.3	0.0	0.0	0.0

Source: Authors' own compilation of data in *National Accounts, 1991–1992*, NIS, Bucharest, 1995

Appendix A.12: Ratio between resources and resource use per product, in 2002 (%, current prices)

L. Chivu et al., *Deindustrialization and Reindustrialization in Romania*,
DOI 10.1007/978-3-319-65753-0

	Resource						Resource use				
	Production of goods and services	Import	Product taxes	Commercial and transport margins	Product subsidies	Total	Intermediate consumption	Final consumption	Gross fixed capital formation	Export	Stock change
Products of the mining industries (coal, coking coal, crude oil, petroleum products, natural gas, ferrous and non-ferrous ores, ores for construction and other ores)	48.7	24.7	11.1	16.5	−1.1	100.0	68.2	20.7	0.0	11.5	−0.4
Textile products, clothing and leatherwear	36.4	44.3	2.9	16.4	0.0	100.0	28.8	13.9	0.0	57.1	0.2
Products of the food industry, beverages and tobacco products	67.8	7.8	8.9	15.5	0.0	100.0	40.3	58.1	0.0	1.5	0.1
Products of wood, paper and printing services	66.7	18.5	3.3	11.4	0.0	100.0	45.5	19.1	3.3	31.6	0.5
Products of the chemical industry	48.8	39.6	4.1	7.8	−0.3	100.0	75.6	3.0	0.0	20.3	1.1
Products of rubber, plastic materials and other non-metallic minerals	56.7	26.5	3.5	13.3	0.0	100.0	80.0	6.5	0.0	12.2	1.3

(continued)

(continued)

	Resource						Resource use				
	Production of goods and services	Import	Product taxes	Commercial and transport margins	Product subsidies	Total	Intermediate consumption	Final consumption	Gross fixed capital formation	Export	Stock change
Products of the metallurgical and steel industries	60.6	27.6	2.5	9.4	0.0	100.0	57.3	0.7	0.0	41.6	0.4
Machine building, manufacture of household appliances, electric and electronic products	40.2	49.7	3.1	7.2	–0.1	100.0	31.1	11.2	32.4	25.1	0.2
Means of transport	54.2	31.3	4.2	10.6	–0.2	100.0	15.2	18.1	42.1	24.4	0.1
Electricity, heating, gas and water	94.6	0.6	4.8	0.0	0.0	100.0	81.4	16.9	0.0	1.7	0.0

Source: Authors' own compilation based on data from *National Accounts, 2002–2003*, NIS, Bucharest, 2006

Appendix A.13: Ratio between resources and resources use per product, in 2005 (%, current prices)

L. Chivu et al., *Deindustrialization and Reindustrialization in Romania*,
DOI 10.1007/978-3-319-65753-0

	Resources						Use				
	Production of goods and services	Import	Product taxes	Commercial and transport margins	Product subsidies	Total	Intermediate consumption	Final consumption	Gross fixed capital formation	Export	Stock change
Products of the mining industries	34.5	52.6	4.3	10.6	−2.0	100.0	98.2	0.1	0.0	1.2	0.5
Textile products, clothing and leatherwear	40.4	39.1	4.4	16.1	0.0	100.0	27.7	19.5	0.0	52.6	0.2
Products of the food industry, beverages and tobacco products	62.3	7.9	10.3	19.5	0.0	100.0	38.4	60.1	0.0	1.4	0.1
Products of wood, paper and printing services	66.3	19.2	4.0	10.5	0.0	100.0	68.0	13.0	0.0	18.9	0.2
Products from coking coal and products obtained from crude oil processing	48.7	7.8	21.0	23.6	−1.0	100.0	18.5	56.3	0.0	26.7	−1.5
Products of the chemical industry	35.8	44.8	6.7	13.3	−0.6	100.0	63.0	18.4	0.0	18.3	0.3
Products of rubber, plastic materials and other non-metallic mineral products	54.9	28.7	4.0	12.5	−0.1	100.0	76.9	10.5	0.0	12.0	0.6

(continued)

(continued)

	Resources					Use					
	Production of goods and services	Import	Product taxes	Commercial and transport margins	Product subsidies	Total	Intermediate consumption	Final consumption	Gross fixed capital formation	Export	Stock change
Products of the metallurgical industry, metal structures and other metal manufacturing industries (except for machines, machinery and equipment)	60.1	31.6	2.7	5.7	0.0	100.0	58.2	3.6	4.1	34.9	−0.8
Manufacture of machines and equipment, including electric machines	33.5	55.7	3.5	8.1	−0.8	100.0	28.4	12.0	34.9	26.6	−1.9
Means of transport	47.1	36.1	4.6	12.6	−0.4	100.0	11.1	26.3	42.4	21.1	−0.9
Other industrial activities	56.2	19.1	3.1	21.5	0.0	100.0	14.7	38.5	10.2	36.2	0.3
Electricity, heating, gas and water	94.6	1.2	4.2	0.0	0.0	100.0	75.5	22.8	0.0	1.7	0.0

Source: Authors' own compilation based on data from *National Accounts, 2005–2006*, NIS, Bucharest, 2009

Appendix A.14: Balance between resources and use per product in 2010 (%, current prices)

L. Chivu et al., *Deindustrialization and Reindustrialization in Romania*,
DOI 10.1007/978-3-319-65753-0

	Resources						Use				
	Production of goods and services	Import	Product taxes	Commercial and transport margins	Product subsidies	Total	Intermediate consumption	Final consumption	Gross fixed capital formation	Export	Stock change
Products of the mining industries	46.7	13.6	2.3	37.5	−0.1	**100.0**	87.3	6.2	0.8	2.8	2.9
Textile products, clothing and leatherwear	43.4	37.3	3.1	16.3	0.0	**100.0**	24.5	32.2	0.0	42.0	1.3
Products of the food industry, beverages, tobacco products	57.8	8.8	9.7	23.7	0.0	**100.0**	25.4	69.9	0.0	4.4	0.3
Products of wood, paper and printing services	66.2	19.9	4.3	9.5	0.0	**100.0**	68.6	10.1	0.0	22.3	−1.1
Coking products and products obtained by crude oil processing	23.5	32.6	19.4	24.5	0.0	**100.0**	57.9	34.5	0.0	13.9	−6.3
Products of the chemical industry	35.3	48.6	4.4	11.6	0.0	**100.0**	67.0	12.2	0.0	19.8	1.1
Manufacture of basic pharmaceuticals and pharmaceutical preparations	13.0	47.4	3.3	36.3	0.0	**100.0**	7.6	80.3	0.0	12.8	−0.7
Products made of rubber, plastic materials and other non-metallic minerals	49.3	26.7	3.6	20.4	0.0	**100.0**	77.3	7.1	0.0	16.1	−0.5

(continued)

(continued)

	Resources						Use				
	Production of goods and services	Import	Product taxes	Commercial and transport margins	Product subsidies	Total	Intermediate consumption	Final consumption	Gross fixed capital formation	Export	Stock change
Products of the metallurgical industry, metal structures and metal products (except for machines, machinery and equipment)	54.6	32.2	2.8	10.4	0.0	**100.0**	68.1	2.2	0.8	26.8	2.2
Computers, electronic and optical devices	30.4	54.4	4.0	11.2	0.0	**100.0**	33.8	8.7	18.0	37.9	1.7
Electrical equipment	32.6	52.3	2.4	12.8	−0.1	**100.0**	37.6	6.6	2.8	55.4	−2.4
Machines, machinery and equipment n.e.c	29.4	54.1	3.5	12.9	0.0	**100.0**	1.9	7.0	62.0	30.4	−1.2
Means of transport	62.3	21.3	3.3	13.1	0.0	**100.0**	27.8	15.4	18.9	38.0	−0.1
Furniture, industrial products, repair and maintenance services for machines and equipment	71.3	12.5	3.8	12.3	0.0	**100.0**	44.1	16.2	13.6	23.7	2.4
Electricity, gas, steam and air conditioning	96.6	0.2	3.7	0.0	−0.6	**100.0**	76.4	22.5	0.0	1.1	0.0
Water supply, waste management, sanitation, decontamination services	94.5	2.8	2.7	0.0	0.0	**100.0**	52.2	39.7	0.0	7.5	0.6

Source: Authors' own compilation based on data from *National Accounts, 2009–2010*, Bucharest 2013

Appendix A.15: Ratio between resources and resource use, by product, in 2013 (%, current prices)

L. Chivu et al., *Deindustrialization and Reindustrialization in Romania*,
DOI 10.1007/978-3-319-65753-0

	Resources						Resource use				
	Production of goods and services	Import	Product taxes	Commercial and transport margins	Product subsidies	Total	Intermediate consumption	Final consumption	Gross fixed capital formation	Export	Stock change
Products of the mining industries	32.1	38.5	2.2	27.2	0.0	**100.0**	92.4	3.3	2.7	3.2	−1.6
Textile products, clothing and leatherwear	34.6	48.0	3.6	13.8	0.0	**100.0**	66.6	14.4	0.0	18.5	0.4
Products of the food industry, beverages, tobacco products	68.6	12.2	3.3	15.9	0.0	**100.0**	15.3	78.3	0.0	5.5	0.9
Products of wood, paper and printing services	79.7	7.8	3.6	8.9	0.0	**100.0**	57.6	2.6	0.0	39.9	−0.1
Coking products and products obtained by crude oil processing	51.6	10.9	19.4	18.1	0.0	**100.0**	59.8	28.3	0.0	12.5	−0.6
Products of the chemical industry	29.0	50.4	3.0	17.6	0.0	**100.0**	65.1	13.8	0.0	20.4	0.8
Manufacture of basic pharmaceuticals and pharmaceutical preparations	9.9	45.9	6.3	37.9	0.0	**100.0**	25.3	56.2	0.0	16.3	2.2
Products made of rubber, plastic materials and other non-metallic minerals	49.3	32.5	3.3	14.9	0.0	**100.0**	58.8	9.2	0.0	30.8	1.2

(continued)

(continued)

	Resources						Resource use				
	Production of goods and services	Import	Product taxes	Commercial and transport margins	Product subsidies	Total	Intermediate consumption	Final consumption	Gross fixed capital formation	Export	Stock change
Products of the metallurgical industry, metal structures and metal products (except for machines, machinery and equipment)	52.8	34.6	2.4	10.2	0.0	**100.0**	71.7	2.2	0.4	25.9	−0.3
Computers, electronic and optical devices	26.3	57.2	1.9	14.6	0.0	**100.0**	34.2	10.2	28.7	27.0	−0.1
Electrical equipment	36.2	50.5	2.0	11.3	−0.1	**100.0**	32.1	7.7	4.9	55.3	0.0
Machines, machinery and equipment n.e.c	29.6	53.6	3.6	13.1	0.0	**100.0**	2.0	3.1	56.4	38.2	0.2
Means of transport	64.6	23.7	4.3	7.4	0.0	**100.0**	20.8	11.5	20.9	46.6	0.1
Furniture	69.3	13.0	3.7	14.0	0.0	**100.0**	27.9	9.7	8.9	53.9	−0.4
Electricity, gas, steam and air conditioning	97.9	0.1	3.4	0.0	−1.5	**100.0**	81.8	17.4	0.0	0.7	0.1
Water supply, waste management, sanitation, decontamination services	91.3	5.6	2.3	0.9	0.0	**100.0**	45.5	29.2	0.0	24.9	0.3

Source: Authors' own compilation of data from *National Accounts, 2013*, NIS, Bucharest, 2016

Appendix A.16: Share held by certain groups of industrial products in the main macroeconomic indicators, 1991 (%)

L. Chivu et al., *Deindustrialization and Reindustrialization in Romania*,
DOI 10.1007/978-3-319-65753-0

	Production of goods and services	Import	Export	Intermediate consumption	Compensation of employees	Gross operating surplus	Product-related taxes	Product and import subsidies
Products of the mining industries (coal, coking coal, crude, oil products, natural gas, ferrous and non-ferrous ores, ores for constructions and other ores)	21.3	43.2	15.7	28.1	4.7	7.5	5.2	8.6
Textile products, clothing and leatherwear	6.1	4.6	8.8	5.6	7.7	2.2	6.7	5.6
Products of the food industry, beverages and tobacco products	9.8	7.6	2.7	6.9	5.7	8.2	4.7	24.7
Products made of wood, paper and printing services	3.2	1.6	10.3	3.6	4.0	1.6	3.8	0.0
Products of the chemical industry	3.2	6.2	7.2	5.5	1.9	1.2	1.4	0.0
Products made of rubber, plastic materials and other non-metallic mineral products	4.2	1.7	3.6	6.5	3.8	2.9	4.1	0.0
Products of the metallurgical and steel industries	4.9	3.2	12.4	8.2	2.4	2.6	2.5	0.0
Machine building, machinery and household appliances, electrical and electronic products	9.2	14.5	14.9	11.4	10.1	4.4	9.5	0.1
Means of transport	3.0	2.0	7.5	2.3	3.0	1.3	2.7	0.0
Electricity, gas, steam and air conditioning	6.9	5.0	0.0	10.8	2.4	4.1	2.4	44.4
Total groups of industrial products	71.9	89.7	83.1	88.9	45.6	36.0	42.9	83.4

Source: Authors' own compilation of data from *National Accounts, 1991–1992*, NIS, Bucharest, 1995

Appendix A.17: Share of certain groups of industrial products in the main macro-economic indicators, 2002 (%)

L. Chivu et al., *Deindustrialization and Reindustrialization in Romania*,
DOI 10.1007/978-3-319-65753-0

	Production of goods and services	Intermediate consumption	Gross added value	Compensation of employees	Gross operating surplus	Production-related taxes	Product subsidies	Import	Export
Products of the mining industries (coal, coking coal, crude, oil products, natural gas, ferrous and non-ferrous ores, ores for constructions and other ores)	5.0	12.9	3.6	5.1	2.5	20.0	38.1	11.9	6.4
Textile products, clothing and leatherwear	3.4	5.0	3.1	5.3	1.4	4.8	0.0	19.8	29.6
Products of the food industry, beverages and tobacco products	9.2	10.2	7.4	4.2	9.8	21.3	0.0	5.0	1.1
Products made of wood, paper and printing services	3.6	4.5	3.5	3.6	3.4	3.1	0.0	4.7	9.3
Products of the chemical industry	1.6	4.6	0.7	1.4	0.2	2.3	3.7	6.1	3.6
Products made of rubber, plastic materials, and other non-metallic, mineral products	2.3	6.0	1.9	2.3	1.7	2.5	0.5	5.1	2.7
Products of the metallurgical and steel industries	2.7	4.7	1.1	2.1	0.4	1.9	0.0	5.7	10.1

(continued)

(continued)

	Production of goods and services	Intermediate consumption	Gross added value	Compensation of employees	Gross operating surplus	Production-related taxes	Product subsidies	Import	Export
Machine building, machinery and household appliances, electrical and electronic products	4.3	6.3	4.0	5.9	2.6	5.9	4.3	25.4	14.9
Means of transport	2.0	1.0	1.7	2.4	1.2	2.7	3.0	5.4	4.9
Electricity, gas, steam and air conditioning	7.4	11.8	3.8	4.3	3.3	6.6	0.0	0.2	0.7
Total groups of industrial products	41.5	67.0	31.0	36.6	26.4	71.1	49.6	89.4	83.4

Source: Authors' own compilation of data from *National Accounts, 2002–2003*, NIS, Bucharest, 2006

Appendix A.18: Share of certain groups of industrial products in the main macro-economic indicators, 2005 (%)

L. Chivu et al., *Deindustrialization and Reindustrialization in Romania*,
DOI 10.1007/978-3-319-65753-0

	Production of goods and services	Intermediate consumption	Gross added value	Compensation of employees	Gross operating surplus	Production-related taxes	Product subsidies	Import	Export
Products of the mining industry	1.9	10.3	1.5	2.9	0.4	3.7	29.6	13.0	0.4
Textile products, clothing leatherwear	2.9	3.7	2.6	5.3	0.3	4.9	0.0	12.3	21.6
Products of the food industry, beverages and tobacco products	8.4	9.7	6.8	4.5	8.6	21.3	0.0	4.7	1.1
Products made of wood, paper and printing services	2.2	4.2	2.0	1.9	2.0	2.0	0.0	2.8	3.6
Coking coal products and products obtained from processing of crude oil	2.6	1.8	1.4	1.4	1.4	17.0	14.4	1.8	8.1
Products of the chemical industry	1.7	5.7	1.0	1.6	0.5	4.9	7.5	9.5	5.1
Products made of rubber, plastic materials and other non-metallic, mineral products	2.4	6.4	1.8	2.1	1.6	2.7	1.0	5.6	3.0
Products of the metallurgical and steel industries	4.1	7.5	2.1	3.2	1.2	2.8	0.0	9.6	13.8

(continued)

(continued)

	Production of goods and services	Intermediate consumption	Gross added value	Compensation of employees	Gross operating surplus	Production-related taxes	Product subsidies	Import	Export
Machine building, machinery and household appliances, electrical and electronic products	3.2	5.0	2.8	4.1	1.8	5.1	20.2	23.1	14.4
Means of transport	2.6	1.1	2.4	2.3	2.4	3.9	5.5	8.8	6.7
Other industrial activities	1.2	0.6	1.1	1.7	0.7	1.0	0.0	1.8	4.4
Electricity, gas, steam and air conditioning	5.9	8.8	2.6	3.3	2.1	4.0	0.0	0.3	0.6
Total groups of products	39.2	65.0	28.1	34.2	22.9	73.4	78.2	93.1	82.8

Source: Authors' own compilation of data from *National Accounts, 2005–2006*, NIS, Bucharest, 2009

Appendix A.19: Share of certain groups of industrial products in the main macro-economic indicators, 2010 (%)

L. Chivu et al., *Deindustrialization and Reindustrialization in Romania*,
DOI 10.1007/978-3-319-65753-0

	Production of goods and services	Intermediate consumption	Gross added value	Compensation of employees	Gross operating surplus	Production-related taxes	Product subsidies	Import	Export
Products of the mining industry	1.7	5.9	1.9	2.6	1.2	1.4	1.8	2.4	0.6
Textile products, clothing, leatherwear	1.9	2.0	2.4	3.0	1.9	2.3	0.0	7.8	10.2
Products of the food industry, beverages and tobacco products	6.9	5.5	6.2	2.8	8.5	19.9	0.0	5.0	2.9
Products made of wood, paper and printing services	1.6	3.1	1.7	1.0	2.2	1.9	0.0	2.3	3.1
Coking coal products and products obtained from processing of crude oil	1.2	5.2	0.4	0.4	0.3	16.7	0.0	7.7	3.8
Products of the chemical industry	1.1	3.9	0.4	0.6	0.2	2.4	0.0	7.3	3.5
Manufacture of basic pharmaceuticals and pharmaceutical preparations	0.2	0.3	0.1	0.2	0.0	1.1	0.0	4.3	1.4
Products made of rubber, plastic materials and other non-metallic mineral products	2.3	6.5	1.1	1.5	0.8	2.9	0.0	5.9	4.1

(continued)

(continued)

	Production of goods and services	Intermediate consumption	Gross added value	Compensation of employees	Gross operating surplus	Production-related taxes	Product subsidies	Import	Export
Products of the metallurgical industry, metal structures, metal products (except for machines, machinery and equipment)	3.6	8.3	2.6	2.8	2.4	3.3	0.0	10.3	9.9
Computers, electronic and optic devices	1.2	2.4	1.8	0.5	2.8	2.8	0.0	10.3	8.3
Electrical equipment	1.1	2.4	1.2	1.0	1.3	1.5	2.4	8.7	10.7
Machines, machinery and equipment n.e.c.	1.0	0.1	1.0	1.0	0.9	2.2	0.0	9.2	6.0
Means of transport	3.6	3.0	3.6	2.7	4.2	3.3	0.0	5.9	12.3
Furniture, other industrial goods, repair and maintenance of machines and equipment	1.7	1.9	2.0	2.0	1.9	1.6	0.0	1.4	3.2
Electricity, gas, steam and air conditioning	5.3	7.6	4.2	3.1	4.5	3.5	14.4	0.1	0.3
Water supply, sanitation, waste management and decontamination services	1.4	1.5	1.6	1.4	1.7	0.7	0.0	0.2	0.6
Total groups of products	36.0	59.5	31.9	26.9	34.6	67.3	18.6	88.9	80.9

Source: Authors' own compilation of data from *National Accounts, 2009–2010*, NIS, Bucharest, 2013

Appendix A.20: Share of certain groups of industrial products in the macroeconomic indicators, 2013 (%)

L. Chivu et al., *Deindustrialization and Reindustrialization in Romania*,
DOI 10.1007/978-3-319-65753-0

	Production of goods and services	Intermediate consumption	Gross added value	Compensation of employees	Gross operating surplus	Production-related taxes	Product subsidies	Import	Export
Products of the mining industry	1.1	1.1	1.2	2.2	0.5	1.3	0.0	7.0	0.6
Textile products, clothing and leatherwear	2.2	2.0	2.5	3.7	1.8	2.0	0.0	5.4	6.4
Products of the food industry, beverages and tobacco products	6.9	7.7	5.8	2.1	7.8	19.3	0.0	6.3	3.7
Products made of wood, paper and printing services	1.8	2.1	1.3	1.0	1.5	1.6	0.0	2.0	3.4
Coking products and products obtained from crude oil processing	2.5	3.1	1.8	0.3	2.6	16.2	0.0	3.0	3.6
Products of the chemical industry	0.9	1.1	0.6	0.6	0.6	1.6	0.0	7.7	3.2
Basic pharmaceuticals and pharmaceutical preparations	0.2	0.2	0.2	0.2	0.2	2.2	0.0	4.8	1.8
Products made of rubber, plastic materials and other non-metallic minerals	2.3	2.7	1.7	1.5	1.8	2.4	0.0	5.5	4.9
Processing of primary metals, metallurgical products (except for machines, machinery and equipment)	3.1	3.8	2.2	2.6	2.0	2.5	0.0	9.8	7.5
Computers, electronic and optical devices	0.8	0.7	0.9	0.9	0.9	1.0	0.0	7.7	4.2

(*continued*)

(continued)

	Production of goods and services	Intermediate consumption	Gross added value	Compensation of employees	Gross operating surplus	Production-related taxes	Product subsidies	Import	Export
Electrical equipment	1.3	1.5	1.0	0.9	1.0	1.2	5.4	7.7	8.3
Machines, machinery and equipment n.e.c.	1.1	1.3	0.9	1.1	0.7	2.2	0.0	9.3	6.6
Means of transport	4.4	6.0	2.2	3.5	1.4	4.4	4.5	7.6	14.8
Furniture, other industrial goods, repair and maintenance services for machines and equipment	1.8	1.8	1.9	2.2	1.6	1.5	0.0	2.0	3.7
Electricity, gas, steam and air conditioning	5.1	6.5	3.3	2.5	3.6	3.0	32.0	0.0	0.2
Water supply, sanitation, waste management and decontamination services	1.2	1.4	1.1	1.4	0.9	0.5	0.0	0.2	1.5
Total groups of products	36.8	43.1	28.6	27.1	28.8	62.7	42.0	86.1	74.5

Source: Authors' own compilation of data from *National Accounts, 2012–2013*, NIS, Bucharest, 2016

Appendix A.21: Physical output of the main industrial products

L. Chivu et al., *Deindustrialization and Reindustrialization in Romania*,
DOI 10.1007/978-3-319-65753-0

	UM	Maximum level of production	Year of maximum level	1990	1996	2000	2006	2008	2011	2013	2014
Electric power	mil. Kwh	75,851	**1989**	64,309	61,350	51,935	62,696	64,956	62,216	58,887.9	65,674.9
Thermal energy	mil. Kcal	182,407	**1988**	168,331	103,986	68,474	48,334	43,847	38,876	32,972.9	28,476.0
Coal extracted, total	thou. tonnes	66,462	**1989**	40,847	47,774	30,924	35,404	36,690	37,342	25,922.6	24,670.5
Hard coal	thou. tonnes	11,693	**1987**	5950	6965	4042	2587	...	...	1874.7	1711.8
Light coal	thou. tonnes	53,980	**1989**	34,220	37,204	26,576	32,754	33,658	35,220	24,047.9	22,958.8
Brown coal	thou. tonnes	910	**1988**	677	605	306	63	...		...	...
Coking coal	thou. tonnes	5870	**1989**	3978	3153	1613	1790	...	0.32	0	0
Crude oil extracted	thou. tonnes	13,337	**1970**	7928	6626	6042	4777	...	...	3983.7	3912.2
Petroleum products	thou. tonnes	1289	**1960**	453	185	266	461	555	502	464.8	509.9
Diesel oil	thou. tonnes	8471	**1988**	6389	4197	3354	4484	4679	3828	4172.5	5138.3
Fuel oil	thou. tonnes	10,231	**1980**	8121	2405	1433	1303	48	0.07	400.4	320.7
Mineral oils	thou. tonnes	664	**1980**	371	217	112	85	...	...	18.7	24.2
Associated gas and methane gas	mil. mc	40,764	**1980**	28,336	18,162	14,607	12,422	11,586	11,174	11,168.9	11,374.6
Raw iron ores	thou. tonnes	2482	**1989**	2002	860	116	123	...	...	....	....
Cast iron	thou. tonnes	9329	**1986**	6335	4025	3066	3946	...	...	...	...
Steel	thou. tonnes	14,411	**1989**	9761	6083	4672	6266	5039	3811	3073.4	3192.9
Finished rolled steel	thou. tonnes	9319	**1980**	4727	4479	3687	5696	4757	4073	2935.3	3170.5
Steel pipes	thou. tonnes	1464	**1980**	510	591	465	580	885	820	478.5	526.1
Aluminium	thou. tonnes	417	**2000**	178	145	417	277	...	...	....	...
Lead	thou. tonnes	44	**1970**	13	14	25	20	...	...	....	...
Copper	thou. tonnes	41	**1986**	28	33	16	22	...	...	...	...
Combustion engines	thou. pcs.	308	**2006**	163	120	107	308	...	...	...	...
Electronic computers	pcs.	512	**1989**	320	...	...	...	...	...	...	..
Electric motors	thou. Kwh	19,187	**1980**	11,,086	1987	1704	1502	1234	700	298.3	308.9
Electric generators	thou. KwA	1111	**1980**	589	2	108	...	...	...	...	...

(continued)

(continued)

	UM	Maximum level of production	Year of maximum level	1990	1996	2000	2006	2008	2011	2013	2014
Electric transformers	thou. KwA	15,939	**1980**	5728	1664	2068	3262	…	5384	2712.3	…
Radio-TV sets	thou. pcs.	1404	**1980**	839	351	32	43	…	…	…	…
Machine tools (lathes, milling machines, rectifying machines, et cetera)	pcs.	12,958	**1980**	5554	1197	654	365	252	71	…	…
Machinery and equipment for oil exploration and drilling	thou. tonnes	166	**1986**	70	21	9	24	49	…	…	…
Machines and equipment for other industries	thou. tonnes	689	**1986**	405	293	69	68	15	12	..	..
Excavators, road rollers	pcs.	1612	**1980**	1048	139	73	6	…	…	…	…
Tractors	thou. pcs.	71	**1980**	22.6	13.0	5.4	3.3	…	…	….	…
Electric and Diesel engines	pcs.	276	**1980**	121.0	1.0	2.0	0.0	0.0	2.0	..	..
Freight rail cars	pcs.	14,060	**1987**	7500	38	1128	2593	4184.0	842.0	…	…
Passenger cars	pcs.	601	**1980**	129	23	…	32	…	…	…	…
Automobiles, vans, autobuses and trolleybuses	thou. pcs.	213.4	**2006**	102.9	119.5	77.2	213.4	…	c	c	c

(continued)

(continued)

	UM	Maximum level of production	Year of maximum level	1990	1996	2000	2006	2008	2011	2013	2014
Lorries and tip-up lorries	thou. pcs.	35.0	**1970**	8.5	3.1	0.8	0.5	…	0.1	c	c
Sea- and river-going vessels	pcs.	144	**1996**	22	144	41	36	…	…	..	..
Ball bearings	mil. pcs.	143	**1996**	101	97	88	75	78.6	80.5	78.6	85.0
Bicycles	thou. pcs.	881	**2011**	136	19	4	137	…	881.0	908.0	584.0
Sulphuric and chlorohydrin acid	thou. tonnes	2437	**1986**	1454	594	328	147	136.7	187.7	111.2	111.7
Chemical fertilisers (100% eauivalent active substance -eas)	thou. tonnes	3097	**1985**	1744	1464	1054	1142	1786.8	1288.3	742.5	785.4
Chemical yarns and fibres	thou. tonnes	303	**1986**	209	78	30	13	…	…	…	…
Plastic materials and synthetic resins	thou. tonnes	834.5	**2008**	473	322	331	791	834.5	658.0	…	…
Synthetic rubber	thou. tonnes	173	**1986**	102	37	20	2	…	…	…	…
Car tyres	thou. pcs.	28,013	**2011**	5142	3739	3226	15,330	18,686.9	28,013.2	28,176.8	23,539.5
Detergents (100% eas)	thou. tonnes	206.7	**2011**	11.6	6.0	11.0	148.0	163.5	206.7	229.6	230.9
Varnishes and paints	thou. tonnes	196	**1986**	134	44	36	110	154.9	136.0	140.5	142.2
Cement	thou. tonnes	14,607	**1980**	9468	6956	6058	8253	10,659.6	8087.3	7450.8	7621.1
Glass panes (2 mm thickness)	thou. sqm	77,504	**1980**	56,649	37,000	30,000	16,000	…	…	…	…
Glassware	thou. tonnes	398	**1986**	307	216	129	126	…	…	…	…
Timber	thou. cm	5144.9	**2011**	2932	1924	1405	3126	3509.0	5144.9	5835.7	5909.2

(*continued*)

(continued)

	UM	Maximum level of production	Year of maximum level	1990	1996	2000	2006	2008	2011	2013	2014
Paper and cardboard	thou. tonnes	822	**1980**	449	327	359	434	399.6	361.8	398.6	414.5
Cotton and cotton-like yarns	thou. tonnes	183	**1980**	131	62	27	29	15.9	18.1	12.4	12.5
Wool and wool-like yarns	thou. tonnes	75.8	**1987**	56.3	32.0	19.0	24.0	22.5	29.1	30.7	27.9
Linen and hemp yarns	thou. tonnes	45.5	**1980**	24.4	7.0	4.0	2.0	1.4	…	0.5	..
Fabrics	mil. sqm	1154	**1980**	841	342	194	154	80.7	44.2	65.4	70.8
Knitwear	mil. pcs.	296	**1980**	203	110	38	39	29.7	27.6	22.9	23.0
Footwear, of which:	mil. pairs	118	**1989**	92	47	38	69	53.1	45.9	49.7	51.6
Made of leather	mil. pairs	59	**2006**	32	36	27	59	47.5	40.3	43.2	46.3
Meat	thou. tonnes	993	**1980**	947	607	259	322	457.5	579.7	631.8	680.3
Meat prepa-rations	thou. tonnes	368.2	**2008**	365	150	127	330	368.2	350.0	325.8	337.7
Fresh milk	thou. hl	5925	**1980**	5223	3491	1608	1665	2028.9	2238.9	2180.6	2594.3
Edible oils	thou. tonnes	392	**1987**	270	236	253	338	157.8	203.8	192.5	273.7
Sugar	thou. tonnes	716	**1989**	538	396	476	605	489.6	384.2	456.3	437.5
Canned meat	thou. tonnes	77	**1980**	48	18	11	28	33.7	25.5	29.9	33.7
Canned fish	thou. tonnes	25	**1980**	18	2	1	10	10.2	9.8	c	c
Tinned fruit and vege-tables	thou. tonnes	540	**1980**	240	163	104	71	79.9	70.4	80.4	76.5
Salt	thou. tonnes	5395	1987	4262	2689	2308	2621	c	c	c	c
Tobacco products	thou. tonnes	49	2011	27	25	33	30	45.3	49.0	48.3	56.8
Soap	thou. tonnes	66	1980	36	10	2	2	4.6	4.3	6.2	8.8

Source: Authors' own compilation of data from *Romania's Statistic Yearbook*, NIS, Bucharest, various editions, and *Tempo online*

Note: Not available data; c-confidential data

Appendix A.22: Net monthly average salary (euro)

	2000	2005	2007	2010	2011	2012	2013	2014	2015
TOTAL	107	206	312	330	341	338	357	382	418
INDUSTRY	111	202	291	330	347	346	363	387	411
MINING INDUSTRY	184	344	541	578	608	625	666	733	777
Hard and light coal mining	206	375	556	566	564	574	583	613	622
Extraction of crude oil and natural gas	199	385	630	680	753	818	893	1051	1124
Mining of metallic ores	151	263	427	472	500	485	481	514	545
Other mining activities	132	209	298	317	339	307	316	314	336
Mining-related activities	163	315	513	624	640	652	735	803	956
MANUFACTURING INDUSTRY	99	180	261	294	312	313	332	355	383
Food industry	77	145	217	225	231	222	231	254	281
Manufacture of beverages	136	259	390	405	421	426	448	454	472
Manufacture of tobacco products	225	474	648	766	845	835	864	936	943
Manufacture of textile products	77	143	209	251	274	273	289	302	327
Manufacture of clothing	75	136	191	204	214	215	228	250	265
Tanning and finishing of hides, manufacture of travelling bags, leatherwear, saddlery and footwear; dressing and dyeing of furs	67	134	186	212	224	223	239	253	278

(*continued*)

L. Chivu et al., *Deindustrialization and Reindustrialization in Romania*,
DOI 10.1007/978-3-319-65753-0

(continued)

	2000	2005	2007	2010	2011	2012	2013	2014	2015
Processing of wood, manufacture of wood and cork products, except for furniture; manufacture of products of straw and other vegetal plaiting materials	69	125	180	193	215	227	228	243	276
Manufacture of paper and paper products	104	188	267	305	318	320	355	380	406
Printing and reproduction of recorded media	111	182	256	305	341	334	371	394	398
Manufacture of coking products and products obtained from processing of crude oil	186	398	575	706	706	692	764	849	937
Manufacture of chemical products and substances	132	249	384	405	443	440	452	471	510
Manufacture of basic pharmaceuticals and pharmaceutical preparations	180	339	523	519	526	526	564	594	636
Manufacture of products made of rubber and plastic materials	100	176	253	300	324	339	360	372	409
Manufacture of other products of non-metallic minerals	109	208	313	359	364	356	375	406	417
Metallurgical industry	147	267	383	410	439	449	477	497	526
Metal structures, metal products, except for machines, machinery and equipment	95	195	280	296	314	310	333	352	384
Manufacture of computers and electronic and optical devices	132	256	342	381	422	439	464	487	514
Manufacture of electrical equipment	108	198	281	342	360	357	380	390	414
Manufacture of machines, machinery and equipment n.e.c.	113	212	306	337	385	384	416	459	484
Manufacture of transport motor-vehicles, trailers and semi-trailers	112	212	312	374	403	415	442	473	504

(continued)

(continued)

	2000	2005	2007	2010	2011	2012	2013	2014	2015
Manufacture of other means of transport	143	276	384	433	462	464	501	536	545
Manufacture of furniture	76	142	203	215	223	224	235	254	289
Other industrial activities n.e.c.	78	149	206	229	263	239	272	283	323
Repair and maintenance of machines and equipment	119	233	322	370	366	352	380	387	403
PRODUCTION AND SUPPLY OF ELECTRICITY, HEATING, GAS, HOT WATER AND AIR CONDITIONING	191	372	535	634	658	652	660	696	692
WATER SUPPLY; SANITATION, WASTE MANAGEMENT, DECONTAMINATION SERVICES	102	185	277	298	315	311	323	340	354
Water catchment, treatment and supply	114	211	330	365	388	382	399	411	425
Collection and treatment of waste water	106	201	300	359	353	364	363	394	408
Collection, treatment and disposal of wastes; collection of reusable materials; decontamination activities and services	84	158	233	239	253	248	256	274	291

Source: Authors' own calculations based on NIS and NBR data

Appendix A.23: Net monthly average salary in industry, by type of company ownership (euro)

L. Chivu et al., *Deindustrialization and Reindustrialization in Romania*,
DOI 10.1007/978-3-319-65753-0

	2008		2010		2014		2015	
	Public ownership	Private ownership	Public ownership	Private ownership	Public ownership	Private ownership	Public ownership	Private ownership
TOTAL	471	309	380	307	444	358	475	398
INDUSTRY	518	297	507	304	530	370	531	398
MINING INDUSTRY	642	604	615	546	676	779	688	847
Mining of hard and light coal	631	351	578	232	620	271	627	309
Extraction of crude oil and natural gas	873	758	885	642	985	1066	987	1160
Mining of metallic ores	449	266	493	313	537	335	560	353
Other mining activities	487	290	478	270	545	268	550	297
Mining-related activities	1064	531	1080	572	1128	771	1161	935
MANUFACTURING INDUSTRY	444	281	441	290	443	353	455	382
Food industry	209	242	229	225	294	254	307	281
Manufacture of beverages	218	361	199	406	291	455	351	472
Manufacture of tobacco products	0	712	0	766	0	936	0	943
Manufacture of textile products	0	232	0	251	0	302	0	327
Manufacture of clothing	106	204	173	204	189	250	214	265
Tanning and dressing of hides, manufacture of travelling bags and leatherwear, saddling and footwear; dressing and dyeing of furs		204	261	212		253		278
Wood processing, manufacture of wood and cork products, except for furniture; manufacture of straw and other plaiting vegetal materials	284	197	334	192		243	369	276

(*continued*)

(continued)

	2008		2010		2014		2015	
	Public ownership	Private ownership	Public ownership	Private ownership	Public ownership	Private ownership	Public ownership	Private ownership
Manufacture of paper and paper products	239	286	333	305	281	380	311	406
Printing and reproduction of recorded media	586	286	482	283	537	377	579	380
Manufacture of coking products and of products obtained from the processing of crude oil	182	626		706		849	235	948
Manufacture of chemical substances and products	494	389	517	396	463	472	448	515
Manufacture of basic pharmaceuticals and pharmaceutical preparations	509	491	512	521	566	598	581	645
Manufacture of products of rubber and plastic materials	338	274		300	381	372	373	410
Manufacture of other products from non-metallic minerals	150	341	216	359	155	407	193	418
Metallurgical industry	505	418	581	405	1051	489	1060	518
Metal structures, metal products, except for machines, machinery and equipment	434	299	321	294	354	352	395	383
Manufacture of computers and electronic and optic devices	403	348	358	382	452	488	441	515
Manufacture of electrical equipment	293	303		342		390		414
Manufacture of machines, machinery and equipment n.e.c.	575	352	397	336	584	457	474	484

(continued)

(continued)

	2008		2010		2014		2015	
	Public ownership	Private ownership	Public ownership	Private ownership	Public ownership	Private ownership	Public ownership	Private ownership
Manufacture of road transport motor-vehicles, trailers and semi-trailers	453	331		374		473		504
Manufacture of other means of transport	438	424	494	429	517	538	570	543
Manufacture of furniture	413	219	489	215	201	254	228	289
Other industrial activities n.e.c.	371	226	339	221	372	279	439	316
Repair and maintenance of machines and equipment	446	311	474	308	395	384	377	410
PRODUCTION AND SUPPLY OF ELECTRIC POWER, HEATING, GAS, HOT WATER, AND AIR CONDITIONING	662	606	649	598	678	746	680	718
WATER SUPPLY; SANITATION, WASTE MANAGEMENT, DECONTAMINATION ACTIVITIES	314	313	312	286	358	320	371	337
Water catchment, treatment and supply	354	412	355	391	395	475	408	499
Collection and treatment of waste water	329	412	354	367	358	483	379	472
Collection, treatment and disposal of wastes; recycling of reusable materials; decontamination activities and services	244	289	211	250	253	280	272	297

Source: Authors' own calculations based on NIS and NBR data

Appendix A.24: Share of the gross operating surplus and compensation of employees in the gross value added, in 2003 (%)

	Compensation of employees	Gross operating surplus
Textiles, ready-mades	76.2	22.9
Food industry, beverages and tobacco products	27.2	71.8
Wooden products, furniture and other industrial products	52.9	46.8
Chemistry and synthetic fibre	82.4	15.9
Rubber and plastic materials	34.5	65.2
Metallurgy and steel making	90.5	8.9
Means of transport	53.3	46.2
Machine building	71.4	30.9
Electrical products and appliances	56.6	42.8
Electricity, heating, gas, water	49.1	50.4
Total economy	42.2	57.9

Source: Authors' own compilation based on data from *National Accounts 2012–2013*, NIS, Bucharest, 2016

L. Chivu et al., *Deindustrialization and Reindustrialization in Romania*,
DOI 10.1007/978-3-319-65753-0

References

Artus, Patrick. 2014. Une nouvelle vague des delocalisations se profile. *Natixis* 425.

Backer, Gary. 1997. *Human Capital—A Theoretical and Empirical Analysis, with a Focus on Education [Capitalul uman—o analiză teoretică şi empirică cu referire specială la educaţie]*. Bucharest: Editura All [Publishing House].

Barry, Bluestone, and Harisson Bennett. 1982. *The Deindustrialization of America*. New York: Basic Books. http://www.d.umn.edu/~epeters5/Cst1201/Articles/Deindustrialization%20of%20America.pdf.

Belhocine, N., and S. Dell'Erba. 2013. *The Impact of Debt Sustainability and the Level of Debt on Emerging Markets Spreads*. IMF Working Paper, WP/13/93, May.

Burritt, Roger, and Katherine Christ. 2016. Industry 4.0 and Environmental Accounting: A New Revolution? *Asian Journal of Sustainability ans Social Responsibility*, December. https://doi.org/10.1186/s41180-016-0007-y

Cecchetti, S.G., M.S. Mohanty, and F. Zampolli. 2011. *The Real Effects of Debt*. Symposium "Achieving Maximum Long-Run Growth". Jackson Hole, Wy (USA), August 25–27.

Chatillon, Alain. 2011. *Rapport d'information sur la deindustrialisation des territories*. No. 403, Senat France. http://www.senat.fr/notice-rapport/2010/r10-403-1-notice.html

Chilosi, Alberto. 1996. *Distributional Consequences of Privatisation in the Economie in Transition: An Analytical Framework*. Dordrecht: Kluwer Academic Publishers. https://doi.org/10.1007/BF02430939.

Chivu, Luminiţa, and Constantin Ciutacu. 2014. About Industrial Structures Decomposition and Recomposition. *Procedia Economics and Finance* 8: 157–166. https://doi.org/10.1016/s2212-5671(14)00076-8.

Chivu, Luminiţa, and Constantin Ciutacu. 2016. *Romania and the Four Freedoms: From Theory to Practice*. In Proceedings of ESPERA 2015. Frankfurt am Main: Peter Lang Academic Research.

Chivu, Luminiţa, Constantin Ciutacu, and Laurenţiu Georgescu. 2015. Consequences of Wage Gaps in the EU. *Procedia Economics and Finance* 22: 141–147. https://doi.org/10.1016/S2212-5671(15)00244-0.

Chriac, Cristina. 2016. *Marea privatizare.Restructurarea proprietăţii*. Bucuresti: Editura Paideia.

Ciutacu, Constantin, and Luminiţa Chivu. 2010a. *Anticipating and Managing Restructuring—National Background Paper Romania*. In 27th National

Seminar on Restructuring, International Training Center-International Labour Office, European Commisssion/DG Employment, Social Affairs and Equal Opportunities, 2010. http://ec.europa.eu/social/main.jsp?catId=819&langId=en

Ciutacu, Constantin, and Luminița Chivu. 2010b. *Anticipating and Managing Restructuring in Romania*. ARENAS, VC/2008/0667, EC, ITC-ILO.

Ciutacu, Constantin, and Luminița Chivu. 2015a. Non-Competitive Evolutions of the Foreign Trade in Romania. *Procedia Economics and Finance* 22: 216–221. https://doi.org/10.1016/S2212-5671(15)00265-8.

———. 2015b. Romania's Deindustrialisation. From the "Golden Age" to the "Iron Scrap Age". *Procedia Economics and Finance* 22: 209–215.

Ciutacu, Constantin, Luminița Chivu, Raluca Dimitriu, and Tiberiu Țiclea. 2013. *The Impact of Legislative Reforms on Industrial Relations in Romania*. International Labour Office, Industrial and Employment Relations Department; ILO DWT and Country Office for Central and Eastern Europe.

Communications from the Commission to the European Parliament, the Council, the European Economic and Social Council, and the Committee of the Regions. *An Integrated Industrial Policy for the Globalisation Era. Putting Competitiveness and Sustainability at Centre Stage* and *A Stronger European Industry for Growth and Economic Recovery*, COM (2010) 614 final and COM (2012) 582 final, p. 4.

Darvas, Z., and P. Huttl 2014. *The Long Haul: Debt Sustainability Analysis*. Bruegel Working Papers.

European Commission. 2014. *Reindustrialising Europe. Member States' Competitiveness Report 2014*. SWD (2014) 278, European Union, Luxembourg, , p. 222.

———. 2015. *Macroeconomic Imbalances. Country Report Romania 2015*. European Economy Occasional Papers, No. 223, EC-DGECFIN, Brussels, June 2015, pp. 12–26.

———. 2016. *European Innovation Scoreboard*. Country Profile Romania.

———. 2017. *Overview of EU Instruments Contributing to the Internationalization of European Business*. DG for Internal Market, Industry, Entrepreneurship and SMEs, EC, 2 March 2017.

Eurostat. 2016. *Estimated Hourly Labour Costs*. http://ec.europa.eu/eurostat/statistics-explained/index.php/File:Estimated_hourly_labour_costs,_2016_(EUR)_YB17.png

Fitjar, Rune Dahl, Martin Gjelsvik, and Andres Rodrigues-Pose. 2014. Organizing Product Innovation: Hierarchy, Market or Triple-Helix Networks? *Triple Helix* 1: 3. https://doi.org/10.1186/s40604-014-0003-0.

Gary, P. Pisano, and Shih Willy. 2012. *Producing Prosperity: Why America Needs a Manufacturing Renaissance*. Boston, MA: Harvard Business Review Press.

George, Georgescu. 2013. Public Debt, Sovereign Risk and Sustainable Development of Romania. *Procedia Economics and Finance* 8: 353–361. https://doi.org/10.1016/S2212-5671(14)00101-4.

———. 2016. *Prospects of Romania's International Investment Position and Financial Stability Risks*. Frankfurt am Main: Peter Lang Academic Research.

Grabas, Christian, and Alexander Nutzenadel. 2013. *Industrial Policies in Europe in Historical Perspective*. Working Paper No. 15, Work Package 306, European Commission, WWW for Europe Project, July.

Häusermann, Silja, and Bruno Palier. 2008. The Politics of Employment-Friendly Welfare Reforms in Post-Industrial Economies. *Socioecon Review* 6 (3): 559–586. https://doi.org/10.1093/ser/mwn011.

Hoareau, Cecile, Jo Ritzen, and Gabriele Marconi. 2013. Higher Education and Economic Innovation, a Comparison of European Countries. *IZA Journal of European Labour Studies* 2: 24.

Il sostegno publico all'internalizazzione delle imprese. 2016. Rome: ICE, p. 307.

Italian Trade Agency. 2016. *Piano della Performance 2015–2017*. Rome: ICE.

Jiwook, Jung. 2015. Shareholder Value and Workforce Downsizing, 1981–2006. *Social Forces* 93 (4): 1335–1368.

Komlos, John. 2014. *Has Creative Destruction Become More Destructive?* NBER Working Papers No. 20379, August. http://www.nber.org/papers/w20379.pdf;https://doi.org/10.3386/w20379.

L'avenir de l'industrie. 2016. Problemes economiques, France, No. 3137/August 2016, p. 5.

Manufacturing the Future. 2012. Global McKinsey Institute.

Meliciani, Valentina, and Maria Savona. 2015. The Determinants of Regional Specialisation in Business Services: Agglomeration Economies, Vertical Linkages and Innovation. *Journal of Economic Geography* 15 (2): 387–416. https://doi.org/10.1093/jeg/lbt038.

Mereuță, Cezar, Ionuț Pandelică, and Amalia Pandelică. 2013. *The Foreign Majority Shareholding in Nodal Companies in the Main Markets of Romania—A Compendium*. Bucharest: Editura Economică.

Migration and Migrant Population Statistics. 2015. Eurostat. http://ec.europa.eu/eurostat/statistics-explained/index.php/Migration_and_migrant_population_statistics

Piano Industriale Gruppo CDP 2020. 2015. *Linee guida strategiche*. In Press Conference, Rome, 17 December 2015.

Piketty, Thomas. 2013. *Le Capital au XXI siècle*. Paris: Seuil.
Problemes Economiques. 2016. France, No. 3137/August 2016, p. 6.
Ranga, M., and H. Etzkowitz. 2013. Triple Helix Systems: An Analytical Framework for Innovation Policy and Practice in the Knowledge Society. *Industry and Higher Education* 27 (4): 237–262.
Results and Performances of Industrial and Construction Companies. 2016. Bucharest: NIS.
Rienzo, Cinzia, and Carlos Vargas-Silva. 2015. *Migrants in UK: An Overview*. In The Migration Observatory at the University of Oxford, 2015 edition. http://www.migrationobservatory.ox.ac.uk/sites/files/migobs/Migrants%20in%20the%20UK-Overview.pdf
Rodrik, D. 2015. *Premature Deindustrialization*. NBER Working Paper, No. 20935, Cambridge.
Schwab, Klaus. 2015. The Fourth Industrial Revolution. What It Means and How to Respond. *Foreign Affairs*. https://www.foreignaffairs.com/articles/2015-12-12/fourth-industrial-revolution
Steel Statistical Yearbook. World Steel Association, Various Editions, 1960–2015.
Stiglitz, J.E., and D. Heymann. 2014. *Life after Debt. The Origins and Resolutions of Debt Crisis*. In IEA Conference, Vol. 152. Palgrave Macmillan.
Structure of the Public Debt, 31 of March 2017. Ministry of Public Finance, Romanian Government. http://discutii.mfinante.ro/static/10/Mfp/buletin/executii/Structuradatorieipublice2000-2017martieRo.pdf
Subran, L. 2013. *The Reindustrialization of the United States*. Special Report No. 1187, Euler Hermes Economic Outlook, 25 January 2013. http://www.eulerhermes.dk/oekonomisk-analyse/Documents/Outlook_no.1187.pdf
Szirmai, A. 2011. *Manufacturing and Economic Development*. UNU-WIDER Working Paper, No. 2011/75, Helsinki, November.
Szirmai, A. et al. 2013. *Pathways to Industrialization in the Twenty-First Century—New Challenges and Emerging Paradigms*. WIDER Studies in Development Economics, Oxford University Press.
Telegdy, Álmos. 2002. *Management—Employee Buyouts in Romania. Privatization Process and Ownership Outcomes*. Budapest: University of Economic Sciences and Central European University. http://www.efesonline.org/CEEEONet/REPORTS%202002/National%20Report%20Romania%20EN.pdf.
Trends in Research, Development and Innovation in Romania and the Requirements of the EU 2020 Strategy. 2016. Joint Roundtable: Institute of National Economy—National Institute of Statistics. Information Bulletin, No. 3 (24), NIS, March 2016.

US Government. 2016. *National Network for Manufacturing Innovation Program. Strategic Plan.* Executive Office of the President National Science and Technology Council, Advanced Manufacturing National Program Office, February 2016. https://www.manufacturingusa.com/sites/prod/files/docs/resource/2015-NNMI-Strategic-Plan.pdf

Vlad, Ionel-Valentin (coordinator). 2016. *Strategia de dezvoltare a României în următorii 20 de ani.* Vol. II, București, Editura Academiei Române (publisher house). http://academiaromana.ro/bdar/strategiaAR/doc12/StrategiaII.pdf

Wnukowski, Damian. 2016 (February 24). Export Promotion Agency: The Experience of Selected European Countries. *PISM Bulletin* 18: 868.

World Bank. 2017. *Doing Business 2017. Equal Opportunity for All.* Washington: World Bank, p. 234.

World Economic Forum. 2016. *The Global Competitiveness Report 2016–2017.* Geneva: WEF, pp. 304–305.

Zaman, Gheorghe, and George Georgescu. 2012. Sovereign Risk and Debt Sustainability—Warning Levels for Romania. In *Non-Linear Modelling in Economics. Beyond Standard Economics,* 228–265. New York: Addleton Academic Publishers.

———. 2016. Provocări în perioada tranziției la economia de piață în România. Creșterea gradului de îndatorare internă și externă. *Revista Studii de Istorie Economică și Istoria Gândirii Economice.* September, Vol. XVII.

Index[1]

[1] Note: Page number followed by 'n' denotes note.

L. Chivu et al., *Deindustrialization and Reindustrialization in Romania*,
DOI 10.1007/978-3-319-65753-0

E

F

W

Z

The manufacturer's authorised representative in the EU is Springer Nature Customer Service Centre GmbH, Europaplatz 3, 69115 Heidelberg, Germany. If you have any concerns regarding our products, please contact ProductSafety@springernature.com

Printed and bound by CPI Group (UK) Ltd, Croydon, CR0 4YY

25/09/2026

02222859-0006